Do
Unto
Others

Do
Unto
Others

Extraordinary Acts of Ordinary People

Samuel P. Oliner

Westview
PRESS

A Member of the Perseus Books Group

Copyright © 2003 by Westview Press, A Member of the Perseus Books Group

Westview Press books are available at special discounts for bulk purchases in the United States by corporations, institutions, and other organizations. For more information, please contact the Special Markets Department at the Perseus Books Group, 11 Cambridge Center, Cambridge MA 02142, or call (617) 252-5298, (800)255-1514 or email j.mccrary@perseusbooks.com.

Published in 2003 in the United States of America by Westview Press, 5500 Central Avenue, Boulder, Colorado 80301–2877, and in the United Kingdom by Westview Press, 12 Hid's Copse Road, Cumnor Hill, Oxford OX2 9JJ

Find us on the World Wide Web at www.westviewpress.com

Library of Congress Cataloging-in-Publication Data.
Oliner Samuel P.
Do unto others: extraordinary acts of ordinary people / Samuel P. Oliner.
    p. cm.
  Includes bibliographical references and index.
  ISBN 0–8133–3984–7 (hardcover : alk. paper)
  1. Altruism—Case Studies. 2. Caring—Case studies. 3. Helping behavior—Case studies.
I. Title.
BJ1474 .O395 2003
171'.8—dc21
                                                              2002153183

10   9   8   7   6   5   4   3   2   1

Dedication

〜

This book is gratefully dedicated to the many heroes and moral exemplars who have exhibited courage, caring, and social responsibility for others in need. We also acknowledge and appreciate the interviewees' time, energy, and insight, which helped us to better understand why some people choose the moral high ground in order to bring about a more caring and compassionate society.

Contents

Acknowledgments

～

This book would not have been possible without the help of many people, including faculty and students. I am immensely grateful to all of these individuals and groups who supplied us with valuable service and support.

I owe a special debt to the following foundations and groups for their financial assistance, which made our research and this book possible: David Hirschhorn, president of the Jacob and Hilda Blaustein Foundation, Inc.; Eli Evans, president of the Revson Foundation, who enabled us to study Carnegie heroes; this research was supported (in part) by the Fetzer Institute; Humboldt State University; and Lois Risling, director of the Center for Indian Community Development. I also want to thank Walter F. Rutkowski, executive director and secretary of the Carnegie Hero Fund Commission, for making available to us a sample of the Carnegie heroes population.

There are a number of individuals whom I wish to acknowledge for their participation in different ways. I begin with Anna LoMascolo, an outstanding graduate student who helped substantially with parts of the book, especially with the earlier parts of the research, and specifically with the interviewing of Carnegie heroes. Kia Ora Zelaney diligently helped us with the early drafts of the book. Several other graduate students dedicated their energy by helping with the editorial work, transcription, interviewing, and other relevant tasks. Among them are Farnad Darnell, Bethaney Weber, and Greg Gibson, who were responsible for making valuable editorial suggestions and the coding of narratives, which helped me to quantify the rich qualitative interviews. I would also like to thank professor Jack Shaffer and graduate student Jodi Kateiva for their input.

Other individuals who were very helpful in the initial stages of the research are Kathy Lee and Mary Farr, who helped by interviewing hospice volunteers, and Jonathon Mermis-Cava, Ali Gross-Hodges, and Will Tift, who did a wonderful job of interviewing some of the respondents for this book. I gratefully appreciate Dr. Vicki Anderson's help in interviewing hospice volunteers and moral exemplars in the Boston area. Her skillful interviews enriched our data for the volunteer and moral exemplar-leaders chapters. I owe a special thanks to Patsy Givens, who tirelessly edited and gave feedback that greatly improved the quality of the manuscript.

I gratefully acknowledge the observations made by professor Franklin Littell, as well as Nobel Prize–winner professor Elie Wiesel, and professors Nel Noddings, John K. Roth, and William Helmreich, who gave their time to make some observations about the values of this book.

Most important, I am thankful for the contributions of Jill Rothenberg, senior editor at Westview Press, who dedicated much time, patience, and energy on the editing of this book, giving me feedback chapter by chapter, and who was able to successfully improve the direction of this book. There are a number of people I may have left out inadvertently, but that does not mean that I appreciate them any less for their assistance.

Preface

∽

Throughout history ordinary people have exhibited heroic behavior. Since September 11 the United States moved from movie-star and sports-hero adulation to others—the uniformed heroes of civil services such as firefighters, police officers, clean-up volunteers, steelworkers, and metalworkers who tried to help save people from the World Trade Center and the Pentagon. These heroic individuals who risk their lives by doing their job on a regular basis were not widely recognized before September 11, 2001. It is important for us to realize that it is not only men and women in business attire who are making a difference in our society but also people in other types of uniforms: police, firefighters, the U.S. Coast Guard, military personnel, and others. These are working-class people who leave their homes to fight in wars and to save lives in other settings. We are now beginning to think of collective heroism and not just individual heroism, such as a man in the military who dives onto a live grenade in order to save his comrades. The example of collective or group heroic behavior was clearly evident in the World Trade Center tragedy when four men on United Flight 93 collectively succeeded in crashing the hijacked airliner into a Pennsylvania field rather than allow it to proceed against what they suspected to be potential targets such as the White House or the Capitol.

It is important to rethink our definition of the term "heroism" to be more inclusive and to give such compassionate behavior more attention. It should also be recognized that in the United States it is not one's duty to rescue someone in trouble; in Europe, by contrast, good samaritan laws exist, and when one sees someone in trouble, one has a moral obligation to help.

Until recently, some said that we have lost our interest and vision about caring for others. Robert Putnam, in his book *Bowling Alone*, laments this idea that we no longer have this ideology or social capital and interest in the common good.[1] However, September 11 reawakened sensitivity to others and put our welfare alongside theirs. This awakening of caring for the other has been shown in a number of activities, including the heroes of Flight 93 and others in the World Trade Center. In the future we should publicize, celebrate, recognize, and praise people who have shown courageous behavior, putting themselves at risk for others. We should also recognize those other moral exemplars who are emphasizing the idea of caring and fairness; among them are whistle-blowers and environmentalists who truly are concerned about the future of our planet and offspring. This renewed and changed civic attitude and behavior was noticed by Putnam in an article published in February 2002.[2] Some of the increased civic behaviors and attitudes were: greater trust in the national and local government; expressed interest in politics; trust of people of other races; trust in neighbors; contributions to religious and secular charities; working with neighbors; giving blood, volunteering, and attending political meetings; and having friends visit your home. Hopefully these changes will last and American society in the future will generally be more caring—not just vigilant against terrorism but also caring for the general other.

Carers, or helpers, become transformed when they have been sensitized to the lack of truth and justice for the other. This transformation becomes associated with a kind of self-identity, involving both the cognitive and the affective realms. Moral exemplars are influenced by other moral exemplars' deeds. Thus, an attribute that our respondents in this book have is moral courage. These individuals are encouraged not only by generativity—that is, helping the other to better himself or herself—but also a certain amount of conviction, positivity, and commitment to the cause of helping. They exhibit considerable treatment of the other out of general respect for all human beings. Although there are risks involved in the undertaking by all helpers, including moral exemplars, that does not stop them. Moral exemplars and other helpers have a history of previous help because they have inculcated the ethic of caring.

September 11 has no doubt sensitized the entire world to the consequences of indifference and how some individuals, previous bystanders, have been moved to help. The important question that arises is: How do we "produce" more people to become helpers rather than bystanders? For every evil person that has committed acts of harm and pain, there are many others who are capable of kindness. What would it take to move more people from the role of bystander and put their inclination of kindness into action? When people are aroused and are given a good reason for helping, they exhibit courage, helping behavior, devote more time to others, and often leave a moral legacy for future generations. In some instances, bystanders have to be educated to see the difference between right and wrong and to take a stand against evil. Thus, caring is teachable and a learnable behavior. As research has shown, kindness is a very important aspect of the human condition. Unfortunately, it is not an aspect that is nurtured to the same altruistic level in all human beings. Some people will help because they see other people's pain and empathize; others will help because they are concerned with how people in history will remember them. Still, some feel there is no escape from duty and that doing nothing (i.e., walking away from a tragedy instead of saving lives or helping others from trouble) will haunt them for the rest of their lives.

Courage is an important aspect of helping, especially in the situation of terrible danger to life. For example, the couriers during the Holocaust—mostly young women—were able to save many lives by doing dangerous work, including carrying food, money, information, and weapons to various ghettos so individuals could defend themselves. In one instance, a woman by the name of Niuta, also known as "Wanda with the Braids," took much risk because she acted as a Polish Christian girl; nobody suspected her of being Jewish. One time she was so angry at what the Gestapo did to her parents and others that she walked in to a Gestapo headquarters in Warsaw and said to the guard she had something "very important and private" to say that would interest the high-ranking officer. The guard let her in; she walked in to the officer's office, took out a little pistol that she had concealed, and shot him to death. Still angry about the brutal treatment of the Jews, she sneaked into another Gestapo official's apartment and secretly hid under the bed covers. When he walked in she took out the same pistol and killed him as well.

This book has a threefold purpose: first, to discuss heroic behavior in different settings; second, to understand what common motivating factors help us explain why some people act altruistically; and third, the moral implication for education, which might help us in understanding what motivates these individuals to help bring about a more caring society. How can we prepare our future generations to be more caring? A climate of helping and caring appears to have been brought about by the tragedy of September 11.

One example of such a climate occurred early on the morning of September 11, 2001, at 7:45 A.M. Virginia DiChiara left her home in Bloomfield, New Jersey, to go to work in the North Tower of the World Trade Center. She worked for Cantor-Fitzgerald on the seventy-eighth floor. She arrived in the lobby of the building at 8:46 A.M., got into the elevator, and went up to her office. At that moment, Flight 11 plowed into the face of the tower twenty-two floors above. The elevator was inoperable, the lights were out, and she was terrified. She dropped her bag, covered her face with her palms, and squeezed her way to the door. With her elbows she pushed the doors back. Behind her was a Cantor-Fitzgerald coworker; she never saw the coworker again. DiChiara was aflame when she went from the elevator. Her hair was on fire, and with her hand she tried to put the fire out. She threw herself to the carpet, rolling over and over trying frantically to put out the flames. She says, "I remember getting up and just looking at myself." She said, "Okay, everything's out, but then I started laughing hysterically. I was so scared because embers on my body were still burning." She crawled some twenty feet down the hallway and propped herself against the wall. She was wearing a sleeveless dress, and her arms were scarred with third-degree burns. She did not feel the pain yet, as she was stunned and in a state of shock. Then she spotted a coworker, Ari Schonbrun, who was head of the global acquisitions and accounts receivable department. When Ari turned around, he said, "Virginia . . . oh my God!" Virginia told him she was badly burned. She was beginning to feel the pain as well. "I'm in so much pain," she said. Schonbrun was mortified. Her skin was peeling off her arms. Ari knew she was in trouble. DiChiara read the expression on his face and knew it was bad. He told her, "Virginia, take it easy. We're going to help you, and you are going to be fine." She said, "Whatever you do, don't leave me." Ari assured her that he would not leave her but would be with her. She held on to him as they went down the stairs, and he covered her because of the tremendous burns on her arms and skin. The stairways were like a black hole, and Ari said, "Virginia, follow me so you don't get hurt."

When she arrived at Cantor-Fitzgerald the year before, DiChiara conducted her first audit in Schonbrun's unit (at that time, it was the business administration department). Schonbrun says they were not friends. Still, he saved her by helping her down the stairs. She was then taken to the emergency room in one of the best burn clinics in New York City. She has expressed public appreciation for Ari's help, and in the December 31, 2001, issue of *Newsweek* she said, "Life will never be the same. Courage is now a full-time occupation." She will need more surgery for her scars, and she may never spend as much time in the sun as she did in the past.

The distinguished Harvard scholar Robert Coles spent much of his academic life gathering stories containing the truth about morality and immorality.[3] This book also contains true stories, many of which were obtained from the respondents in personal interviews, others gleaned from extensive reading in the growing literature of good and evil. In the course of our research we gathered hundreds of inspiring stories of people acting to help others. We highlight examples here because they illustrate a particular aspect of caring behavior toward others. Some of the stories narrate behaviors that can only be described as heroic, a type of altruism that involves high risk to the actor, or helper. Among the helpers/heroic altruists are rescuers during September 11, the Holocaust, Carnegie heroes, and military heroes. The events of September 11 provided us with a new vocabulary of heroism that balances the theories and brings them to the present in graphic immediacy.

"You Must Live and Tell the Story"

How One Heroic Act Saved My Life

How can one seek Truth or cherish love without fearlessness?
—**Mark Shepard,** *Gandhi Today*

In June 1942 my family, including my grandparents, was ordered by the Nazis to move to the ghetto in the small town of Bobowa, situated near the Slovak border in southern Poland. We had seventy-two hours to get there, and we had to leave all our worldly possessions behind except for what we could carry, mostly bedding and utensils. The Bobowa ghetto was approximately eighteen kilometers as the crow flies from my grandfather's and father's villages, Mszanka and Bielanka, respectively. We stayed in the ghetto for two months, and as a twelve-year-old boy, I experienced great fear and hunger, sadness and deprivation. In Bobowa we were crowded with other families into a room twenty-five feet by thirty feet and slept on straw covered with some blankets that we had brought. My biological mother had died of tuberculosis when I was seven, and my father had married a woman named Esther, with whom he had two more children, a girl and a boy, Shayia and Jaffa. With the five of us in that room were my grandfather, Herman, and his wife, as well as two other families—a total of at least twenty people. It was a world of total misery and hunger.

From time to time I would sneak away from the ghetto, go to nearby villages, and try to get some food from the peasants. I traded needles, watches, pens, and other items that these farmers needed in exchange for potatoes, fruit, eggs, bread, and other edibles. At night I would sneak back into the ghetto, and all of us in the house would eat. Sometimes we would cover up the windows when we were eating because beggars would come by and knock on the window. And although we did not have enough food to share, if they saw us, we would give them some slices of bread and potatoes.

Life continued like this until August 14, when the Nazi soldiers in mobile killing units called *Einsatzgruppen* surrounded the ghetto early in the morning and drove the people out of their dwellings to military trucks that were parked in the middle of Bobowa's town plaza. The *Einsatzgruppen*, made up of Germans and Ukrainians serving under the Nazis, went from house to house banging on doors and yelling *"Alle Juden—raus . . . raus!"* (All Jews—out . . . out!). Still in pajamas and terrified, I saw Esther rocking back and forth holding Shayia between her breasts. She stared at me for a moment and then said with a determined sadness, *"Antloif mein kind und du vest bleiben beim leben"* (Run, my child; run away so that you may live and save yourself). I did not know what to do or where to go, and yet an adult had given me permission to run and hide. Esther understood that something bad was going to happen to the Jewish people of the Bobowa ghetto. I heard her sad, pleading words, and with tears in my eyes I ran and hid on the roof. From the roof I saw a soldier throw a small child out of an upper window of a tall house nearby. Another grabbed a girl by the arm; she was fighting back, begging him to leave her alone. People hurried past the end of the alley, clutching their few belongings. In groups and in pairs, they hurried past, pushed from behind by the uniformed Germans. A young girl broke away from the rest. She threw down the bundle she was carrying and ran down the alley. A Nazi guard saw her and aimed his rifle. . . .

The flat, sloping roof had been used as a storage place, and I covered myself with old boards and pieces of rubbish. The sun climbed slowly and the tar paper got warm and soft. Gradually, the shouting, screaming, and occasional gunshots subsided. All day long there was the sound of heavy trucks. I felt sick. Dust made my throat and chest hurt, and the smell of tar paper heated by the sun made me dizzy and frightened. I drifted into a daze, a sort of dreaming wakefulness, and flies crawled on my ear. Whenever there was a noise close by, my heart beat so hard I thought it would burst.

By late afternoon the ghetto was quiet. The people had stopped crying, the Nazis had stopped shouting, and the trucks had stopped roaring in the streets. The ghetto was like a ghost town. A gentle, quiet breeze drifted dust on my neck from the thin planks that covered me. At one time—long, long ago—these breezes had been redolent with animal smells and alive with the sound of human voices; now I felt sure there was no one left for the breezes to touch. Like the blood flowing through my veins, a feeling of great loneliness filled my body, and I wondered if I was actually dead. Maybe I *was* dead, and my lot through eternity was to lie under these boards in absolute stillness and listen to the breeze.

I began to hear quiet sounds. I heard Polish words and muffled laughter, some shuffling and scurrying. Slowly, I crawled out from under the boards. I was as still as I could be, and I was aching with an awful longing. At the edge of the roof I looked down in time to see two Poles emerging from a house about half a block away. I recognized one man as a Pole from a neighboring village. Before the war, my father had done business with him on market day. I watched him emerge from the house with some curtains in his hand. The other man was carrying a mattress behind him.

I waited until they had gone out of sight. Then, making sure no one else was on the street, I climbed down from the roof. My pajamas were a dead giveaway that I was a Jew, and so I searched through some houses until I found some clothing. A strange feeling crept over me as I put on a pair of pants with neat patches sewn on the knees. A breakfast was laid on the table—bread, baked under crude conditions and with black crust on the sides. The floorboards were splintered but swept clean; in the corner was a forgotten prayer book. My mouth was dry, my knees weak. I felt like a grave robber and prayed for forgiveness. The ghosts of the people who had lived here spoke to me with their unseen eyes as if to say they had no further use for the material and that it was all right to take the clothes, that it was better to keep a fellow Jew warm than to clothe a rampaging Pole. A wooden shutter creaked outside the broken window, and my body filled with fear. I could not stand to remain in the house another moment.

The Bobowa ghetto consisted of wooden and brick buildings with narrow alleys of cobblestone or dirt. The nearby roofs of tin glinted in the late afternoon sun; it was a sight with no one but me, it seemed, to see. Then I heard the sound of boot heels, and I peeked cautiously around the corner of a building. Six Germans, or Ukrainians in the service of the German army, were walking down the street.

They split up and searched from house to house, cellar to cellar. Flattened, I hid again on the roof (which was very easy to climb up), and I watched a soldier approach one particular house. Moss grew on its roof, and moisture made dark streaks down the wood of the outer wall. As he pushed open the door, a young woman rushed out. She threw herself at him, insisting there was no one else in the house. He laughed and grabbed her waist, pulling her to his chest. Her body sagged, and she did not fight him, but I could see her eyes squeezed tightly shut. Then there was the cry of a baby. The soldier hit the woman and knocked her down, then he turned and strode into the house. The woman jumped to her feet and rushed after him, but as she reached the doorway a pistol shot went off inside the house. She fainted right there on the threshold.

I left my rooftop hideaway and ran. Bile was coming up in my throat. I was in a daze. I ran and ran, stumbling on the uneven streets. Finally I stopped and leaned against a wall to catch my breath. In front of me was an old shop with boards nailed over the windows. My chest hurt, my knees were weak, and I started to slide along the wall. Suddenly I remembered the picture.

Of all my possessions, I valued most the picture of my biological mother. It was in my father's temporary house in the ghetto. In the confusion of my mind, the picture stood out as being of vital importance, and I was sure I could not take another step without it. The ghetto was a very dangerous place to be, and my stepmother had said "Go!"—yet I simply had to retrace my steps to get the photo. The marketplace was on a sort of plateau in the middle of Bobowa. Shaped like a square, it consisted of cobblestones and trees. I avoided this area because it was where the Jews had been loaded onto German military trucks. Keeping an eye open for the Nazis and Polish looters, I arrived at my father's vacant temporary house. It was a sad-looking structure with a low roof and rotting doorposts. Saddest of all was the stillness in it. Swallowing my fear, I entered the door I had gone through so many times in the past two months. Only twisted bedding and a wreckage of personal belongings remained in the otherwise empty room. Some looters had been there already. My chest felt crushed with the agony of an entire people. On my hands and knees, blinded by tears, I searched for the photograph. It was nowhere to be found. I had lost my entire family, and now I had lost the irreplaceable picture of my mother.

As I wormed through hedges and crawled along the sides of buildings, one thought filled my mind: *escape*. As I neared the barbed-wire fence that

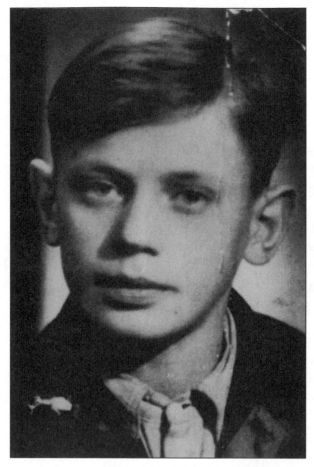

Samuel P. Oliner

partially surrounded the ghetto, I saw a young Polish boy. He had a fat, white face and crooked teeth, and I'd had several fights with him in the past. Of course, he spotted me and immediately sounded off—*"Jude! Jude!"* Frantically, I searched for a way of escape, but I was at the edge of the ghetto, and there was no going back, no way out. Trapped, I rushed at the boy, desperately intent on choking the voice that was giving me away. The boy's eyes widened with fear. He dodged me and ran off screaming that a Jew was trying to kill him. Shaking like a leaf, I stumbled into one of those old, broken-down houses on the edge of the ghetto and hid in a small closet.

Very quickly it grew dark outside, and I spent the night in that house. There were dark and fearful sounds to keep me awake: the wind kicking garbage about, the noise of a board turned over, or of a door pushed open and then closed. Once I heard a sob and then, sometime later, a small, thin laugh in the darkness. Loudest of all was the pounding of my heart as I waited for some Nazi to open the door of the closet with the cold, blue steel of his rifle barrel. Only toward dawn did I manage to drift into and out of sleep.

But sleep was not more comforting than reality. It was filled with the faces of my family staring at me: not just my father and my stepbrother and stepsister but also my real mother, my oldest sister, Feigele, and my oldest brother, Moishe, whom I had not seen since I was sent into the ghetto. All the while the dark, sad eyes of Esther stared at me as she clutched her children and said, "I love you."

In the morning I realized I should have escaped during the night. The golden opportunity had come and gone. Now the Nazis were up and about, once more mopping up the ghetto. If I were killed, it would be my own fault. I was so scared that I could barely open my mouth, but I practiced being calm in case I had to speak to anyone.

I opened the closet door and looked out into the room. Through the windows the sun made yellow squares on the floor. The window panels were filmy and glared in the sunlight. I sneaked to the door of the house, pushed it open, and peeked outside. Mist was rising from the lane, which was dark and muddy. My clothing was caked with dirt from the day before, and the cool air made me shiver. The buildings along the lane were black and empty.

I left the house cautiously. I breathed deeply, and my belly growled. The ache of hunger was intense, making my feet numb and my head empty. As I stood there, wondering which way to go, a Nazi came around the corner of a building.

"Halt!" he said, yanking the rifle off his shoulder and pointing it at me. "Who are you?"

"Oh, I'm not Jewish."

Astonished at my own voice, I waited, holding my breath and expecting the Nazi to pull the trigger at any moment. He was a big man with short blond hair and slightly brown teeth. Looking me over from head to foot, he tried to make up his mind. Just then, another kid ran from the tangled hedge next to the house crying for his mother in Yiddish, "Mama, Mama, Mama!"

The guard took off after him, and I ran in the opposite direction. The shots rang out very clearly. I ran along the barbed-wire fence and then ducked down a narrow lane. The somber windows of the empty houses stared at me as I slipped and skidded in the mud. The main road was across a narrow footbridge and past a rickety wooden fence covered with vines. Throwing caution to the wind, I ran toward the fence. It was my luck to notice it, and I broke through it and ran into the Polish sector of Bobowa.

The Poles were conducting their business as if everything were normal. Dogs barked, and wooden carts creaked along the road. A man in a homespun shirt was harnessing his horse. Noticing my hurry, he stopped and looked at me: "Hey, are you a Jew?" He came toward me, and so I dodged down an alley. Dogs ran after me, barking at my heels. I stopped long enough to throw rocks at them, and then I went through town as quickly as possible without arousing further suspicion. After what seemed to me like a lifetime, I ran away into the countryside.

The country surrounding Bobowa was mildly hilly with small, scattered villages in the valleys. The Carpathian winters were very cold. Roads were poor year-round, deeply rutted, and, at certain points, sloped into ravines. And although it was now August, it was a little cold and the roads were muddy. My feet were bare as I followed the road away from Bobowa. I did not look back. I wondered what had happened to my parents and to the Jews of Bobowa. Where could they have been taken? Then I remembered the rumors in the ghetto about resettlement somewhere in the East. But where in the East? I kept wondering if I would ever see my family again. I kept hoping. My mind felt empty and dead. Wild grasses grew green along the hillsides. Cattle were in the high pastures. I trudged along, wishing I were a cow with food and shelter and nothing in the world to worry about.

Toward noon I came upon a farmer digging a ditch along the road. He wore a coarse homespun jacket and wooden shoes. His face was brown from exposure to the weather; a rough, gray stubble was on his chin. Taking courage, I approached him.

"Please, sir, could you give me some bread? I haven't eaten in two days."

He leaned on the shovel he had been working with and sized me up. I was certain he could tell I was a Jew. But I was too tired and hungry to run. Besides, where was I to go? The world seemed nothing but a cold and muddy road cut through hillsides of green and brown grass. When the farmer smiled, I saw that many of his teeth were missing.

"Come to my house and I'll give you some bread."

We walked toward a farmhouse on the side of a hill. A little trail of smoke came from the chimney. Behind the house was a shed for the animals (*stodola* in Polish).

"It looks like the Germans have cleaned out the wretched Jews from Bobowa," said the farmer. His footsteps were slow and methodical, but I had to hurry a little to keep up with him.

"What did they do with them? Where did the Germans take the Jews?" I asked.

"Oh, Jacek, my neighbor, told me they took them all to Garbacz."

"Where's that?" I tried not to sound too interested. The farmer squinted a little as he strode along.

"About fifteen kilometers up in the woods, not far from the village of Mszanka."

"And there, what are they going to do with them?"

The farmer laughed as if I had said something funny. "The Germans took care of everything," he said. "They shot every last one."

I stumbled and nearly fell and heard my voice burst out: "They shot them all?"

"Yes. Every one."

"But how can they shoot so many people?"

"They kept shooting them with machine guns all day long, and some of them just fell into the graves from the planks that were put across the mass grave."

"Does that mean that some people were alive when they fell into the grave?"

"Naked bodies, both dead and alive, were piled up one on top of another and covered up with chemicals and earth. Some, who were still alive and were on top of the pile of bodies, crawled out and ran away. A peasant saw one of these people; he looked totally insane, as if his brain had snapped."

Later I learned about Garbacz and that the trucks loaded with Jews— old men and women, young men, mothers, children—took them to a pre-dug mass grave in Garbacz, a small forest near the town of Gorlice. The people were forced to undress in the most vile and humiliating way and made to march about sixty feet across huge planks that were laid across the grave. The *Einsatzgruppen* shot them and watched them fall into the grave. Some were only wounded, but as the bodies piled up on top of each other, the wounded were trapped under the dead. There was absolute chaotic madness in the little forest of Garbacz; there was such fear and screaming that many Polish peasants living nearby escaped into the hills and woods because they did not know what to expect from the killers. It took eighteen hours to kill a thousand people, then bury them with a thin coat of soil. Some time later there was a movement in the grave—one Jewish man crawled out from under the thin layer of soil and escaped. He was totally out of his mind, and while he was wandering aimlessly from place to place, the Gestapo caught him and executed him in the same little forest of Garbacz.

I could not believe that such cruelty and evil was possible. I did not understand why innocent people would be murdered in such a humiliating and terrible way. The indignity of being undressed in front of these brutal, uniformed soldiers was beyond my comprehension. What did the soldiers feel as they were killing innocent men, women, and children? How did they relate to their own families? Were they able to love their wives and children?

After the man gave me some bread I wandered around the countryside for a while, dazed and in disbelief. I slept in barns or in fields and ate food off the land—carrots, apples, pears. I thought hard about what to do next, and I decided to go across the hills into another village adjacent to Mszanka, called Bystra. Balwina Piecuch, her husband, Jacek, their son, Staszek, and their daughter, Zosia, lived there. Balwina knew my family from before the war and had gone to school with my father in the local village of Mszanka. One night I knocked on her door, and she immediately recognized me. She already knew about what had happened at Garbacz. She saw how scared and disheveled I was, took me in, comforted me, hugged me, fed me, and let me go to sleep in the attic because it was unsafe for me to sleep downstairs. She knew that there was a traitor located nearby who made his living turning in to the Gestapo non-Jews who hid Jews. In exchange he was rewarded with food, clothing, and money. Very few people of that region will ever forget Krupa—this traitor, a murderous peasant.

Balwina informed me about the fate of the Jews. "In the cities," she said, "there are bands of Jews fighting the exterminators. There are fugitives hiding in the country." She thought me too young, at twelve years old, to fight with the partisans, that I would probably get killed very quickly. She told me about some peasants who keep their eyes out for Jews because the Gestapo will reward those who capture fugitives with boots and money and things like that. But if I did as she told me to do I would live. "Only by living will you honor your family, and I will help you. And some day, when the war is over, you will be a grown man; then you will be able to do things to remember your family and tell the world what has happened to your people."

"What type of name . . . who will I . . . what shall I take?"

"How about Jusek? Jusek . . . Polewski?"

"Okay. If you think—"

"Do you know Polish *pacierz* [prayers]? Daily catechism?"

"No, I don't."

"Do you know how to read?"

"No. Polish I cannot read."

"Then I will teach you, and you will memorize as much as possible." Then I was to go around to the villages nearby and look for a job. With what I learned, I would be just like a Polish Catholic boy. I would look around for a job and tell everyone who asks that my name is Jusek Polewski. And I would remember to be careful when I undressed so that no one would see the circumcision that would give me away. I knew by now what would happen if someone realized I was Jewish.

"I will watch myself," I told Balwina. I was so grateful to her for doing all this for me, for helping me. I do not know what I would have done without her. I was scared, though, really scared. Maybe someone would recognize me. I have been in many of the villages around here, and it was possible that someone would recognize my true identity.

"Don't be afraid," said Balwina. "You will act like a Polish gentile boy, and if you see anyone you know, avoid that person and watch yourself. Be careful. Now have breakfast."

Realizing that the egg was burned, she made another one and put it on the table. Her husband came in from outside. He was much younger than Balwina, uneducated and simple. Balwina wore the proverbial pants in the family, and whatever she said was the law. The man walked through the kitchen and into the other room. A boy about eleven years old came into the kitchen, followed by a younger girl.

"Staszek," said Balwina, "Sit at the table by Jusek. I might need you to help me. Yes, that's right. Now, Jusek, for that will be your name, let me try to teach you catechism. Okay, repeat after me and memorize what I say. After you get a job, try to go to church every Sunday."

"Our Father, who art in heaven, hallow'd be Thy name. . . ."

A boy of twelve has lots of imagination. But reality was quick and sharp to cut these fantasies in half. Tears are a funny thing—you imagine things, and the horror makes you cry until you think there are no tears left. Then you find out the truth, and there are plenty of tears all over again. Balwina told me of the execution at the forest of Garbacz, where my family and my people were stripped of their clothing that frigid June day and told to walk the wooden planks. And for days, it seemed, I cried. A thought or a word—

anything at all—sparked the feeling of agony. Balwina was always there, moving about like the mother I did not have. I'd had two mothers, and both were dead. Life seemed unbearably cruel. Balwina said Jewish fugitives were doing whatever they could just to stay alive. So as quickly as I could, I learned the Lord's Prayer.

The agony never went away, but the tears stopped, and only rarely after that did I cry again. Just to survive each day took supreme effort, and there was no time for tears. The Germans were everywhere, and Balwina was afraid I would be found out if I stayed with her. I kept practicing the Lord's Prayer, and I memorized it well. She showed me how to genuflect and make the sign of the cross when I walked by the numerous Catholic shrines. Balwina was very religious, and I thought, naively, that she sought the religious reward of converting an infidel. Really she was a humanitarian woman with a great, kindly heart. In order to help save another person's life, she was risking her own and her family's safety during the entire period I stayed with her.

The days passed, and early one morning Balwina climbed the stairs to the attic. She was still in her nightshirt. The roosters had not yet crowed; she gently shook the shoulder of Jusek Polewski. "Wake up, Jusek. Wake up. Remember now, your name is no longer Shmulek Oliner. Jusek, it will be dawn in just a short while, and if you hurry no one will be able to recognize you. I want you to leave soon. Go to some of the nearby villages across the hills and look for a job. Go from house to house and ask if anyone needs a *pastuch* [cowhand or stable boy]." She began to cry. "I will miss you. Be careful. If you ever . . . if it's safe—but only if it's safe—try to come back some night and visit and tell me where you are. Now be very careful because you know what that means for us."

"Of course," I replied. "I know what would happen if anyone found out, and I will be very careful. I am grateful to you for letting me stay. I am very, very grateful. And someday, if I ever survive this, I will never forget you."

As I was prepared to leave with some bread for the road, Balwina cried, "You poor boy. I will help; you must live." Yet, she and the family determined that it would be safer for me to be on the outside—less likely to be betrayed and caught. As I left, she hugged me and insisted that I let her know when I found a job as a stable boy, and which village I was in across the hills.

The premature death of my mother had saved her much sorrow, and I wondered if she was watching over me. It began to occur to me that death was, indeed, forever. In fact, it seemed death was the only certainty there was. And if death was forever, then there had to be some meaning to the shortness of life—there must be some hope in living. I tried to remember what my mother looked like, but there was just an impression, the smell of *Shabbat* bakings. Even the face of my stepmother was sliding away into the sound of a harsh voice, the look of fear, the touch of last-minute tenderness. Also sliding away was Shmulek Oliner. He was a thing of the past, buried in the memories of people now dead.

I was certainly not an unusual sight walking barefoot on the road leading away from Bystra, the village where Balwina lived. Since the Germans had entered Poland, a lot of homes had been broken up. Orphaned children were frequently seen on the roads, and the Poles generally treated them well. I hitchhiked along the road, and peasants would pick me up in their old wooden carts. They shared with me their black-crusted bread and joked in a friendly manner.

In spite of their kindness, I lived in constant fear of being found out. I imagined how glad these poor, friendly Poles would be for a pair of boots or a few hundred *zlotys* (Polish currency). Some Poles, such as Krupa, sometimes crippled a captive just for fun before delivering him to the Gestapo, and I vividly imagined this being done to me.

I prepared a story that I had a brother and a very poor mother who could not keep me around the house, and so she had asked me to find a job. Ironically, I found one right away at a Jewish farm in the nearby village of Biesnik. The Jews who owned it had been exterminated, and the farm was rented to a childless non-Jewish couple called Podworski. After I told them who I was—the new me—they hired me—but they insisted on meeting my mother. I kept making excuses about how my mother could not come anytime soon. During the Christmas of 1942—my first Christmas spent with the Podworskis—they sent me back to visit my mother. So I sneaked back over the hills through the snow and ended up at Balwina's house. There I was received with love, assurances that the war would come to an end soon, and encouragement to have hope so I might survive to tell the world what had happened to my family and to me.

Staszek, acting the role of my brother, came from time to time either to warn me of danger because the Gestapo was searching for Jews or to pass on encouraging information from Balwina. I worked for the Podworski's for approximately two and a half years as a stable boy, taking care of the cattle while continuing to conceal my identity. After liberation by the Soviet army in March 1945, I left the childless couple for whom I worked, and who I believed did not know I was Jewish, and I went back to Balwina because now it was safe.[1]

What made Balwina take the heroic high road and risk her life for me? Balwina was a simple peasant, a religious woman who lived the Christian teaching of love, charity, and compassion. She knew to help a Jew was a very risky act from which she had nothing to gain except tragedy, but she also felt we all belonged to a human community. Balwina's acts of kindness have remained with me to this day and have had a substantial influence on my personal and academic life.

For the last thirty years my academic interests have concerned two major topics: the nature of evil, and the nature of goodness. As a result of my experience during the Holocaust, I became interested in exploring the roots of evil, studying and teaching about racism, anti-Semitism, genocide, homophobia, ageism, and similar oppressions. However, most of my efforts have focused on goodness. What made Balwina care about me enough to risk her life and that of her family in order to hide me, to teach me about the dangers that might befall me (including that of my circumcision being discovered), instruct me to go to church like a good Catholic boy, and show her continued caring by keeping in touch with me throughout the three long years of my hiding out in the open in Biesnik?

I have long reflected on this question and, in recent years, have revisited her family several times. I see in Balwina a religious, compassionate, and strong woman. Balwina and her family were awarded the Righteous Medal from Yad Vashem in Israel, which to this date has recognized approximately 16,000 non-Jews, designating them the Righteous of the World. On the medal is inscribed a saying from the Talmud: "He/she who saves one life is as if he/she saves the entire universe."[2]

Although there are many instances of injustice and cruelty that occur in the world (such as the killing of my family by the Nazis when I was a young boy), there are also many acts of compassion, kindness, and caring. This book is motivated by the belief that informing ourselves about the lives and acts of caring and compassionate individuals can restore to us a sense of hope and a positive image of humankind. In writing it, I sought to gain a deeper understanding of these compassionate (small *h*) heroes and their acts of altruism—and especially what lessons we can learn from them to carry into the future.

Throughout the book we will use true stories to illustrate the various types of altruism and illuminate the early lives of those whose altruism has brought them to our attention. We need to see that heroes, altruists, and good people of all sorts live among us—and always have.

Stories have an important moral impact because they not only explain an event and arouse emotions about moral and immoral acts but also inform the reader about what reality is. The narrative story serves as a general metaphor for understanding human conduct, and people remember episodes and stories better than abstract ideas or semantic memory.[3]

The purpose of *this* book, then, is to examine heroism and altruism in different settings and to draw conclusions about its role in the world we live in now. There are everyday heroes among us, both trained and uniformed like the firefighters who risked their lives in the World Trade Center on September 11. In a post–September 11 world we recognize that the importance of altruistic acts—understanding altruism's various characteristics and motivations and teaching them to future generations—is especially vital.

There are abundant stories of heroic acts of September 11, some uniformed and trained, as well as others who risked their own lives for the welfare of others. What was the motivation of these people to be with and comfort others during such crises? Why did they not save themselves but risked their life to save others? The following two examples shed light on their motivations, and that they had internalized certain habits of the heart, consisting of compassion and social responsibility for their fellow human beings.

Abe Zelmanowitz's heroic decision to die rather than abandon his wheelchair-bound friend was typical of him, say friends. At his funeral, his act was considered to be that of the ultimate *mensch*—a descent human being. He and Edward F. Beyea, a disabled man in a wheelchair, had worked for Blue Cross on the twenty-seventh floor of the North Tower for about twenty years. They became very good friends. After the hijacked airliner was crashed into the tower, Zelmanowitz stayed at Ed's side; he could have easily escaped and saved himself. Relatives say he was a kind, compassionate, and generous human being. His sister-in-law, Evelyn, maintained that September 11 was an extraordinary day. It was his choice not to desert his helpless friend; it would have never entered his mind. Zelmanowitz, an Orthodox Jew, and Beyea, a Protestant, shared an incredible amount of respect and devotion for one another. Abe would always phone ahead and make sure that the restaurants they went to were wheelchair-accessible. Abe's rabbi, Rabbi Halberstam of Sharei Zion Synagogue, said, "Abe could walk out on his own two feet. Every one of his coworkers is alive, but Abe had a different purpose. He was not leaving another human being to die alone."[4]

Police Officer Nancy Ramos was nearly buried alive when the South Tower collapsed; court officer Edwin Kennedy was her hero. When the first plane hit the World Trade Center, each officer had had only two years on the job. Blocks away from each other at the time, they rushed to help evacuate dozens of people before the South Tower collapsed. But the force of the collapse blew them both into a ruined Borders bookstore. Ramos remembers, "It was pitch black. I fell to the ground." At first Kennedy thought he was dead because of the deadening silence, but then he heard voices call out, "Anybody alive?" and then he realized he was alive. He remembered Ramos having been near him moments before, and he began to search in the darkness and rubble to look for her. Although she had sprained her ankle and was blinded by the dust and darkness, she soon felt her hand in his, and then she knew he wouldn't leave her. He said to her, "I got you. Don't worry. Remember your training. Remember your training." After he dragged Ramos to safety, he realized the extent of his own injuries—his lungs were seared and his left shoulder damaged. Eventually they both went back to work. Ramos got married, but she wanted to find her rescuer. After finding out who he was, she arranged a surprise reunion with the help of his coworkers and TV cameras. He shied from being called a hero and rather felt bad about three of his colleagues who had perished. To her, "He's my hero. He's part of my family now."[5]

The word "altruism" is derived from the Latin root *alter*, which means "other." To Auguste Comte, the father of sociology, "altruism" meant the discipline and eradication of self-centered desire and a life devoted to the good of others, particularly selfless love and a devotion to society.[6]

I have been that *other*—the recipient of selfless love—and had it not been for the altruistic instincts of one person, I would have died almost before my life had really begun. Over the years I have tried to understand altruism, to discover what leads to caring and compassion, to name what gives an individual a sense of social responsibility, and what it means to put the welfare of others alongside one's own. This book is equally personal and interpretive. Balwina Piecuch's act of compassion was the spark that led me here. Had it not been for her abiding love, caring, and specifically focused advice about how to survive and what to do, I would not be here. Her acts of kindness put me on the road to researching (see Appendix A) and trying to understand goodness.

Why are some people able to help whereas others are simply bystanders when they notice someone in need? The stories included in the chapters that follow will help us understand the nature of heroic and conventional altruism.

2

❧

"Let's Roll!"

Heroes of 9/11

I begin this journey with two heroes—Rick Rescorla (a 9/11 hero) and an anonymous Carnegie hero—to illustrate a single type of heroic behavior by civilians.[1] Later in the chapter, I will also describe other altruistic activities, which include individuals in a variety of situations, from those who are uniformed, trained, and paid, who perform acts of great courage beyond the call of duty, to rescuers during the Holocaust, as well as those who help in other settings. I begin by telling the story of this 9/11 hero.

Rick Rescorla was a security officer for the brokerage firm Morgan Stanley, which occupied twenty-five floors (1.5 million square feet) in the South Tower of the World Trade Center. While the South Tower was collapsing, someone yelled over the loudspeaker that people should return to work because the North Tower was safe and secure. Rescorla ignored the orders and hurried all the employees out of the tower. Rescorla had a varied life. He was born in Hayle, Cornwall, England, some sixty-two years before to a single mother, but he was raised as her younger brother. For a long time he did not know that his grandparents were *not* his parents and that his biological mother was *not* his older sister. He was involved in military service in Britain, taking part in a number of different war zones. He was an extremely brave man and strong leader, participating in all kinds of battles for England, including Cypress, and serving with Scotland Yard as a detective. But by age twenty-four he was bored by his work at Scotland Yard, so in 1963 he came to the United

States and took basic training at Fort Dix, New Jersey. He was sent to Officer's Candidate School at Fort Benning, Georgia, and there again Rescorla emerged as a swaggering leader, belting out Cornish and English songs with his powerful voice. After graduating as a second lieutenant in 1965, Rescorla was assigned to platoon leader in Bravo Company of the 2nd Battalion of the 7th Cavalry division. In 1965 he was sent to Vietnam, where he distinguished himself. He was a powerful, courageous, and confident soldier who was involved in a variety of very dangerous battles. His courage was so pervasive that morale in his unit was quite high. He appeared on the front cover of the book *We Were Soldiers Once . . . and Young*, which was made into a movie staring Mel Gibson. The book was written by General G. Moore and war corespondent Joseph Galloway and dealt with the Battle of Ia Drang, in which Rescorla played an important role. Even though there were times when U.S. soldiers were in bad shape because the enemy was shelling them, Rescorla went from foxhole to foxhole joking with soldiers and encouraging them to hold on. One of the soldiers said of him, "What a commanding presence he had." During the battle he saved a number of his men by lobbing grenades at enemy machine-gunners. In 1968, when he came out of the war at the rank of a colonel, he attempted a number careers, including studying at the University of Oklahoma, with the help of the G.I. Bill. He became interested in many different topics, including Shakespeare and the law. Although he was well read, he felt that he was not cut out to be an academic. In 1985 he moved to New Jersey and became director of security for the Wall Street brokerage firm Dean Witter, which later merged with Morgan Stanley and took offices in the South Tower of the World Trade Center. In his work, he established a military kind of procedure to ensure that security was well handled. Several times he warned the management of the Twin Towers that there would be attempts to bring trucks loaded with explosives into the underground garages of the towers. Later on he was even predicting that there would be cargo planes loaded with explosives and bombs flying into buildings. His ingenuity was for anticipating danger, and that's what made him so courageous. On September 11, when a plane struck the North Tower at 8:48 A.M., Morgan Stanley had 2,700 employees working on more than two dozen floors spanning the middle floors of the building. Some supervisors were urging employees to stay calm and to continue working, but Rescorla contradicted these orders and quickly moved employees out of the building. After all the employees left, he telephoned to Morgan Stanley headquarters located in Midtown Manhattan that he was going back to search for stragglers. Earlier John Olson, Morgan Stanley's regional director, saw Rescorla reassuring colleagues on the tenth-floor stairwell and said to him, "Rick, you've got to get out, too." He answered, "As soon as I make sure everyone else is out." It was reported that he said to some Morgan Stanley employees, "Today is a day to be proud to be Americans, and tomorrow the whole world will be talking about you." He was also heard saying, "God Bless America" and singing Cornish folk tunes in the stairwells. At home his wife Susan watched anxiously as another airplane crashed into her husband's tower, and she became terrified. After a while the phone rang; it was her husband. He said to her, "I don't want you to cry. I have to evacuate my people now." He added, "If something happens to me, I want you to know that you made my life"—and the phone went dead. Rescorla did not make it out, and neither did two other security officers who were at his side. Only three other Morgan Stanley employees died as the building disintegrated, the second to be hit but the first to fall.[2]

Why did Rescorla act so courageously? Why did he have an overpowering concern for the safety of others? It is clear from various narratives and reports, including those of his wife, that throughout his life he was a risk-taker and did not fear death. He was a man who was prone to singing and joking in dangerous situations. He kept his wall photos and medals in the closet and told his wife that he did not want to see the film *We Were Soldiers* when it was released. His heroic undertakings throughout his adult life, including British and U.S. military service, was typical of his overwhelming sense of the Code of Honor and caring. He cared greatly for his fellow soldiers and for the 2,700 employees who worked for Morgan Stanley. After Rick Rescorla perished, there was a petition to President George W. Bush to honor him with the Presidential Medal of Freedom. Many thousands of signatures have already been collected, including mine, and sent to the president.[3]

Courage and caring were motivating factors in the case of Rick Rescorla; what does he have in common with the 24-year-old printer, a Carnegie hero-rescuer, who saved several women from drowning after their van swerved off a windy road into a lake? The printer was on a cross-country team that went to Canada for a weeklong vacation every year before the school semester started. He was in his Jeep, and there were two vans—one full of guys, one full of girls. The three vehicles were going along, his Jeep in the middle, the guys' van in front and the girls' van behind. They were about five miles from the cabin where they were staying, and the road got windy at that point.

There was a very sharp curve coming up, so he slowed down, went around it, then sped up again to go on the straightaway. He then looked into his rearview mirror just to see how the van behind him was going to take this curve. To his astonishment, it went through the roadside barricade. The barricades were short lengths of telephone poles laced together with cable. There wasn't much to hold the van on up the road; it snapped through the railing, flew over an embankment, and crashed into the water, which was about ten feet deep. He stopped the Jeep and rushed to the embankment.

According to his account:

> I got to the van it was rolling in the water, doing belly rolls. And the windows on one side of it broke because when it rolled it hit rocks in the bottom so the windows on one side all gave out. . . . I got there, and two girls . . . were both screaming their lungs out. I pulled out Jen as it came rolling around . . . and it went down with Annie still hanging out of the window. So I went down to get her as it went under, and then she came back up. . . . She got out by herself, then I pulled her to shore—it was like one yank. Then there was a ten-second period where [the van] just sank, it disappeared. . . . I couldn't imagine not doing it. You know, I was right in the middle of it. I couldn't imagine not doing it. . . . I imagined going to ten different funerals at ten different times and talking to ten sets of parents. . . . When I pulled the first girl out, [I thought] one down, nine to go. I've got to do the best I can.

Looking through the interview transcript for explanations for risking his life to save the women from drowning, I found that the young man was a good swimmer and felt self-confident in the situation and sure that he could help. From his parents he learned the virtue of caring, courage, self-reliance, and helping others in need.

Learning to Care

What are the conditions that produce altruistic people? We have learned that happy preschoolers who have higher empathy are more altruistic than sad ones. Children and adults who easily sense what others are feeling and vicariously share that feeling are more likely to be altruistic than children and adults who do not. Preschoolers who readily express their feelings to teachers or peers when they are distressed are more likely to be helpful than inexpressive children. Children who are more popular and helpful express a stronger need to belong or to be connected with others. Adults who have a generally positive view of human beings are more apt to offer help to those in need than are misanthropes.[4]

In order to raise caring and moral children, parents have to provide emotional support and love, inculcate in children the difference between right and wrong, teach them to be responsible and feel empathy for others, develop self-esteem, make children feel that they matter, and discipline in a loving manner.[5]

Dennis Krebs and Frank van Hesteren advise us about the developmental stages that children go through. Their prosocial behavior may encompass such things as *smiling and cooing* in response to stimulation. This stage is followed by *egocentric accommodation,* behaviors oriented to fulfilling their own needs. Next is the *cooperative stage,* doing one's share in concrete exchange with others. Then comes *mutual altruism,* being sensitive to the audience of the generalized other (to other people). This is aimed at fulfilling shared roles of obligation and avoiding social disapproval and even sustaining a good reputation and upholding friendship; in a word, securing a place in the community. *Conscientious altruism* is oriented toward fulfilling an internalized obligation to assist in maintaining the institutions of the society and not violate the expectations of one's group. *Autonomous altruism,* the next stage of altruistic development, is based on a more internal higher order of principles. This stage is guided by internally held values such as upholding human dignity and the human rights of liberty and justice for all. *Integrated altruism,* then, transcends self and integrates with humanity in general. Finally, there is *universal love,* also known as *agape.* This stage is the most mature and most inclusive. It is an ethical, responsible, universal love, encompassing service and sacrifice for humanity and upholding the dignity of the recipient of such help.[6]

It is useful for the sake of discussion to categorize altruistic behaviors into types. Behavior is *heroically* altruistic when (1) it is directed toward helping another; (2) it involves a high degree of risk or sacrifice to the actor; (3) it is accompanied by no external reward; and (4) it is voluntary. It is *conventionally* altruistic when it does not involve a high degree of risk or sacrifice to the actor.

Within the heroic category, I discern three different types of heroic altruists. The first one consists of 9/11 heroes—professionally trained individuals such as Rick Rescorla who are paid to help in emergency situations. Examples are firefighters, police officers, members of the U.S. Coast Guard, military heroes, and the like. The second type of heroic altruists are nonprofessional, nonpaid individuals who respond to emergency and life-threatening situations and are involved for a short duration. Examples of these are World Trade Center and Pentagon rescuers and the heroes recognized by the Carnegie Foundation for risking their lives to save victims in very serious situations (see Chapter 5). The third type of heroic altruists are also nonpaid but are involved for long duration and the involvement can be life-threatening to them. Rescuers of Jews in Nazi-occupied Europe and resistance workers against injustice are examples of the third type of heroic altruists (a detailed discussion follows in Chapters 3 and 4). The fourth type of altruist is conventional, which is of long duration and not life-threatening to the helper/altruist.

Conventional altruism differs from the heroic only in that it does not usually entail risk to the life of the helper.[7] This category includes general volunteers, hospice volunteers, moral exemplars, and philanthropists. Moral exemplars are individuals who have a moral commitment to achieve justice, equality, and fairness for those in the community who are in need of loving kindness, compassion, and caring. Philanthropists are individuals who desire to help humankind, especially shown by gifts to charitable or humanitarian institutions and individuals.

Throughout the book, we will use stories to illustrate the various types of altruism and illuminate the early lives of those whose altruism has brought them to our attention. We need to see that heroes, altruists, and good people of all sorts live among us and always have.

Philosophers have told us that human beings in almost every culture have the capability of both evil and good. Humans possess both the nature of *evil* and *evil inclinations* as well as the nature of *goodness* and *loving kindness*.

Earlier in this chapter, I mentioned some familial behaviors that generate goodness. But what are the roots of evil? What might cause humans to be evil, to commit acts with bad moral consequences, consequences that cause pain, injury, or trouble to others?

Among the important explanations for causes of evil is this: When a person or group feels that they have been mistreated and wronged they will find an enemy, real or imaginary, that has wronged them. They retaliate against that enemy, buttressed by the ideology of hate and uncritical evaluation of the cause of their grievance. Some grievances are all too real. Economic deprivation, cultural and political invasion by a stronger power, oppression of various kinds are all, sadly, part of human heritage. This perception of being wronged is frequently a justification for striking out at the perceived enemy. Thus, Adolf Hitler, Osama bin Laden, and others have defined some cultures, groups, and individuals as the enemy that has caused them problems that can only be met with murder and violence. In the case of Germany, Hitler articulated an enemy who "stabbed them in the back." These enemies were the victorious Allied powers of World War I, as well as Jews, Bolsheviks, and Slavs.

Why are ordinary people who profess to love their wives, children, and their own community able to perform extraordinary acts of violence without moral restraint? Some psychologists talk about the process of *doubling*, which separates the personality and thus makes the killing possible. This process creates two opposing bands of the self, which are walled off from each other to avoid internal conflict. In the case of the Nazi doctors, doubling was buttressed by anti-Semitic Nazi ideology and dehumanization of the Jews, which then made it easier for the perpetrators of mass murders to accomplish their missions.

In order to murder others, one has first to define them out of the human race or as diabolic oppressors. This seems to be the way Americans are perceived by radical fundamental Islamic groups such as Al-Qaida and Islamic Jihad. Second, the role of leaders is vitally important. Evil leaders, through their abilities to arouse popular sentiment, are able to define the outsider as the enemy and find a following with blind obedience to their power and authority. Hitler and his henchmen, or people obeying Al-Qaida directives from fanatic leaders such as bin Laden and others, are able to persuade their followers to destroy "the enemy."

Humans are enemy-making animals. They construct a portrait of others as unworthy and define them out of the human race. This has caused many millions of deaths in the twentieth century alone as a result of wars, rebellions, and genocidal massacres. Modern technology distances killing and mass murder, and it is too often covered up by euphemisms such as "collateral damage." It is very difficult for "normal people" to fathom the evil acts of destruction of which some people are capable.

September 11 will be remembered. It may not be the largest mass murder in one day in the history of the world—Hiroshima, Nagasaki, and the bombing of Hamburg have taken larger tolls on life in a single day. Still, this happened to the United States, a superpower secure between two oceans, and it was the most unexpected surprise in U.S. history, the attack on Pearl Harbor notwithstanding. Why such *evil* occurred at all is a question that historians, sociologists, economists, political scientists, philosophers, poets, and playwrights will be debating and attempting to explain for many decades. It is a sad fact of modern society that ideology, competitiveness, and position drive people into a busy whirl where some cannot discern the difference between good and evil.

The well-planned attack on the Twin Towers and the Pentagon has shocked Americans. The wounds are deep in the people. I have read a substantial amount of material on the topic since September 11 and have visited Ground Zero in New York several times. Articles still appear in the press daily about the tragedy and how individuals behaved in the face of terrorism. Many of these individuals acted courageously. They exhibited a sense of *goodness* and *caring*, which we define as virtuous, kind, and benevolent. *Courage* can sometimes be a necessary element of loving kindness, agape, empathy, and ethical care for the other. Indeed, sometimes social responsibility in extreme situations will require the sacrificing of one's life for the other. The words "heroic altruism" are certainly appropriate in many cases of 9/11 rescues and attempted rescues in which firefighters, policemen, and port authority officers perished trying to save others.

There were many heroes during and after September 11. Individuals in both the North and South Towers refused to leave their comrades even though they could have easily saved themselves. They stayed with the disabled, the elderly, or others who could not make it out—and some paid with their lives. A great number of other firefighters and police officers rushed into those exploding towers in order to save lives. Some were successful, but many perished. It is estimated by now that in all 2,931 people died, including 319 firefighters, 50 police officers, and 27 port authority officers. We can say that because they were paid to do it—it was the *duty* of the firefighters, port authority police, and other police officers to save lives. Yet many of those brave individuals did not have to go beyond the regulation call of their duty. And it is clear now that many did. They did not have to climb to the top floors knowing that they would not return alive; yet they did just that.[8]

Thus, the definition of "heroism" must include acts of bravery beyond the call to save a life even though the actor was paid and trained for it. It is not only an unpaid volunteer who is a hero. The Carnegie hero who dove into the river to save a life, or the numerous other acts of bravery in rescue that the Carnegie award recognizes, are heroic acts. These citizens were neither trained nor paid nor were they expected to do what they did. They saw a tragedy occurring and acted heroically, because to them life was sacred. So, too, the police officers, firefighters, and port authority officers in the September 11 tragedy deserve the moniker "hero" for their courage beyond the call of duty. [9]

Uniformed Heroes: Trained in Courage

Recalling the types of heroic altruist, the first type designates heroes who are *trained uniform and paid professional emergency rescuers involving high risk*. These are firefighters, police officers, and Coast Guard personnel. Although these people are trained professionally and are expected to save lives, they perform acts beyond the call of duty at all times. Another example is military heroes, who are expected to honor the code of courage and bravery and to protect their comrades. At times, they go beyond what is expected of them, for instance, by throwing themselves on a grenade in order to save their colleagues. These acts of bravery are heroic, and it is expected of them to take risk, but it is not expected that they should lose their lives in the process. No Western army demands that sort of ultimate sacrifice of its soldiers.

The most common heroes among us are trained, paid, and uniformed civil service employees like police officers and firefighters. Occasionally, they sacrifice themselves for the welfare of the stranger, but they accept this possibility, for it "comes with the job." The following are a few examples of such heroes:

- Matt Mosley, a thirty-year-old Atlanta firefighter, saved the life of Ivers Sims, a construction worker perched atop a construction crane looming 220 feet above a burning building. The smoke and flames were engulfing Sims, and he had started praying to God to save him. Mosley was harnessed to the end of a fifty-foot rope tied on to a helicopter and appeared like an angel out of the heavens. Mosley was not fond of heights, but he nevertheless volunteered to rescue Sims. He harnessed Sims to the rope, and both men were flown to safety. On ABC-TV's Good Morning America, Mosley denied being a hero, saying he was just doing his job. He also said he was more scared of morning talk shows than he was of the firefight and rescue.

- Policeman Stephen Driscoll was in the World Trade Center heading up to save people when the tower collapsed. People who were attending his funeral services would say that he was an individual that if one percent of all the people Steven helped showed up, they would fill Madison Square Garden and people would still be in the parking lot. His friends thought of him as having one of the greatest hearts in the world. Caring and loving were essential parts of his personality. Reverend William Kalaidjian, former New York Police Department chaplain, said of Driscoll, "There wasn't anything he couldn't do for anyone else if they needed it. He would be the epitome of helpfulness."[10] His concern and friendship with all he came in touch with was spoken of over and over by many people at the funeral service.

- U.S. Coast Guard personnel are another example. The Coast Guard consists of 40,000 personnel and is the fifth part of our defenses; it receives about 70,000 distress calls annually and saves more than 3,600 lives in the process. Other ordinary people jump into rivers and ditches in order to save drowning people. In the press recently we saw the statement that we should stop promoting athletes to inappropriate levels and start looking elsewhere for inspiration. Let us begin to look at other uniforms—those of ordinary people performing extraordinary feats. Let us look in the mirror and hope that we might be so brave should the occasion ever arise.

Nontrained Heroic Helpers

The second type of heroic altruist is *not paid but is also short duration and involves risk to one's life*. These kinds of heroes are mostly civilians (and include Carnegie heroes discussed in Chapter 5) like Michael Benfante and John Cerqueira, who carried a disabled woman strapped in a special chair down sixty-eight floors in a World Trade Center stairwell to safety at a time when the buildings around them were melting. There was tremendous smoke, and they were being asphyxiated in the stairwell. Benfante, thirty-six, who was a manager in an office, ordered everyone out of the stairwell and with the help of Cerqueira saved the woman in the wheelchair. They did not know her name. They put the wheelchair into a special chair in the stairwell designed for such emergencies, strapped her in, and began a long journey down as the building continually blazed. Others around them pitched in to help carry from time to time, but Benfante and Cerqueira never let go. When Cerqueira was asked why he helped, he said that in the back of his mind he could hear his mother tell him to get out of there quickly and save himself— but instead he decided to help save a life.

Sometimes heroes act because the opportunity demands it. During United Flight 93, the hijackers took over the plane and were probably flying either to the Capitol or to the White House. There were four men that we know about aboard the flight: Todd Beamer, who made the phrase "Let's roll" famous, Thomas Burnett, Mark Bingham, and Jeremy Glick, each of whom got in touch with loved ones and informed them that they were being hijacked and were going to take action. They managed somehow to overcome the hijackers and caused the plane to crash in a field in Pennsylvania instead of into its intended target. Thus, the situation in which these heroes found themselves is an excellent example of people voluntarily arising to act in a specific situation of short duration.[11]

We also know that other passengers tried bravely to help. Flight attendant Barbara Bradshaw identified the hijackers and then called her husband in Greensborough, North Carolina. She had been moved to the back of the plane, and she said that she and other passengers planned to rush the captors. Another passenger, Honor Elizabeth Wainio, also apparently had plans to rush the hijackers. In a call she made to her stepmother using a mobile phone lent to her by Lauren Grandcolas, she said, "I've got to go now, Mom, they are breaking into the cockpit."[12] Those who were involved in trying to storm the hijackers on Flight 93 had never been heard of before that day as particularly heroic individuals. Therefore, we conclude that the situation made them act that way.

Another example is Father Mychal Judge, who was a chaplain in the New York Fire Department. He was a priest in love with helping, expressing his sense of brotherhood, comradeship, family, altruism, and religious faith at all times in his relations with others, especially firefighters. One particular parishioner/firefighter said that he was scared to be in the world without Father Mike. Father Mike was trying to help administer last rights to a dying firefighter as objects and debris were falling. Father Mike removed his helmet and was struck and killed by falling debris.

Consistent stories of heroes have informed us that there is a touch of nobility among those individuals; they have certain personality traits of courage, caring, and empathy. People involved in the tragedy said that they could not just simply stand by. One particular example of an act of courage and caring was by a man, Austin Anderson, of Lakewood, Colorado. Before September 11, he was driving down Interstate 25 and saw a man in a car drifting back and forth, getting close to the center rail. Anderson realized there was something wrong. He was thinking of his grandfather, who had had a stroke while driving the freeway five years prior, and he thought that this might be a similar case. The driver was drifting to the left, and the sixty-nine-year-old man swerved into the median three times. Anderson called emergency 911, pulled behind the car, and jumped from the truck that he was driving. The driver could have killed many people on the road. As it turns out, the elderly driver was diabetic, had forgotten to take his insulin, and went into a coma. Due to the action of Austin Anderson, the man's life was saved. Recently, the Denver Fire Department awarded Anderson commendations for his actions. When people praised Anderson as a hero, he stated that he was not; he just saw a guy in trouble and helped. He was more in disbelief that no one else had bothered to help. Many brave men and women that we interviewed also did not regard their risky helping behavior as being particularly heroic.

After September 11 at Ground Zero, there were numerous volunteers who were digging the sad and tragic ground for bodies, and doing it around the clock. Many of these volunteers were firefighters and police officers who took off-duty time to help, and many were ordinary citizens who felt the need to help at this difficult time. It is reported that so many people volunteered that after three days the rescue teams had to stop accepting volunteers because there were so many.

One of my colleagues demonstrated to me another example of a situation that aroused in him the need to help. He said that he and his young son were sitting by a huge rock near a river in Southern California when they suddenly noticed a child who was drowning. Although my colleague was not a very good swimmer, he jumped into the river to rescue the boy. He grabbed the panicked child, who tried to pull him down, then quickly turned the boy's back toward himself, preventing the child from drowning them both. Only when they had reached the shore were others there to offer assistance. His explanation for his brave act was, "What would my young son think of me if we both stood there and watched a tragedy in progress."

Long-Term Heroic Altruists

The third type of heroic altruism is also *unpaid and voluntary and involves great risk, but it is over a long duration.* Jewish and non-Jewish rescuers of Jews in Nazi-occupied Europe fit this category. There are many of stories regarding these events, some of which will be discussed in Chapters 3 and 4. During World War II, the Nazi regime in Europe was methodical in its quest to exterminate all Jews. Squads of soldiers searched homes and created great fear and paranoia among all the villagers and city-dwellers. They wanted to instill a sense of suspicion among the people in order to reach their goal. However, there were many Jews and non-Jews who resisted the Nazis and wanted to save the lives of those who could not help themselves. The following story illustrates long-term heroic altruism, which involved high risk to the helper during the Holocaust. In fact, in Poland approximately 2,000 Catholics lost their lives when the Nazis discovered that they were hiding Jews.

In Warsaw a young couple saved two young Jewish brothers from the Warsaw ghetto. Soon after the Warsaw ghetto was established there was misery, hunger, and deprivation. Mr. Roslan, whom I interviewed, knew a Jewish woman who had three young sons. Mr. and Mrs. Roslan had a boy and a girl of their own. When he found out that the Warsaw ghetto was going to be liquidated, he sneaked into the ghetto and asked the Jewish woman to let him save her three boys. What mother would want to give up her children even to a man whom she knew well and trusted? (They had traded food for cloth, watches, and other items in the past.) Finally the Jewish mother was convinced that she should give her boys up for safekeeping. One night, Mr. Roslan came and sneaked one child at a time through a hole in the ghetto wall and took them to his apartment. Not long after, one of the Jewish boys became very sick, and even though Mr. Roslan tried everything possible to help him, he died. Mr. Roslan did not know Jewish burial ritual; he put the boy into a basket and covered him with a white cloth. Because it was too dangerous for him to take the dead body out to bury it in a Jewish cemetery, he dug a hole in the dirt basement of the building and buried the child there.

When the second Jewish boy became very sick, the Roslans were determined not to let him die. They tried everything possible, including hiring a non-Jewish doctor who secretly came to their apartment to examine him. The doctor told them that if the child were not taken to the hospital right away he would also die of the infection. Mr. Roslan wondered how he could get the boy to the hospital without anyone betraying him. Because he traded old furniture, he cut out a big hole in one of the stuffed couches, stuck the boy in there, and told him to be very quiet. Mr. Roslan and his brother-in-law put the couch on a horse-drawn wagon and took him to the hospital. To the neighbors it looked like he was trading furniture, and at the hospital it looked like he was delivering a couch. The boy was given treatment and then returned home in the same manner. Due to the courage of the Roslans, two boys survived. When I interviewed the Roslans in Los Angeles forty-five years after the event, tears welled up in their eyes as they told me of the boy who died because they could not save him. They, too, exhibited courage and determination to keep a promise to the mother at the Warsaw ghetto.

One of the righteous during the Holocaust was Janusz Korczak, about whom Pope John Paul II recently said, "For the world today, Janusz Korczak is a symbol of true religion and true morality." In Betty Jean Lifton's *The King of Children* she discusses this courageous pediatrician, author, philosopher, and humanist advocated a Magna Carta for children's rights.[13] His most famous book, *King Matt the First*, tells of a young child trying to reform the world. This story is as beloved in Poland as *Peter Pan* and *Alice in Wonderland* are in the English-speaking world. He also wrote *How to Love a Child* and, in the 1930s, had a radio program called *The Old Doctor*, through which he dispensed homely wisdom and humor. Critics proclaimed him a new voice in Polish literature.

He was born Hersch Goldszmit in 1879 but adopted Korczak as his pen name when he submitted a manuscript in competition with other authors and used it for the rest of his life. His grandfather was a glazier and his father an eminent lawyer who went mad and died at a relatively young age. Korczak supported his family by tutoring students and then went to medical school, specializing in pediatrics and doing his residency at a Jewish children's hospital in Warsaw. In 1905 he was conscripted as a doctor to the czar in the imperial army to serve in the Russian-Japanese War. He returned from the war in 1906 and found that he was quite well known as a result of his books, including *The Child of the Drawing Room*. Because of his father's madness, he feared passing on the genes of madness and decided not to marry. Instead, he wanted to help children, which he did for most of his adult life.

After Polish independence in 1919, the minister of education asked Korczak to set up an orphanage for children of Polish workers in the small town of Pruszkow, fifty kilometers south of Warsaw, which he did. Thus, he became a director of two orphanages. The one in Pruszkow was Catholic and known as "the orphans home," but it also housed youths who had broken the law. The other one, in Warsaw, was known as "our home" and was for Jewish orphans.

By the 1930s, his efforts on behalf of children were legendary, and people from all over the world came to listen to his views on raising children, how to love them, how they had human rights, and how to nurture them to be morally responsible. In fact, his research on child development largely preceded studies conducted by other child psychologists in the West. In the mid-1930s, vicious anti-Semites discovered Korczak's Jewish identity and accused him of being part of a Jewish plot to ruin Polish children. In December 1935 his radio program was cancelled, the station reluctant to keep a Jew in such a prominent position. In the late 1930s he lost his directorship of the Catholic orphanage. One non-Jew who witnessed this dismissal situation later wrote that he shall never forgive himself for his silence at that time and asked how it was possible that no Jew could be in charge of orphans and juvenile offenders. But Korczak experienced some rays of hope when in November 1937 the Polish Academy for Literature awarded him the Golden Laurel for Outstanding Literature Achievement. He was called the greatest humanist and intellectual on the air, according to his friend, Jan Piotroski, editor of the magazine *Antenna*. At the beginning of World War II, Korczak also served in the Polish army for a short time until Poland surrendered to the Germans in 1939.

When the Nazi's invaded Poland and established the ghetto in Warsaw in 1941, the Jewish orphanage had to move to the ghetto—and Korczak went with the children. Because of his name and fame, a lot of his colleagues wanted him to leave the ghetto and save himself. They provided false papers, places to live, and advice on how to get out of the ghetto, but he refused because he wanted them to also save the children. That was impossible; thus, he turned his friends down. He said, "You do not leave a sick child in the night, and you do not leave children at a time like this." He also refused to wear the Star of David, which caused him to be thrown into jail by the

Nazis; but as a result of the influence of his non-Jewish friends, he was allowed to return to the orphanage. The sadistic Gestapo chief, Dr. Blutenau, humiliated Korczak, calling him a "Jew pig"; yet Korczak stood up and faced him. In the Warsaw ghetto, Korczak found many children on the streets crying, so he would take them to the orphanage, even though there was no room.

He tried to observe the Jewish holidays, wrote Hanukkah plays for the Jewish children, and danced with the Catholic orphans around the Christmas tree. He was a man of ecumenical belief, very much loved by the children and respected by his colleagues. Every time Korczak came out of his office, he was smothered by children like chicks around a hen. The orphanage had a magazine called *Little Review*, which published articles written by children. The children also had a right to vote on which teacher to teach them; this was a democratically constructed orphanage. As suspicions of deportation rose, they began to observe Passover and tried to live normally as long as possible.

The Nazis played games with the Jewish leadership of the ghetto, confusing and deceiving them. When the rumor that they were going to start deporting people surfaced, the head of the ghetto (*Judenrat*), Adam Czernikow, a friend of Korczak's, went to the Gestapo to see if there was anything to the rumor. He was told there was nothing to it, although the Gestapo knew there was. Soon thereafter the deportation started. Czernikow could take it no longer and committed suicide, leaving a note to his wife apologizing that he had no choice.

Innocently, Korczak clung to the hope—as I did as a young boy working on a farm in Biesnik—that the Allies might defeat the Germans quickly. It was an unfulfilled dream. Throughout this misery in the ghetto, he wrote books and articles about kindness, compassion, and caring for children. He also wrote the *Ghetto Diary* (which was later found by one of the orphaned children who had avoided being deported and was delivered to Maryna Flaska; this wonderful non-Jewish rescuer hid it in her attic by cementing it into the wall so that nobody could find it). In it Korczak talks about his philosophies, his dealings, his optimism, and his regrets. The book was not published until 1956, when communist censorship in Poland was reduced.

Children all over the ghetto were dying of typhus. Dr. Korczak kneeled beside them, warming them with his hands and giving them encouraging words; most were beyond response. His own fatigue was a symptom of malnutrition, but rather than eat he gave his food to the hungry children.

He was well aware that when the ghetto was being evacuated the orphanage would be, too. He prepared the children by talking about death being a part of life, that life took on a different form. He produced a play even though the Gestapo chief forbade it. *The Post Office*, by Rabindranath Tagore, the Indian philosopher and poet, conveys a powerful notion of gentleness and peace. In the play, a young orphan boy named Amal is dying. His nature was so pure and good that he enriched the lives of all who came into contact with him.

August 6, 1942, was a tragic day. The Nazis yelled, *"Alle Juden raus!"* (All Jews out!). He and Stefa—his assistant who was like a mother to the children—were prepared. All the children lined up according to age. He was not quite sure where they were going, but he marched into the street with the children, four in a row, carrying the flag and singing. There was a rumor spreading that they were going to a cottage called "Little Rose" where they had spent summer vacations. The diabolical deception was that the Nazis had established an infirmary at the *Umschlagplatz* (railroad station), but this was a cover to allay any suspicion about "resettlement" or being shipped to death camps. Nahum Renba, who was in charge of the infirmary, records in his memoirs that Korczak was at the head of the first group of children, Stefa at the second. Unlike other groups, who were being driven with whips, the orphans walked with dignity. Renba burst into tears, saying, "I shall never forget this scene as long as I live."[14] Korczak walked with head held high, with a characteristic gaze as if looking far off ahead. They were taken to the trains and shipped to their death in Treblinka. Korczak entered the gas chamber with the children and comforted them as they died.

Korczak had so profound an influence on several people who had been in his orphanage, or otherwise associated with him, that they later became social workers. Because he was a totally assimilated Jew with a Polish name, Poles claim him as one of their great moral heroes of all time. So does the state of Israel, as he was born Jewish. Both countries have cooperated to commemorate this brave human being. After the war, Poland built a statue of Korczak in Warsaw at the Jewish cemetery, which I visited while in Poland during my research trip.

Helping — A Way of Life

The fourth type of heroic altruism I call *conventional altruism*. This is *voluntary and over a long duration, but it does not involve high risk to the helper.*

These are volunteers of various kinds who on a regular basis help and aid
other individuals, including Hospice volunteers. These are altruists who are
trying to comfort people as they are dying, whereas the heroic altruists described above are trying to save lives. These acts require dedication, compassion, and courage. But conventional altruists are relatively safe from pain in
one's own life for the act of helping. These types of altruists include moral
exemplars, who over a long duration have helped not only individuals but
also communities and nations. These individuals (discussed in Chapter 7)
have a profound influence in the community or society; one example would
be Nelson Mandela. But they are also ordinary people in the community
whose acting and caring for others exemplifies their behavior. In addition,
conventional altruists include philanthropists. These are individuals who are
voluntarily helping in various ways, especially in the area of financial support for groups and individuals in need of help. These philanthropists try to
heal the community in which they live, especially in the areas of health, education, and moral redemption. Dr. Jonas Salk, who discovered a vaccine for
polio, was one such person (see Chapter 7).

Helping manifests itself in many ways. Hospice volunteers (see Chapter
9) help terminally ill patients by being present when they need them, establishing human contact, and providing comfort and care to make their remaining days of life easier. They also comfort the patient's loved ones.

One hospice volunteer we interviewed in Northern California stated she
learned to be caring from her parents, especially her mother, who volunteered
in her community for many years. She had begun her volunteer work as an
English tutor to foreign students and their parents, and later she volunteered at
the local Northcoast Literacy Project, helping people learn to read and write.
These initial helping experiences as a young person made her feel very positive
about later joining the hospice volunteers. She says about her motivation,

> I think it is mostly from the experiences when I was nursing and
> some of my patients died, it made me feel that patients die a
> rather lonely death. Doctors, nurses, families, and patients never
> talked about it and never took the opportunity for preparing the
> person to die. Death is one of those things that you never talk
> about, like sex. As a result of hospice being present in hundreds of
> communities throughout the United States and England (where it
> originated) people feel like talking about it a little bit more.

She continues, "My experience at hospice did a lot for me. I am no longer afraid of death, and because I think that way, I am helping people who are in the process of dying." Her hope is that in the future nursing and medical schools will take up the practice and philosophy of hospice and introduce classes on the subject. It is time that physicians (who are still afraid to talk about it even now), when they have a terminal patient, do something about it by showing compassion for their dying patients. She says, "It is . . . educational, and more focus should be put on caring." When asked why she became involved in hospice, she told us that it was not only her parents' background but also her religious background to help others; the encouragement of friends also led her to become involved. "Taking care of older people who are dying is one of the most loving things to do." She added that her grandfather's and grandmother's deaths were another reason for getting involved with hospice.

Another hospice respondent, when asked why she got involved, said she felt guilt for not doing enough in her community. "So this was something to make up for that. I am sure most people don't even think of that. There are other reasons, like my mother's volunteering, and the fact that my sister was getting a Master's degree in Social Work and helping alcoholics, even though she has four children to take care of."

Heroes All

Heroes are necessary because they are a great influence on the outcome of issues and events, the consequences of which would have been profoundly different if they did not act as they did.[15] Thus, if Balwina Piecuch did not act, I would not be here today; if my colleague did not jump into the river, a child would have drowned; if a Carnegie hero didn't jump into the lake, the women would have drowned; if Janusz Korczak had not helped the many hundreds of orphans who survived the Holocaust, many more innocent lives would have been destroyed; had Korczak not accompanied the children who were deported to the gas chambers in Treblinka, they would have experienced a more terrifying death.

What do Mr. and Mrs. Roslan have in common with my own rescuer, Balwina Piecuch, and what do they both have in common with the Carnegie hero who jumped into the lake to save the lives of drowning victims, or with

Janusz Korczak? Why did Korczak not save himself? He was famous, and he had the means to get out of the ghetto.

When we interviewed Mr. Roslan, I probed why he and his wife did this, and he answered, "How could I . . . I saw those poor hungry boys and I saw the desperation of the ghetto—I just could not walk away from this. I knew that my wife and I would have to help."

All of these stories illustrate that people help in different ways and different settings. What motivated them to act on behalf of victims or those in need? The explanations for why such people risk their lives or commit their time and energies will be discussed in greater depth in the chapters that follow.

The first part of this book will focus on the three types of heroic altruists, including September 11 heroes, military heroes, Carnegie heroes, and non-Jewish and Jewish rescuers and resisters during the Nazi occupation of Europe. The second part will address conventional altruists such as moral exemplars, philanthropists, and volunteers—including hospice volunteers—in an attempt to better understand their reasons for putting forth so much effort to better humanity.

In Chapter 3, I will discuss the actions and motivations of non-Jewish heroic rescuers who risked their own lives and those of their families to save Jews during the Nazi occupation of Europe.

3

Saving the Jewish Baby

Non-Jewish Rescuers in Nazi-Occupied Europe

Without love what have you got—a world without a heart.
                    —Gentile rescuer during the Holocaust

Can you see it? Two young girls come, one sixteen or seventeen, and they tell you a story that their parents were killed and they were pulled in and raped. What are you supposed to tell them— "Sorry, we are all full already."

                    —Stanislaus, a Polish rescuer

World War II brought cruelty, injustice, and persecution of the innocent—unspeakable horrors that must be spoken. One way that a social scientist—especially one as closely connected to events as I—manages to confront such horrors intellectually is to quantify, to characterize, to analyze the events and participants according to scholarly criteria, and this is some of what I have done. I divided the 300 million people under the Nazi occupation between 1939 and 1945 into four groups: (1) killers—executioners and collaborators; (2) victims—Jews, political prisoners, and prisoners of war (POWs); (3) bystanders—the bulk of the population; and (4) heroic rescuers—those who risked their lives to save people. This chapter deals with the heroes/rescuers of Jews by non-Jews. The stories are true, and they illustrate the decency, caring, courage, and humanity shown by individuals and groups. The central question throughout this chapter and the book is: What motivates men and women to take the moral high road and risk their lives and the lives of their loved ones on behalf of others, frequently total strangers?[1]

In 1943, the Nazis were liquidating the ghetto in Krakow, Poland. Approximately a thousand Jews were being led to the *Umshclagplatz* (a concentration point from which people were then sent to their death) to be transported to their death in Treblinka. An anxious Jewish woman carrying an infant in her arms realized the tragic end in store for them both. She noticed a blonde woman—a Catholic Pole—standing on the sidewalk along with other onlookers, and she sneaked away from the marching column for a split second and begged the woman to save her child.

The blonde woman took the child from her and carried it to her third-floor apartment. She was neither married nor had she ever been pregnant, and her neighbors soon became suspicious. One neighbor informed the Polish police who were now in the service of the Nazis. The police arrived, arrested her and the baby, and brought them to the police station for interrogation by a Polish police captain. Other policemen were at their desks in the room. The Polish captain pointed a finger at the child and said, "This is not your baby, is it? This is a Jewish child, isn't it?" As if by divine inspiration, the blonde woman burst into tears, pounded on the desk, stared at the captain, and in a rage said, "You should be ashamed of yourselves. Do you call yourself Poles? Do you call yourself gentlemen? There is one man sitting in this office here who is the father of this child, but he stoops so low that instead of admitting paternity, he would rather see his child labeled a Jew and exterminated!" The rescuer survived, and the child was saved and grew to become a scientist as an adult. When she was interviewed, the blonde woman's response was, "How could I stand by and ignore the poor mother's plea to save a child? This was a beautiful little boy, and I've learned that what the Nazis were doing to the Jews was unjust, cruel, and I just couldn't be a bystander and ignore this woman's tears." She clearly shows compassion and creativity, as well as feelings of being unable to live with herself had she failed to save the child's life. A similar sentiment was expressed by Stanislaus, as relayed in the following story.

Stanislaus was born in 1920 into a poor Polish Roman Catholic family. His mother had come to Warsaw from the countryside, where she worked as a domestic and part-time midwife. His father, who had some high school education, was disabled by an accident when Stanislaus was eight years old and

lived on a pension thereafter. He had one brother four years older than himself. Stanislaus graduated from high school in 1939 but was unable to continue his studies until after the war, when he completed a degree in the
Diplomatic Consular Department of the Academy of Political Science in
Europe. During the war, he and his family lived near the Warsaw ghetto,
and his helping activities continued over a period of several years.

The first incident he recalled involved Isidor, a "formerly rich merchant
from Gdansk":

> He told me several times how the SS men [*Schutzstaffeln*, or pro-
> tection squads] had drowned his son. He settled in the ghetto
> and used to visit us at night. The ghetto was situated in
> Krochmalna Street, and we lived on Chlodna Street, so that be-
> tween our house and the ghetto there was a kind of *Niemands-*
> *land* (no-man's-land). At night it was possible to bring that Jew
> in, and we treated him very cordially. Commercial transactions
> began between us. He used to come and say, "Stanislaus, listen"
> (he had a funny way of speaking), "could you buy that? Might
> you bring something else we could sell and make some money?" I
> remember that whenever he came at night with his socks on (he
> had his socks on regardless of the temperature), he always
> checked the pots to see if there was anything to eat. Naturally, he
> sat down and ate because he was simply hungry.

This contact, however, did not last long; Stanislaus says that he and his
mother were almost the witnesses of Isidor's death:

> My mother tried to help in every possible way. I still remember
> how we stood by the barbed wire on the corner of Krochmalna
> and Ciepla Streets—the wire ran in the middle of the street. On
> one side of the wire was that unfortunate Isidor, pale as death—
> and on the other side was my mother and me, my mother hold-
> ing a loaf of bread with tears in her eyes. She threw the loaf over
> the wire, but others took it. These were our last moments, the
> last contact.

The daughter of a well-known Jewish antiquarian also used to come to
see them and stay overnight:

With her, however, we had no trade relationship. Her father was unfit for any trade, and so was she. In that case, it was purely and solely providing help. She came to us, stayed overnight. Very often she went out in the street with my mother, and later with me.

But she, too, suffered a tragic end:

Their fate was a terrible one. The ghetto border limits were changed in the meantime, and we had to move. One day she came with her friend whom we did not know—quite slim and very pretty, with very Semitic facial features. They told us a terrible thing. The Germans had come at night, collected all the families, and drove them to the *Umshclagplatz*. The girls hid somewhere and later in the evening crossed the barbed wire in order to get to us. On the way they were accosted by two or three Polish males who pulled them into their place, raped them, and threw them out into the street. . . . They stayed with us for about one month, and later on they left one day and never returned; there is no doubt that they perished.

Stanislaus and his mother were responsible for the entire household:

> My mother did not work, and my father was in the hospital several times during the occupation. He was a complete invalid—a living creature, but unable to help with anything. My brother had moved out; he could not stand the psychological pressure of living with all those people under threat of death twenty-four hours a day. He was unable to sleep or eat. So there were two people to run the house—my mother and me.

A total of twenty individuals—an elderly married couple, two sisters, a young man who had escaped from a concentration camp, among many others—stayed at Stanislaus's place, or at places he arranged, for periods of time ranging from several days to several years.

> I made hideouts—not only in my own place but also in some other places in Warsaw. There were double walls that were made of bricks at that time, or of material called Heraklit [cement and flax board]. It was three to four centimeters thick and properly treated. Then it was covered or painted or wallpaper was put on it—over some hidden entrance. My first hideouts were very awkward because I knew nothing about masonry. I laid the bricks

wrong and the whole wall collapsed. But then I got professional advice from a bricklayer and learned how to do it right.

Stanislaus told us that he managed to supply food for them from his own resources and those of one of the Jews he was keeping.

> First of all, the living standard was much lower then. Staple food was based on groats or the like. My mother did the shopping, buying in small quantities. Some of the people we helped were poor as mice; I don't know how they supported themselves. Professor T. was involved in underground life, and he had contacts abroad from whom he got money and that he distributed among those he was in charge of. He contributed, and so when peas or beans were boiled, my mother cooked for all. I worked for an accounting office and made as much as an average Pole earned then; I got an allowance in kind. I contributed my share; sometimes I got an allowance, some peas or the like. But it was partly the professor who supplied the money.

It was not by chance that so many people came to him. Stanislaus went to the ghetto often, even after the ghetto walls were sealed. When we asked him why, he said:

> I had my friends there. Besides, when you went to the ghetto, everybody was buying and selling so that they could sustain themselves. Those people were sentenced to death even more than we were—of simple starvation. If somebody had colossal reserves of cash (I did not know such people), then he might be able to survive. But a workingman, like the man who worked in the slaughterhouse, had to do something to get a piece of bread.

Clues to Stanislaus's motivation are found in his recollection of details regarding almost all the individuals he helped—details not only of their physical appearance, but also their psychological condition. He remembers what Isidor did before the war, how he spoke, what he wore, and what he looked like as he stood on the opposite side of the barbed wire. He remembers his mother with "tears in her eyes." He tells us not only the fate of the two girls before they arrived at his house, but also what happened to them afterward. He is mindful that the Jew with resources has an advantage compared to the "workingman." He tells us about his invalid father and about his brother, who could neither eat nor sleep. He makes few references to himself; sentences that begin with "I" quickly change to focus on others. "I had my friends in the ghetto," he says, and then he begins to describe what life in the ghetto was like.

Understanding others, taking their perspective, and anticipating their futures may have left Stanislaus little psychological room to consider his own needs. He speaks little of his own or even his mother's wartime deprivations. He understood how others felt, and that left him with "no choice." His empathy is reflected in the reasons he gives for his rescue decision:

> Human compassion. When someone comes and says, "I escaped from the camp," what is the alternative? One alternative is to push him out and close the door, the other is to pull him into the house and say, "Sit down, relax, wash up. You will be as hungry as we are because we have only this bread!"

Friendships transcended ethnicity, religion, and social class, and once formed, were enduring. Born in a district inhabited by many Jews, and "the street on which we lived was 80 percent Jewish," he lived among Jews, went to school with them, and had many Jewish friends before the war. "I was so involved with Jews," he said, "that I had even learned to speak Yiddish."

Stanislaus also appeared to have considerable ego strength. His brother chose to leave the maternal home to escape the constant suffering. Stanislaus chose to stay. It was not that he did not feel fear. "I don't want to say that we were not afraid—we were afraid, too"; and he is sympathetic toward those whose fear immobilized them. Stanislaus, however, did not dwell on those risks but rather on the needs of those he helped.

How did such ego strength develop? His family was not particularly close while he was growing up, but his mother influenced him greatly, emphasizing three basic values throughout his youth and mature years: education, care for others, and universal tolerance.

Stanislaus's mother valued education as a means to social position and a worthy end in itself. "She wanted to educate us and give us knowledge, so that we would be competitive with others and get a good job and position." But knowledge was also a means for "understanding and interpreting the world," and because of his mother's attitudes, "my brother and I learned how to appreciate knowledge." He was "spanked" frequently by both parents when he didn't study hard enough, failed to prepare his lessons, or was "hanging around with bad boys." Although not an exceptional student, Stanislaus eventually earned a master's degree.

Caring and respect for others were taught by his mother explicitly and by example. "I learned to respect the world from my mother," he said. His mother modeled caring behaviors in many ways. His childhood and adolescence were spent in a household filled with his mother's relatives, who sought her support as they looked for work or studied in the big city. His mother herself occasionally worked as a maid and midwife to earn the money necessary to provide for the boys' education. Stanislaus credited her with initiating his wartime helping activities.

The great risks undertaken by Stanislaus offer important insight that informs my research (see Appendix B). Was rescue primarily a matter of opportunity? Did external circumstances and the situation make rescue possible? Was it important to have specific knowledge and material resources? Was the rescuer specifically asked for help? Or was rescue primarily a matter of character? Were personal attributes such as values and moral principles the primary motivator to rescue? If so, what were these attributes, values, and principles? Were they primarily learned characteristics and, if so, how were they acquired?

We found that both rescuers and bystanders possessed similar material resources that might have facilitated rescue, such as food and hiding places; rescuers and bystanders had relatively similar occupations and homes. Both groups perceived similar risk. The circumstance that distinguished rescuers from nonrescuers was that although the opportunity appeared to be similar, the rescuers were asked for help. At best, opportunity to help may have facilitated rescue but did not, by any means, determine it.

Many values were expressed-values that represent ethical, empathetic, normocentric, or principled belief.[2]

The overwhelming majority of rescuers cited at least one reason that was founded in their *ethical* beliefs. Their ethics included justice and fairness, and the belief that persecution of the innocent could not be justified. But the ethic that mattered most was the ethic of care and compassion, both clearly evident in Stanislaus's story. For most rescuers, helping was rooted in the ethic of care and the need to assume personal responsibility to relieve suffering and pain. Some rescuers felt this for special individuals—Jews for whom they had a particular affection, for example—but most rescuers felt an obligation to others in general. Pity, compassion, concern, and affection made up 76 percent of the reasons rescuers gave for extending help to strangers. It is easy to understand why we help those for whom we feel affection, but why help a stranger? People who had helped at least one stranger, as well as friends, gave these sorts of responses:

- When you see a need, you have to help.

- Our religion was part of us; we are our brothers' keepers.

- We had to give our help to these people in order to save them. Not because they were Jews, but because they were persecuted human beings who needed help.

- Care compelled action. It meant assuming personal responsibility—not because others required it, but because failure to act meant acquiescence.

- I could not stand idly by and observe the daily misery that was occurring.

- I knew they were taking them and they wouldn't come back. I didn't think I could live with that, knowing I could have done something.

Parents played a very influential role for both rescuers and nonrescuers; however, significantly more rescuers perceived their parents as benevolent figures, modeling values conducive to forming close, caring attachments to other people, including diverse groups of people who might be different by virtue of status, ethnicity, or religion. When rescuers were disciplined as children, they had been talked to, and the consequences of their misbehavior had been explained to them, rather than being disciplined physically. Nonrescuers were more likely to have been spanked, kicked, punched, and verbally abused by their parents.

Parental values were very important. Values that rescuers remembered learning from their parents differed extensively from those of nonrescuers. One aspect of such values related to ethics; the other related to people acting on or feeling ethical obligations. Considerably more rescuers made the point that it was to all people that they owed an obligation. Additionally, significantly more rescuers than nonrescuers emphasized learning from parents the value of helping others in the spirit of generosity, without concern for reciprocity. Rescuers as well as nonrescuers thus emerged from their parental homes with fundamental attitudes of caring toward other persons and themselves. They had a sense of who they were, had a capacity to relate to others, and understood the nature of their relationships and the basis of such relationships. In short, the core of their personality was largely formed early in life.

Significantly more rescuers during the Holocaust felt a sense of responsibility toward others—feeling obligation to help even when nothing could be gained. By contrast, significantly more nonrescuers felt exempt from such obligations, depending on others to assume responsibilities. Although rescuers and nonrescuers shared similar sensitivities to others' moods and worries, appreciably more rescuers felt particularly empathic toward others' pain. Others' sadness and helplessness aroused their emotions. Rescuers got angry when others were hurt.

However, many nonrescuers who we interviewed were less affected by others' suffering, less emotionally receptive to helplessness and pain.

Such attitudes and feelings may well have resulted from the rescuers' general appraisal of others' similarities to themselves. More frequently, they perceived themselves as being like other people, sharing fundamental similarities with others—regardless of their social or economic status, ethnicity, or religion. Significantly, a greater number of rescuers had friends from diverse ethnic groups, and more rescuers felt themselves as being similar to other human beings.

For about 38 percent of the rescuers, helping Jews had less to do with any authoritative social group than with an event that aroused their *empathy*. In many cases it was a direct face-to-face encounter with stress, as is revealed in the following narratives of rescuers whose empathic motivations were central and consistent.[3]

Education, tolerance, and caring remained all-important to Stanislaus. When we asked him what he would tell young people if a party with goals similar to those of Nazis came to power again, he replied: "I would tell them two things—about being tolerant, and about human relationships, the relationship of one man to another." Asked to describe the people he most admired during the war, he characterized one as "having knowledge and being wise," the other as being of "good heart, open-hearted, honest, powerful, and a person of strong beliefs."

Stanislaus felt most similar to Catholics and poor people, but Jews continued to have a special place in his life. He'd lived in a predominantly Jewish neighborhood in his youth and had many Jewish friends (his grandmother was born Jewish but gave up her religion and her wealthy family out of love for his poor Polish Catholic grandfather). Sacrificing all on behalf of people one cares about is something Stanislaus understands well, even if the other is an "outsider."

At the time we interviewed him, Stanislaus remained a helpful person, regularly extending himself on behalf of the ill and the disabled. He was currently very involved with providing life assistance to an older Jewish man, "an old and disabled person who lives by himself. I shop for him and I visit him—I take care of his problems. I help him clean his apartment, wash windows, and so on."

Sometimes direct interaction with victims arouses empathy, as we see in the following example. Because he recognized the victims' humanity, a German military officer could not allow innocent people to die; here is the story as he relates it:

> In the spring of 1942, I was assigned to Tunisia as a paratrooper. We were to support the safe retreat of [then-Major General Erwin] Rommel's African troops because the war in Libya was being lost. SS men were gathering up Jews, not to send them away from the area, such as to concentration camps, but for field work at the front.

> We had taken a position, facing the Americans, forty kilometers south of Tunis. The Americans, provoked by our troops, made a paratroop attack. Many prisoners were taken. An Italian came to us with a report of spies hidden on a farm between the lines; he claimed that the spies had disclosed our positions to the Americans. I was assigned to direct the assault on the farm. We captured five young Jews; the Italian told us they were Jews. Two were sons of a physician in Tunis. All five were friends—their ages between sixteen and twenty.

> The Jews were interrogated; they were very scared. We were monsters to them. They were afraid of anyone wearing a German

uniform. The interrogation was conducted by an SS captain. He had been assigned to our unit, as it was already customary at that time to assign Nazi party members to military units. The decision was that these Jews were to be shot because they had been found in the front lines. I was in a leading position [regiments—*gefechtsfuhrer*], and they were assigned to me.

In the evening when they came back, quite by chance I entered into a conversation with one of the physician's sons. He spoke German. His father had studied in Germany; they grew up in Sicily but had gone to a German school there. I was told of the threats by the noncommissioned officer. As I had all the documents, I knew that these five men had only come into the present situation by chance, and I knew they were to be shot merely because they had been found in enemy territory. I decided to help them somehow. I told them that I would release them from custody and help them to flee. They were very scared, suspecting we would shoot them during their escape. But I convinced them that I would help them. I provided them with food supplies and gave them a map, explaining the military frontier and how they needed to pass through the lines. I also gave them a pistol. I sent the prison guard away for a while and let them out of the prison. They began their flight in the dark of the evening.

This officer's interaction with other human beings had aroused empathy and compassion within him, and that empathy made the killing of the young men unjustifiable in his eyes. Empathy, it would appear, is a very powerful force indeed.

Unlike the German officer who found his motivation internally, Ilsa was triggered to action by the *normocentric* values that mattered most to her— her religious upbringing, as well as the direction modeled by others whom she esteemed, especially her husband.

Ilsa told us she was born in 1907, the daughter of a German Lutheran minister. Her mother died when Ilsa was just eight years old, and she and her younger sister were sent to a missionary school in Basel, Switzerland. When she was twenty-five years old, she married a Lutheran minister, and they went to live in a small German town. Their rented parsonage had six rooms and two attics. During the war, her husband served with the German military, and she lived with her three children in two rooms of the parsonage. The other rooms were rented. Other renters in the parsonage included a relative and a family with five children. In the fall of 1944, the young minister of her district asked her to take care of a Jewish couple who were being moved from house to house:

> There would be no food stamps for them. Because a district school of the NSDAP [the Nazional Sozialistische Deutsche Arbeiter Partei—the official name of the Nazi party] was in the town, and our parsonage was being observed, I had some concerns. My husband was in the service in Italy, and I was alone with the children. He had been harassed before he became a soldier. When I told the minister of my concerns, he said, "Please keep them [the Jewish couple] at least for a few days." The large, deep cellar of our parsonage was used as an air-raid shelter. I wondered what the neighbors would say when they came to the air-raid shelter.

Ilsa was German, and so her acts were against her own national authorities, not an external oppressor; thus, the question of *why* she helped should be preceded by the question of *what* made her reject those authorities. When asked if she felt any similarity to the Nazis, she said "not at all." She can speak only negatively of Nazis. Asked about groups of people toward whom she had strong positive or negative feelings, she repeated "Nazis—negative, rejection." But, in fact, she supported the Nazis in the beginning "because of their strong opposition to the communists." What accounts for Ilsa's change?

Ilsa based her fundamental evaluations on what was happening to her group—her husband and her church. "My husband," she said, "suffered on account of the Nazis, and I was there with him." Her rejection of communists was based on the same type of reason: "My husband suffered on account of the communists, too," she said. Strongly embedded in her religious community, the daughter and wife of Lutheran ministers, she perceived the NSDAP as "persecuting the church."

"Helping one's neighbor" was an important religious norm for Ilsa. The most important things Ilsa learned about life from her religious leaders were "acquaintance with the word of God, participation in the church community, respect for other people, complete honesty, helping one's neighbor."

How did the concept of "neighbor" develop to include Jews? Unlike in the situation of Stanislaus related above, for Ilsa, Jews had been rather remote. Before the war she neither knew any Jews nor was aware of any Jews living in her district. She learned about Jews only when the minister asked her to hide people being transferred from one locality to another—Jewish people being sheltered among trusted church members.

Ilsa did not perceive herself as an independent person. In childhood she "always went along with what was happening, I never objected to anything. . . . I am not a leader." She saw her role in life primarily as that of wife and mother.

Her subordination to others had its roots in her early years. In talking about what she had learned from a meaningful figure in her childhood—a schoolteacher—she mentioned "consideration of each other, honoring adults, modesty, contentment with what was provided, and subordination." She was very grateful to her mother for teaching her "unconditional obedience, honoring others, including one's peers." From her father, she learned to "believe in God, prayer, and religious participation." This type of upbringing emphasizes obedience to authority.

For Ilsa, the relevant authorities were her husband and her church. When the latter applied some degree of pressure, she was able to draw strength from her feelings of belonging to her religious community and the conviction that it was essential to fulfill the group's goals. Thus, her rescue actions were taken in response to an authority; and the continuation of the activity depended on the continuing presence and support of the group.

In other cases, however, norms were internalized, and the behavior assumed more of a voluntary and independent character. Sometimes norms were so strongly internalized that the behavior appeared to be highly independent of any specific authority. Ilsa's normocentric "compass," as it were, existed within the self, and the obligation to act derived from this self-concept.

After the Japanese surprise attack on Pearl Harbor, many Americans felt animosity toward the Japanese—and for good reason. Sempo Sugihara, a Japanese diplomat running a Japanese consulate in Kovno, Lithuania, was inundated with hundreds of Jews begging for transit visas so they could leave the horror of the war and head east toward Siberia.

Paul Blustein relates Sugihara's story. "Haunted by the pitiful sight outside the consulate, Sugihara cabled Tokyo three times for permission to issue transit visas en masse and was turned down each time." But he made up his mind and went against the foreign ministry, issuing transit visas for nearly 6,000 Jews, primarily Polish refugees, during the weeks before all the foreign consular representatives were removed from Lithuania by the Soviets. "For a few days in the summer of 1940 . . . Sugihara granted as many transit visas as he could write, producing hundreds of documents a day as his wife massaged his hands and fed him sandwiches."[4] Recalling the events of 1940, he explained, "I really had a hard time, and was unable to sleep for two nights. I thought as follows: 'I can issue transit visas. . . by virtue of my authority as consul. I cannot allow these people to die, people who had come to me for help with death staring them in the eyes. Whatever punishment may be imposed upon me, I know I should follow my conscience.'"[5]

In 1941 the Japanese government attempted to halt the entry of Jewish refugees to Japan, and many ended up in Shanghai for the duration of the war.

Upon his return to Japan in 1947, Sugihara was dismissed as a diplomat. According to government officials, he was asked to submit his resignation not because of the part he played in this incident, but rather as part of a reduction in staff. Both Sugihara and his wife felt this was merely an excuse, but they finally settled down in Moscow, where the former diplomat worked for a Japanese trading company. He was virtually forgotten until 1968, when he was tracked down by a survivor who wanted to thank him personally for saving his life. After the initial recognition of his righteousness, he was invited to Israel in 1984 by Yad Vashem and awarded the title Righteous Among the Nations.

Carl Lutz was born the ninth of ten children in Switzerland in 1895. In his youth he observed his mother's example of helping, and he learned that one should always be ready to assist a fellow human being without self-interest. This teaching stayed with him throughout his life.[6]

As a young man he worked as an industrial apprentice in Saint Margrethen in the Rhine Valley, eventually traveling to the United States, where he first worked in a factory in Illinois, fought the draft of the U.S. Army, and later served in the Swiss consular corps in St. Louis. The consular corps seemed to have suited Lutz, and he served as Swiss consul in Philadelphia and later (1935–1939) in Joffa, Palestine, where he was an eyewitness to the atrocities of the Arab-Jewish conflict.

From 1939 to 1940, at the outbreak of World War II, Lutz became the Swiss representative in Palestine, where he was promoted to vice consul. In this role he had protected German citizens, who were considered potential enemies by the British mandatory authorities there and imprisoned. Lutz took humanitarian actions to assist the German prisoners and got the British to treat them better. This intervention put him in good stead with the Germans, particularly Dr. Edmund Veesenmayr, who was Germany's ambassador to Hungary.

In 1941 Lutz was commissioned as the Swiss vice consul in Budapest, Hungary. He would use this position to do much good. From 1942 to 1944 he aided in the movement of 10,000 mostly orphaned Jewish children to Palestine. But this was just the beginning of his resourcefulness and courage.

He obtained permission from the German and Hungarian puppet authorities to keep 8,000 Jews under his protection. Through his own ingenuity, Lutz devised a document, the *Schutzbriefe*—or protective pass. The pass would multiply the number Lutz could help many times over. The pass was for the use of Swiss citizens in Budapest, were in sequential numerical order, and allowed 8,000 citizens to be protected under Swiss authority. Lutz could name the 8,000 émigrés—but only if he did not ask for more permits.

Lutz provided the 8,000 names and gave them each a *Schutzbriefe*. Then he started the sequence of numbers all over again and assigned 8,000 more names, and so on, again and again. The Germans were led to believe only 8,000 Jews had left Budapest, but in the end Lutz aided in saving 62,000. On occasion he would ask for the assistance of Edmund Veesenmayr to get German and Hungarian approval of the legitimacy of emigration certificates.

It should be noted that Carl Lutz was the first diplomat from a neutral country to issue the passport of safe conduct to Jews who were threatened with deportation to extermination camps. He insisted throughout his time in Budapest that all bearers of the Palestinian certificate should be regarded as British citizens and therefore entitled to Swiss protection, as Switzerland was officially acting on behalf of the British Empire. Unfortunately, on frequent occasions Hungarian police did not recognize the passes, would brutalize Jews, and eagerly help Adolf Eichmann transport them to their deaths (Eichmann headed the Nazi resettlement office that administered the Final Solution).

The times were very traumatic for Lutz; a great number of people were asking him for help, lining up before the Swiss legation. It was impossible for him to forge so many protective letters, so he enlisted the forgery experts of the Jewish Pioneer Movement to help. As a result, fake protective letters reached approximately 120,000 Jews in all. Often, the Hungarian fascist and anti–Semitic Arrow Cross government disregarded these letters, and they captured some 27,000 able-bodied Jews from Hungary and marched them to Germany to work. Later, a second contingent of 40,000 was also captured. News reached Budapest that many of these had died of starvation, exhaustion, and brutality during the marches.

Representatives of the Vatican, Switzerland, Sweden, Spain, and Portugal protested vigorously and demanded that the German authority and the new Ferenc Szalasi regime in Hungary stop these inhumane deportation marches immediately. It did not help, so Lutz gave orders to print more protective letters.

The *Auschwitz Protocol*, a manuscript informing the world of the horrors in the Nazis' largest extermination camp, a document that had strongly influenced Lutz's decision to act, had also been smuggled to Switzerland to George Mandel-Monteilo, a Hungarian Jew who became the El Salvadoran diplomat in Geneva. He sent a large quantity of blank entry visas to Lutz, who then filled in the names of Jews who were already on the march to Germany. With his wife, Lutz drove westward, caught up to the marches, and gave out the signed documents on the spot. Together, Lutz and Mandel-Monteilo issued Salvadoran papers to Hungarian Jews and saved thousands of lives. Mandel-Monteilo also launched a press campaign in Switzerland, which spilled over to Sweden, Great Britain, and the United States. In all these countries it was the public protesting and rallies against the genocide that forced the hand of silent governments.

Throughout his time in Hungary, Lutz was determined to save as many Jews as possible, despite the lack of support, noncooperation, and disapproval from the Swiss government. Time and time again he asked his government to intervene, to give Jews transit visas to Palestine, something the Swiss government had initially approved but continually failed to do. In a way, then, he fought a triple enemy: Eichmann and the Germans; the Hungarian fascist Arrow Cross; and his own government. Despite this triple danger, Lutz, Gertrude (his wife), and Peter Zürcher (his assistant) accomplished much. After the war, he returned home to face disciplinary measures from the Swiss foreign office. In their opinion, during his time as vice consul he had repeatedly disregarded authority and overstepped orders from Berne.

Lutz, Gertrude, and Zürcher, as well as the secretary of the Swiss legation, Harald Feller, were recognized in 1964 as Righteous Among the Nations, and Lutz has received honors from many countries, including Israel, the United States, Germany, Switzerland, and Hungary.

When the Germans invaded Denmark on April 9, 1940, the Danes offered little resistance—they were no match for the German army. As a reward for nonresistance, Hitler made them a model protectorate, which meant they retained their own government, foreign offices, and armed forces. The Germans pledged not to control the internal and external affairs of Denmark and promised not to interfere in Denmark's political independence, assuring the Danes that their constitutional protections and bill of rights—including the rights of Danish Jews—were to be upheld. This arrangement lasted from 1940 until October 1943. During that period the German army lost the Battle of Stalingrad, and resistance movements intensified in Denmark and other parts of Europe; in 1943 the Germans took over the Danish government.

Georg Duckwitz was born to a patrician family in Bremen, in the Hanseatic City, and pursued an international career in the coffee trade, residing in Scandinavian countries for several years.[7] In 1939 the Nazi foreign ministry assigned him to the German embassy in Copenhagen as the German shipping attaché and expert in maritime affairs. He was already well acquainted with local conditions and enjoyed good connections with Danish leaders.

In 1942 he became a close confidant of the Third Reich's representative, Dr. Werner Best. Best, a former deputy chief of the Gestapo and hardcore Nazi ideologue, adhered to the moderate policies of his predecessors. However, during the time of uprising, Hitler demanded an iron-fist policy toward the increasingly rebellious country and the immediate implementation of the Final Solution. When Best sent a telegram to the German authorities to start rounding up Jews on October 1–2, 1943, the telegram was intercepted by Duckwitz, and he, placing himself at great risk, immediately informed his Danish Social Democratic friends, who alerted Dr. Marcus Melchior, chief rabbi of Denmark, who then exhorted the Danish Jews to run and hide as quickly as they could. With help from some 4 million Danish citizens, who hid Jews in the countryside and in their homes, as well as Swedes, who hid them in fishing vessels and took Jews to Sweden, some 7,200 lives were saved. When the Nazis started searching Jewish homes, most were empty, and they managed to capture only 450—those who had not been notified in time to disappear.

Duckwitz is considered one of the major heroes and rescuers of World War II and was recognized by Yad Vashem as Righteous Among the Nations in 1971. His moral principles and humanity forced him to action, and his position made that action effective.[8]

Italian-born Giorgio Perlasca is credited with saving thousands of Jews from annihilation by placing them under the protective flag of Spain.[9] He fought with an Italian contingent supporting Francisco Franco in the Spanish civil war and had earned an official document entitling him to protection at any Spanish embassy. After he was demobilized, he took a job as a merchant with an Italian company selling beef to the German military in Budapest. When Italian dictator Benito Mussolini fell in 1943, Perlasca refused to return to Italy; and in October 1944, he approached Angel Sanz-Briz, the Spanish envoy, and applied for a job. Sanz-Briz had been issuing protective passes to Budapest Jews for several months, and Perlasca helped in that effort. On the morning of November 30, 1944, he learned Sanz-Briz had left Budapest. Perlasca changed his first name from the Italian Giorgio to a more Spanish Jorge and boldly established himself as chargé d'affaires. In this capacity, driving a car with diplomatic plates and the flag of Spain, he deceived the officials of Hungary's highly anti–Semitic Arrow Cross government, established safe houses, and continued to issue passes predated to Sanz-Briz's time.

Perlasca's bluff was no doubt helped by the fact that Spain under Franco was the only fascist neutral country in Europe and Hungarian authorities were anxious for Spanish support.

Adolf Eichmann returned to Budapest in October 1944 to expedite exportation of Hungarian Jews to Auschwitz. By this time, helped by the Arrow Cross, Eichmann had succeeded in deporting 18,000 Budapest Jews to their deaths. One day a group of Arrow Cross men broke into one of the safe houses, lined up all the adults in the large foyer, and prepared to march them to the Danube to shoot them. According to Ernie Meyer in the *Jerusalem Post International*, "Perlasca walked into the hallway and shouted in his broken German, 'How dare you behave like this on the property of a friendly country? If I have to cable Madrid about this violation of Spanish interests, there will be grave consequences.'"[10] An officer from the fascist Arrow Cross apologized and ordered his men to let the people go. Perlasca saved these Jews from certain death.

On another occasion he was at a railway station with Raoul Wallenberg helping Jews out of a transport. Perlasca picked two children from a group and told them to go to his car. An SS major threatened him with a pistol and tried to take them back. Wallenberg told the SS officer, "This man is my colleague." The SS man said, "But he disturbs my work," to which Wallenberg responded, "You call this work?" At that moment SS Colonel Adolf Eichmann approached and ordered the major to "leave the youngsters, their turn will come." The Nazis went away, and Perlasca got the children. From then on his fellow Italians referred to him as "the Italian Wallenberg, the embodiment of the 'Banality of Good.'"[11]

In April 1945 Dr. Hugo Dukesz, one of the people Perlasca saved, wrote to him:

> We are sorry to learn that you are about to leave Hungary for your native Italy. On this occasion, we want to express the affection and gratitude of the several thousand Jews who survived thanks to your protection. There are not enough words to praise the tenderness with which you fed us and with which you cared for the old and the sick among us. You encouraged us who were close to despair, and your name will never be omitted from our prayers. May the Almighty grant you your reward.[12]

Giorgio Perlasca returned to Italy after the war and lived in relative obscurity until his story was published in the *Jerusalem Post*.[13] At that same time, Perlasca was mentioned as one of the great heroes in *The Black Book: On the Martyrdom of Hungarian Jewry*. The poet Eva Lang, one of those he saved, dedicated her poem "Homage" to him. In 1989 Giorgio Perlasca visited Israel and received the Righteous Medal from Yad Vashem. When asked why he rescued thousands of Jews, he responded, "What would you have done in my place?"[14] His social responsibility and empathy were the driving forces behind his acts of rescue, and his efficacy was helped by the circumstances of his position and his sheer audacity.

As a young woman in the early days of German occupation, Irena Sendler was aroused by the suffering of her Jewish friends and acquaintances.[15] She was employed at the social welfare department of the Warsaw municipality and obtained a special permit allowing her to visit ghetto areas for the purpose of "combating contagious diseases." But unbeknownst to the occupiers, Sendler was also a member of a Polish underground organization in Warsaw called Zegota—the Council for Aid to Jews. Her job with the municipality gave her unique access and enabled her to supply many Jews with clothing, medicine, and money. She wore an armband with the Star of David when going about in the ghetto as a sign of solidarity with the Jewish people and as a ploy to divert attention away from herself. She recruited a large number of people to Zegota and become a valuable asset to the movement. The sheltering of families in the ghetto was supported by funds from Zegota, and each of her recruits was responsible for several blocks of apartments. She, herself, oversaw approximately ten apartments where Jews were hiding. She also had a companion, Irena Schulz, with a network of contacts both in the ghetto and on the "Aryan" side, so Sendler was able to smuggle children out of the ghetto and place them with non-Jewish families around the region.

In October 1943, Irena Sendler was arrested by the Gestapo and taken to the infamous Pawiak prison in Warsaw, where she was questioned and tortured. Because they were unable to secure information from her, Irena's interrogators told her she was doomed. However, on her execution day, one of her underground companions bribed a Gestapo agent, and she was freed. Because she was still listed on public bulletin boards as being among the executed, she was compelled to stay in hiding for the remainder of the German occupation. Even so, she continued working secretly for Zegota. In 1965 she received the Righteous Among the Nations Medal, on which is written a line from the Talmud, "She who saves one life is as if she saved the entire universe."[16] When we interviewed her in Warsaw, she exuded confidence and courage, and said, "I wish I could have done more to help during these dark years."

Jan Karski, whom we interviewed in Washington, D.C., was born Jan Kozielewski in Poland in 1914. He was first a Polish army officer, then a diplomat and a secret underground courier, and an outstanding hero of World War II.

Karski's heroism stemmed from risks he took on dangerous missions as a courier to Poland for the Allies and for the Polish government-in-exile in London. Karski witnessed firsthand the massacre of Jews in Poland. He was arrested as a Polish officer and accused of participating in the underground. Although tortured, he survived to continue informing the world of the tragedy that was occurring, trying to influence Western leaders to stop the genocide of the Jewish people.

His secret missions took him from Warsaw to Berlin, Paris, Madrid, Gibraltar, and finally to England. The Jewish leaders in exile and the Polish government-in-exile asked him to report on the German war machine and to alert the world of the enslavement of the Poles and the destruction of the Jews. Before he went to give testimony, he approached different underground organizations for messages to take with him. One of them organized a dangerous and secret trip to the Warsaw ghetto and to a transit camp where he saw the misery, massacres, and deaths that were occurring. Then only twenty-eight years old, Karski later wrote of that night, "It was an evening of nightmare, but with a painful, oppressive kind of reality that no nightmare ever had."[17]

Karski gave U.S. President Franklin D. Roosevelt and British Prime Minister Winston Churchill a full report of what he had seen happening to Jews—and they did nothing. In London, Anthony Eden and others did not believe him. Karski said, "Those people honestly didn't believe me. They thought I was exaggerating out of hatred of the Germans. That this was just propaganda."[18]

Karski visited Washington, and Supreme Court Justice Felix Frankfurter came to the Polish embassy and asked what was happening to Jews in Europe, especially in Poland. Karski told him, and the jurist listened in silence. Then he said, "I am unable to believe you."[19] Roosevelt summoned him to the White House, where Karski made a short statement and then answered Roosevelt's questions. The president made no comments or asked any questions about Jews. After an hour and twenty minutes, the president held out his hand. Karski said, "Mr. President, I am going back to Poland. People will know that I was received by the president of the United States. Everybody will ask me: What did President Roosevelt tell you? What am I to tell them?" Roosevelt said: "You will tell the leaders that we shall win this war! You will tell them that the guilty ones will be punished. Justice and freedom shall prevail. You will tell your nation that they have a friend in this house."[20]

Jan Karski died in 2000 and will be remembered as one of the great moral and courageous Polish heroes for informing world leaders about a genocide that was occurring right under their noses.

Herman Graebe, whom I interviewed in San Francisco, was the only German national witness to war crimes who voluntarily testified at the Nuremberg war crimes tribunal.[21] During the war he was a Christian engineer. A meticulous organizer and supervisor assigned to manage the development of Nazi railroad services in Germany, he was subsequently transferred to work on railroads throughout Ukraine. To do his work he needed many laborers and workers with special skills for building; and he needed assistants fluent in at least four Eastern European languages. He hired two Jewish women: Maria Bobrow as secretary, and Claire (last name unknown) as translator.

When Maria Bobrow told Graebe of her husband's death at the hands of an SS mobile killing unit, Graebe was shocked.

He tried to help one Jewish family living in Rovno, Ukraine, by hiring the husband as a carpenter and supplying him with a work permit. But the city of Rovno was sealed off, and after two attempts to save the man's family he had failed; they were lost. He heard shots and understood what was taking place. He became outraged and wanted to right this wrong. Graebe experienced firsthand the annihilation of Jews and was an unwilling witness to mass killings. He remembered the people standing near the edge of large pits passively waiting—their faces, the naked emotions, the last hugs and kisses for families before they were shot into the mass grave. These images were etched into his eyes, changing him forever. Anger transferred into action, and Graebe was compelled to save the lives of as many innocents as he could.

With the help of his two assistants, he developed a complex rescue network in villages all over Ukraine. He fed the people out of his own pocket, gave them nonexistent jobs on the railroad, and provided them with forged work papers, internal passports, and food-ration cards. At the end of the war he saved more Jews, taking them by train through Poland and Germany and then through the Allied lines, delivering them to the safety of the U.S. Army.

Reflecting on what he had accomplished during the war, Graebe said,

> Most of the Jews I had saved [in Rovno] were dead. I found it very hard to accept the limitations imposed on me by fate. My cunning should have been more effective than all the rifles of the Reich. My only consolation—and it took me a long time before I could accept it—was the knowledge that I gave some people a reprieve, an opportunity, a moment of life in a sea of death. Sometimes, now years later, I think of more things I could have done to save more people. I am not sure that anything would have worked better. I only wish that the people I had rescued could have been saved to see life on the other side of the war.[22]

In 1954 Herman "Fritz" Graebe was honored by Yad Vashem for his acts of compassion and help in rescuing Jews. I am honored to have had the opportunity to meet Mr. Graebe—a truly righteous man—and shall never forget the hospitality and kindness he showed me during my long interview with him.

When the Nazi's invaded France, a peace was negotiated between Marshal Philippe Pétain and Hitler. Northern France was to remain under German occupation, and southern France was to be free of German occupation—as long as it was obedient to Nazi rules. The southern part of France under the Vichy government was relatively free of German interference, though the leadership did the Nazis' bidding, and some bureaucrats were fascists. Fearing that the Allies were going to invade France—after the success of the African campaign against General Rommel's forces in 1943—the German command decided to occupy southern France and send the Nazi army to defend against any potential attack from the south. Southern France came directly under Nazi supervision, and fear was felt by the French people of the region. It was under these conditions that the Trocmés rescued Jews and other refugees.

Magda Trocmé, her husband, André, the pastor of the Huguenot church in the French village of Le Chambon, and other Chambonnaise people, including religious leaders such as Édouard Theis and Daniel Trocmé, rescued some 5,000 Jews by turning the churches in the village into a community of rescue.[23]

As the German army invaded France, a flood of Jewish refugees fled the danger in the north and arrived in the mountains of southern France, a land of Protestants who believed in helping their fellow human beings. With the Vichy government convincing French citizens to turn in Jews, there were few places Jews could take shelter. Pastor Trocmé was a pacifist and a conscientious objector whose philosophy was based simply in the principles of right and wrong. His concern was with protecting human life. There was no excuse not to. With the agreement of the church council, he spread the word to rescue Jewish men, women, and children and bring them in to safety. Slowly, the Jews seeped into the village, and the people hid them at their homes and farms. André Trocmé, Theis, and others were imprisoned in a Vichy detention camp for being uncooperative with the government and unwilling to give up the names of the Jews or the villagers hiding the Jews. But all the time they were held, Magda continued the work of saving Jews. All the toil and sacrifice of the Trocmés and their fellow villagers are seen in Magda's words:

> It is important, too, to know that we were a bunch of people together. This is not a handicap, but a help. If you have to fight it alone, it is more difficult. But we had the support of people we

knew, of people who understood without knowing precisely all that they were doing or would be called to do. None of us thought that we were heroes. We were just people trying to do our best. . . . In the end, I would like to say to people, "Remember that in your life there will be lots of circumstances that will need a kind of courage, a kind of decision of your own, not about other people, but about yourself." I would not say more.[24]

Why did the Trocmés help others? Philip Hallie, in his 1979 book *Lest Innocent Blood Be Shed*, said: "André Trocmé was too energetic, too surprisingly creative to be categorized neatly. But there was one description of himself that even he accepted, which was that of *un violent vaincu par Dieu*—a violent man conquered by God."[25] André felt a great tension between anger and love. In his childhood this tension grew out of his mother's death; in his youth it was because of his intense admiration for Kindler, a German soldier who taught him nonviolence; and in his parishes it took the form of passionate mysticism controlled by Magda's compassionate common sense. But ultimately, "Only his complex love for Jesus, for commitment itself, and for the fresh, the 'interesting,' could overcome this anger in him against Hitler, who was doing such harm to God's precious human lives."[26]

When I interviewed Magda in the French village of Le Chambon, she impressed me as a creative, loving, compassionate woman. When I asked why she and her husband risked so much to save others, she replied, "To help means to be human; it's that simple." Magda and André Trocmé, Édouard Theis, Daniel Trocmé, and other Chambonnaise people were all recognized by Yad Vashem for their courageous and righteous acts of rescue.

The Moral Behavior of Nations: Denmark, Bulgaria, Fascist Italy, and Others

Sometimes many members of a nation became rescuers who were triggered into action because their *principles* of justice and equity, derived through largely autonomous means, were being challenged in fundamental ways. Only a small minority (about 10 percent) acted out of consideration largely for independently derived overarching *principles*—a belief come to as a result of their own thinking and chiefly without reference to what others might think. When we asked an Italian rescuer why he helped, he said:

> It was all something very simple. Nothing grandiose was done. It was done simply without considering risk, without thinking about whether it would be an occasion for recognition or to be maligned. It was, in effect, done out of innocence. I didn't think I was doing anything other than what should be done, or that I was in any special danger because of what I was doing. Justice had to be done. Persecution of the innocents was unacceptable.

One Danish man told us the story about how on August 29, 1943, he and others heard that the Nazis were going to make a *razzia* (roundup) and put Danish Jews into German concentration camps. Together with friends from the police department, they organized a refugee organization and began to ferry Jews by taxi and even by police cars down to the commercial fishing harbor, arranging for them to go across to Sweden.

The harbors were controlled partly by the German navy but also by the coast police—a special department of the Danish police force. Our informant told us, "We had to be rather careful to do our 'shipments' from places where controllers would not stop fishing boats and where we knew German navy patrol boats would not be present. After a week's time, we managed to get all the people of Jewish extraction out of the country— 7,000 of them."

Some nations—notably Denmark, Bulgaria, and even fascist Italy— helped Jews and other victims of Nazi persecution as a function of, if not state policy, at least daily practice. Many other nations gave lip service to helping the refugees of Nazi Europe but did little to save lives. For instance, during the Evian conference of 1938 in France, delegates from thirty-two nations met and spent nine days discussing the plight of refugees from Germany and Austria, but little was done. When the German government heard about talk of sympathy for Jewish refugees in Germany, it replied that foreign countries criticized Germany for their treatment of the Jews, but none of them wanted to open their doors when the opportunity presented itself. Sadly, this seems to be true.

During the war various attempts were made to bring Jewish and other persecuted children to the United States. After *Kristallnacht* in 1938, U.S. Senator Robert Wagner and U.S. Representative Edith Rogers introduced a bill in Congress that would enable 20,000 children over and above the German quota, but not necessarily only Jews, to enter the United States over the course of the next two years. After a struggle, the bill was taken off the congressional agenda. However, in the summer of 1940, when the Battle of Britain was at its height, the idea of bringing British children to the United States on a temporary basis was broached. Within a few weeks the U.S. State Department made it possible for British children to enter this country as visitors, although Jewish children from Germany were denied the opportunity to come (as per standing immigration laws). There is also the suggestion of anti-Semitism at the State Department.

Sometimes entire villages were recognized as Righteous Among the Nations, such as the Dutch village of Nieuwlande. During 1942–1943 the entire village resolved that in every house it would hide at least one Jew. All 117 villagers were recognized. The small town of Le Chambon-Sur-Lignon in France, where the residents rescued 5,000 Jews under the moral leadership of Pastor Trocmé and his wife, Magda, was recognized as Righteous Among the Nations.

It is well known that Denmark implemented various rescue techniques during those dark years. Georg Duckwitz, the German diplomat in Denmark, warned Danish and Jewish leaders that the Nazis had decided to round up Danish citizens. As a result, most Danish Jews were rescued by the Danish underground and the general population. Denmark, along with Norway, attempted to save their Jewish citizens by helping them into Sweden. This great nationwide rescue effort in Denmark was recognized among the Righteous of the World. Initially, Italy and Hungary were very slow to cooperate with the Nazis, and by dragging their feet they managed to save many of their citizens.

Albania was also saving Jews. Though Albania never had a large Jewish population—in 1930 there were fewer than 300 Jews in the country—during the Holocaust 1,800 Jews fled to Albania from nearby Serbia, Croatia, Macedonia, and northern Greece.

In speaking about Albania and Kosovo, Dr. Mordecai Paldiel said, "In Pristina, the capital of Kosovo, several hundred Jews were deported to concentration camps. Jews in other areas were not harmed, but Jews faced deportation from Albania proper when it came under direct German rule. However, the overwhelming majority of the Albanian population, Muslim and Christian, gave refuge to 2,000 Jews in their midst, resulting in almost total rescue of the Jewish community."[27] Dr. Paldiel, the director of Yad Vashem, has catalogued the reasons given by rescuers for why they risked their lives on behalf of Jews. Among the responses were: "I did what I could. I'm sorry I could not do more." "What I did was the most natural thing to do; it would have been unnatural not to do what I did." "It was something had to be done." "I could not do otherwise."

I find in these stories a number of motivating factors that differentiate the gentile rescuers from their bystanding neighbors. The rescuers included the Holocaust victims as part of their own moral community. They exhibited the altruistic spirit in thought and in deed. They rescued others because they had a high degree of empathy and compassion toward the victims. They couldn't bare to see their own principles of justice, fairness, and equity violated. They possessed internalized moral authority and the moral precepts of their communities. And almost uniformly these rescuers exhibited courage, moral conviction, and behaviors learned from significant role models while they were growing up. Values of caring and prosocial behavior were instilled in them from infancy, and they believed that the mistreating of others for ideological or any other reason was never justified and could not be tolerated. Rescuers, by and large, exhibit a commonality with all human beings and do not create dichotomies between themselves and the other. Although these motivating characteristics were to some extent found in all rescuers, some were triggered to action by their empathic predisposition, some by their normocentrism, and some by the principles of justice. By their deeds, these rescuers managed to diminish evil in the world. The welfare of the other became the rescuers primary concern, regardless of risk.

4

"Have Courage and Remember"

Jewish Rescuers in Nazi-Occupied Europe

> You shall not fear the terror of the night, nor the arrow that flieth by day. . . . Only with your eyes shall you behold the reward of the wicked.
>
> **—Psalm 91:5, 8**

I n 1943, at Auschwitz-Birkenau, SS officers were separating people into two groups at the selection platform—those with children to be exterminated right away in the gas chambers, and those who looked healthy enough to be sent to slave-labor camps. Luba Tryszynska's family was executed by the Nazis. Her husband's mother made a promise to her son that no matter what happened, she would save Luba's life. When she saw what was happening on the platform—that it was mothers with children who were being taken—she grabbed Luba's son and stayed with the child, knowing that she would be exterminated with him and Luba would be sent to work.

A lucky event occurred inside Auschwitz. Ola, a prisoner doctor, recognized Luba and requested that she be her maid and assistant. Luba and her closest friend, Hermina, made a promise to themselves that they would help each other or they would die together. It is generally accepted that people who supported each in concentration camps had a better chance of survival. While at Auschwitz, Luba Tryszynska heard that nurses were being sent to a camp in Germany, so she volunteered to go, and in December 1944 she was sent to the Bergen-Belsen concentration camp. There were no gas chambers in this camp, but malnutrition, diseases, and summary executions made it a very gruesome and efficient extermination center. In fact, one of Luba's jobs at Auschwitz was to drag the dead bodies to the crematorium. As the Allied forces were closing in and order was breaking down, the already wretched conditions worsened. Transferees kept arriving, jamming more people into the vermin-infested barracks.

The month Luba arrived, a desperate group of children stood in an open area in Bergen-Belsen, crying and shivering in the wind. "They had watched mutely as their fathers and older brothers were loaded aboard a convoy of SS trucks and driven away," says Lawrence Elliott, who interviewed Luba for his *Reader's Digest* article "Heroine in Hell."[1] Soon thereafter the trucks returned for the mothers and sisters to be taken to their death. The children did their best to comfort one another as Luba, nearby in the darkness, listened to the sounds of their crying. Luba suffered. She closed her eyes tight, trying to shut out the terrible memories and noises, but she heard and could not stop thinking about the children.

When Luba and other women opened up the barrack doors, two truckloads of children were being unloaded into a waiting area near the barracks. Luba inquired as to who these children were and learned the were the Dutch children of diamond workers. The Nazis were making plans to open a diamond factory in Bergen-Belsen, but when this did not work out, the parents were sent to labor camps, the women to salt mines (where the munitions factories were housed); the children were left alone. The children were crying and making noise, so the guards brought some sandwiches. But after a while, when the noise and crying continued, they loaded the kids back onto the trucks and took them into the forest. After the first truck stopped, the drivers argued about what to do with the kids, then decided to return to the camp and unload them again.

Luba, who became known later as "the Angel of Bergen-Belsen," approached a child and asked, "What happened? Who left you here?" One of the older boys explained that they were brought there without being told where they were going. The oldest of the fifty-four children was fourteen and was carrying a two-and-a-half-year-old girl. There were other children who were even younger. Seeing this, Luba gestured for them to follow her to the barracks. Some of the women tried to stop her from bringing the children inside because they knew that this meant tremendous trouble and would provoke the SS. But Luba would not give up. She shamed the women by asking them, "If these were your children, would you turn them away? Listen to me; they are somebody's children," and she led the ragged group in. When the children told her what the Nazis had done to their parents, she was determined to save them. Her own son had been murdered, so she would particularly make sure that these children would not suffer the same fate.

Knowing that you could not hide dozens of children, she told an SS officer what happened and said, "Let me take care of them," and added, while putting her hand on his arm, "there will never be a problem, I promise." "You are a nurse—what do you want with Jewish trash?" he inquired. "Because I was a mother, too," she said. "Because I lost my son in Auschwitz." The SS officer suddenly realized that her hand was still on his arm; prisoners were not supposed to touch any German personnel. He struck her full in the face with his fist, knocking her to the ground, making her lips bleed. She persisted, "You are old enough to be a grandfather," she said. "Why do you want to harm innocent children, babies? They will all die without someone to look after them." Luba thought that he was moved, or perhaps he just did not want to decide what to do with the children. He barked, "If you want these lousy children, you can have them. Keep them. To hell with them."

Now the problem was how to feed them. Obtaining food was a major difficulty and a cause of anxiety. The *Blockowa*—the non-Jewish female guard in charge of the barracks—would look the other way as long as the bribes continued. After a while the guard wanted more, and the task became more difficult. Every morning Luba went to the kitchen to beg, barter, or steal food for the children. The boys were sometimes able to steal some bread. The children were subsequently dubbed the "diamond children," and they lovingly called her "Sister Luba" and cherished her as they had their own lost mothers. It was Luba who procured the food, nursed them when they were ill, and sang lullabies through the long dark nights. Communication was a problem because these were Dutch kids, and Luba didn't speak Dutch, but they understood the universal language of love. In the midst of all of the horrors caused by the Nazis, Luba kept her fifty-two children alive.

After some months, Bergen-Belsen inmates knew that the Allies were closing in. It had been an awful winter, and as the spring of 1945 arrived the

Germans tried to dispose of all of the old corpses that littered the camp. It had been a losing battle against diseases such as typhoid and dysentery, which had left the children dehydrated and exhausted. Lawrence Elliott says that Anne Frank was dying in one of those barracks. Good news arrived on Sunday, April 15, 1945, when British tanks rolled into the camp. Loud speakers boomed "You are free! You are free!" in a half-dozen languages. The Allies brought doctors and medication; what they saw was thousands of corpses lying unburied in the camp.

Nearly a quarter of the 60,000 inmates died after liberation, mostly because they were either too ill to recover or because they overate. Of the fifty-two children Luba found and looked after, only two died in her care after liberation. Luba stayed with the children and gave them encouragement that some day they might see their parents and relatives. The British authorities decided to send them to Holland, and after a very sad good-bye she left the children behind. A Dutch official said, "It is thanks to her that these children survived. . . . We owe her much for what she has done."[2]

Luba found a new life for herself in Sweden, where she met Sol Frederick, also a survivor. They married there and moved to the United States, where they had two children of their own. But Luba never forgot about her other fifty-two children. Some of those children blossomed in the United States, others in Australia and elsewhere. One of the diamond children, Jack Rodri, kept thinking about Luba and wondered where she was. In the early 1950s he went on an American television show and told the story of Luba—the Angel of Bergen-Belsen—and said that he was trying to find her. Contact was made soon thereafter, and in 1991 forty-eight of the diamond children were brought together; the Dutch Royal Family awarded Luba the Humanitarian Award.

Not only was there armed resistance in the ghettos and concentration camps of Eastern Europe; we also know that in Western and Southern Europe there were massive rescues and resistance by individuals and groups in the Netherlands, Germany, France, Yugoslavia, Italy, Greece, and Bulgaria. Historical accuracy demands that we dispel the commonly held belief that Jews walked liked sheep to the slaughter. The image of European Jews passively accepting their fate is one of the most powerful myths of World War II. Historical myths exist because they serve a purpose; the myth of Jewish passivity has served many. To anti-Semites, it has provided proof of the lack of Jewish character, reinforcing the historic stereotype of the passive, cowardly Jew. To the Allies who refused to intervene to halt the extermination of

Jews, the myth has served to mitigate guilt: If the Jews themselves were passive, were the Allies really to blame for not intervening?

Faced with the determination of the Third Reich to exterminate them, European Jews had three behavioral options: collaborate fully with the Nazis in hopes that by doing so they could save themselves; adopt a "defensive acquiescence," hoping that by complying with all Nazi requests the Nazis would exempt them from destruction; or choose to resist.[3]

The definition of "resistance" is complicated and has been discussed much by scholars. In my view, resistance implies a variety of dangerous activities by groups and individuals to save lives. Such activities include hiding and transporting victims, sabotage against the Nazis, morale-building operations, underground political work, active unarmed resistance, and armed resistance.[4] Taken in the broader sense, then, resistance can be divided into four types: revolts and underground activities inside ghettos and camps; revolts and underground activities outside ghettoes and camps; partisan activities; and actions in defense of lives and human dignity.[5]

Resistance against the Third Reich was difficult for anyone, but it was nearly impossible for Jews. Scattered in the midst of a largely indifferent and frequently hostile Gentile population, the obstacles seemed insurmountable, and yet many Jews resisted—they fought those who tried to round them up, they escaped to the forests to join the partisans, they caused revolts in camps and ghettos, they engaged in sabotage, they hid.[6]

Regardless of the particular form of resistance described, success was determined by three factors. First, the character and skills of the individuals played a crucial role. Individuals who were assimilated into non-Jewish culture had a better chance of passing as Aryan. Courage and the ability to adapt to unforeseen circumstances, non-Jewish physical appearance, and German language skills all helped. Second, the social environment, or the historical attitude of the local population toward Jews, could spell the difference between survival and death. Surviving without assistance from the non-Jewish population was next to impossible.[7] Third, the physical environment also played a crucial role: Those who escaped to the forests of Byelorussia had a better chance than those fleeing on the open steppes of Ukraine.

The following stories illustrate the courage of the men and women who risked their lives individually and in groups to escape the horrors of the ghettoes, the concentration and extermination camps, and the tyranny of the Nazi regime.

Inside Ghettoes and Concentration Camps

Besides Luba Tryszynska's rescue in the Bergen-Belsen camp, there were attempts in a hundred ghettos in Poland, Lithuania, Byelorussia, and Ukraine, underground organizations to wage armed war against the Nazis from within the ghettoes, or to break out by use of armed force to engage in partisan operations outside. Resistance in the ghettoes became more intensified when the Nazis invaded Russia in 1941 and started murdering Russian Jews en masse. Despite the fact that some conservatives and cautious *Judenrats* (Jewish councils) opposed armed resistance, young fighters started organizing. Knowing full well that they could not win against such overwhelming odds, they were willing to fight until death.[8] Thus, there were uprisings in Auschwitz-Birkenau and in many smaller camps and ghettos. Young Jewish men and women sabotaged crematoriums. They broke out and fought back. When they finally knew that the Nazi design was for total extermination, they fought back, striving to restore the reputation of a heroic Jewish people.

Chaika Grossman

By 1942 many of the ghettos in Poland—including Bobowa, my ghetto—were being liquidated, but the Bialystok ghetto, which served as an important industrial center for the Nazis, was relatively stable. Nevertheless, the Jewish political factions within the Bialystok ghetto were organizing for resistance. In January 1942 the Jewish underground sent Chaika Grossman to Bialystok, her hometown. She posed as a Polish Christian so that she could live outside the ghetto and was instrumental in organizing a leftist-Zionist united front, providing weapons to the ghetto occupants. Differences in ideology and strategies had separated various factions, but by the end of July 1943 all the Jewish underground groups in the ghetto finally agreed to form a united front, and Grossman was elected as a member of the command staff. She undertook dangerous missions to the Warsaw, Vilna, and Grodno ghettos to share information with Jewish leaders.

On August 15, 1943, the SS units surrounded the Bialystok ghetto. They sent troops into the factory area and ordered the remaining Jews to assemble for deportation. With few weapons at their disposal, the ghetto fighters went into action, carrying out acts of sabotage and inciting the Jews to revolt and escape. Against overwhelming forces, they held out for almost a week. During the uprising, Grossman fought alongside her comrades. She also managed to escape to the Aryan side of the city, where she continued providing supplies to partisans in the forests. In 1948 she settled in Israel and later served for twenty years in the Israeli parliament. She died on May 26, 1996.

Abba Kovner

Abba Kovner, who became the poet laureate of Israel, is one of the great heroes of the Vilna ghetto in the Lithuanian capital. He, along with a group of young women including Vtka Kempner, Ruzka Korczak, and other members of the Young Guard, had realized that Jews were in great danger, being exterminated in various places. They decided to take action to avenge these killings and became part of the guerilla movements in the Baltic forests that since 1942 had been undertaking acts of sabotage against the Germans, including blowing up German troop trains and railroad tracks. They were up against great odds and lacked the much-needed support of the ghetto president, Jacob Gens, who felt that by cooperating with the Nazis he would save the majority of the Jews under his supervision. The two young women, Vtka and Ruzka, served as couriers. Because the Germans normally did not suspect women to be dangerous, these two partisans, with their hair dyed, could pass as Polish girls. A band of these guerilla partisans, known as "the avengers" and led by Abba Kovner, emerged from the Baltic forest and joined the Russian army in an attack on Vilna.[9] Later on he and Vlatka Kempner married and moved to Israel.

Virtually every one of the numerous ghetto uprisings ended in defeat. The Jews faced overwhelming power from the Nazis, and they brought inexperience and a lack of arms.[10] What they did not lack was courage. Jews fought for various reasons—to avenge the murders of other Jews, to ensure that future generations would know that Jews had resisted the Nazis, for the sake of Jewish honor, and, of course, to save their own lives.

The Jewish resistance groups were divided for various ideological and political reasons. Little help was received from the Poles, yet Zegota was one of the exceptional groups—Jews and non-Jews—that organized to try to save lives in Poland.

One of the most heroic and unequal fights in the history of European war was the Warsaw uprising.[11] On August 28, 1942, the Bund movement, a Polish underground organization to aid Jewish victims, set up a Jewish fighting force established by a young man named Mordekhai Anielewicz. In October and November 1942 most of the underground parties moved into the Warsaw ghetto and started organizing. The fighting began on April 19,

1943, with approximately 700 poorly armed and poorly trained Jewish fighters holding out for three weeks against an army of more than 3,000 trained troops commanded by General Juergen Von Stroop. Although most of the fighters died, they also took Nazi lives. Some scholars consider this resistance by civilians in Warsaw as the longest fight against a powerful army in all of Nazi-occupied Europe.

Jack Werber

In his autobiography, Jack Werber describes how 700 Jewish children were rescued from certain death in Buchenwald in late 1944.[12] Werber was from Radom, Poland, where most of the Jews were killed during the Nazi Holocaust. He led a fairly normal life until the German army entered Radom in 1939 and arrested him. A rumor had circulated in the city that the Germans needed workers in the fatherland and were gathering up young Jewish men. A number of Jews, fearing the worst, left just two days before the Germans arrived; Werber was not among them. The German army, which, according to Werber, initially behaved well in order to fool the Jews, was soon replaced by Hitler's storm troopers—the SS—who "stole, robbed and beat the citizens indiscriminately and stopped paying for everything," according to Werber. He describes brutality, beatings, and forced labor designed to humiliate the Jews and end any resistance.

Werber was arrested and beaten, thrown into a truck, and taken to prison. He was moved about to various camps and eventually ended up in Buchenwald. In 1942 another inmate—a political prisoner named Emil Carlebach—approached him to join the Buchenwald International Underground. Initially, it was made up of German Communists and Social Democrats, including German Jews and other Germans such as Jehovah's Witnesses who had been imprisoned for being conscientious objectors. Eventually it admitted non-German Jews as well.

Carlebach was a German-Jewish Communist and the *Blockaltester* (head of the block) in Barrack No. 22. Because of his political activity as a teenager, he had been arrested a few times, had spent time in other prisons before, and was sent to the newly established Buchenwald in 1937. Also in the camp there was a group of criminals who were sworn enemies of the underground. They had come to Buchenwald about the same time as the political prisoners and were initially put into power positions. The SS could rely upon them to control and brutalize the inmates. Werber relates that the underground eventually took control of the camp, but not before hundreds of resistors lost their lives in the struggle with the criminal element. Slowly the underground managed to put its own people into leadership positions in the camp. Food was in short supply, leading to a tremendous source of conflict; some fared better than others. It was Werber's job to report people who stole food and sold it outside for other commodities.

In the summer of 1944 it was learned that a transport of several thousand Jews was coming from Skarzysko, a town near Radom. In Skarzysko was a large ammunition factory that employed many Jews as slave labor. As the Red Army approached Skarzysko, the camp was liquidated and the inmates dispersed, the bulk of them transported to Buchenwald. Among the several thousand were 700 boys between the age of six and sixteen. One of these boys was Sidney Finkel, who became my good friend after the liberation and who confirmed for me Jack Werber's account. Realizing that the children would be murdered, Werber and others knew immediate action must be taken.

Several factors contributed to Werber's success. The Nazi-created infrastructure of the camp required a minimum number of German officers; at least some of the day-to-day operations of the camp were delegated to inmates who by the end of the war were mostly underground operatives. A second factor was that inmates at Buchenwald (which had been a work camp for political prisoners and not primarily an extermination camp for Jews) were allowed a bit more leeway in terms of their actions and were sometimes able to receive packages from outside. Also contributing to their success was that in the last months of the war German officers became more afraid for their own personal safety and less concerned about what was happening in the camp.

Just before the arrival of the boys on the Skarzysko transport, Werber learned that the Nazis had murdered his entire family—wife, daughter, parents, seven brothers and sisters—and at first he felt that there was no reason to go on. But seeing the children transformed his outlook. Others in the underground, too, were determined not to allow the children to be destroyed. Werber, at very great personal risk, made the saving of these children his special mission.

With consent from the supervisors of the underground, Emil Carlebach called a meeting of Jewish members. The non-Jewish faction did not oppose saving the boys but was not involved in the action. It was up to the Jews to save those 700 lives. Werber describes the leader of Block 23, Karl Seigmeyer, a German Communist from Leipzig who was extremely helpful with concealing the boys in that block: "Calling him a good person isn't adequate. He was a saint," he said to me when I interviewed him.[13] Hans Reines, who was an assimilated Czech Jew and the deputy block leader, was also an outstanding individual and very helpful with the rescue.

Werber did his best to show the children love, compassion, and understanding. This was especially important because most of them no longer had living parents. Werber states that the very act of doing this gave his life meaning. The kitchen *kapo* (a prisoner who was in charge of other prisoners) set aside food for the youngsters, and quite a few blocks had special bowls or baskets in which inmates would put food scraps—although most did not know that these scraps were going to the children. Some inmates were unwilling to give up their scraps of food, but a great amount of pressure was put on them to do so. Werber made arrangements for the children to be hidden in various barracks and be given false work papers. Collectively, the underground started a school where the children were able to study Jewish history, music, and the Hebrew language. This activity offered a great deal of hope for all that they might survive. Ultimately, most of them did.

A decision was made to disperse the children to different barracks: the majority went to the adjacent Small Camp and was housed in Block 66, where they did not have to work. Werber notes that "Elie Wiesel, Rabbi Israel Lau, the chief rabbi of Israel, and his brother Naftaly Lavi, who was an Israeli diplomat, were also in this block. Of course, we had no idea at the time who they would become. They were simply part of a larger group of children whose lives we helped save."[14] The children were almost always kept inside the barracks and out of sight, and perhaps it was simply luck that the SS men were so busy trying to avoid being sent to the Russian front that they didn't pay close attention to all that was happening in the camps. When soldiers did try to visit a barrack, they were told horrifying stories of illness and epidemics.

On April 3, 1944, camp commander Herman Pister made a speech to the prison leaders, saying, "We know that you have ammunition. We know everything that you're doing. But don't provoke us. And if you don't revolt, I give you my word as a soldier to turn over the entire camp to the Americans at the end."[15] Obviously, their luck was holding; the commandant saw the defeat of the Nazis on the horizon, and the Americans soon liberated the camp. Most of the 700 children were saved.

Roza Robota

By September 1944 Auschwitz-Birkenau was the only Nazi killing center still in operation, and liberation seemed close at hand for the prisoners there.

The Soviet army had moved deep into German-occupied Poland, and Allied planes had begun bombing nearby German factories. For months, three slave laborers named Ester Wajcblum, Ella Gartner, and Regina Safirsztain had been stealing small amounts of gunpowder from the German munitions factory within the Auschwitz complex (Weichsel-Union-Metallwerke) and smuggling it to the camp's resistance movement. Among these in the camp movement was Roza Robota, a young Jewish woman who worked at the clothing location at Birkenau. Once she received the gunpowder, Robota passed it to her comrades in the *Sonderkommando*—the special squad of prisoners who worked in the crematoria. They were planning to destroy the crematorium and the gas chambers and spark a general uprising. Then rumors spread that the SS was going to exterminate the *Sonderkommando*. The SS had done this previously in order to get a fresh crop of workers; it was safer for the Nazis to exterminate the workers on a regular basis. The *Sonderkommando* at Crematorium IV set fire to the crematoria and attacked the SS guards with hammers, axes, and stones. The flames were the signal for the camp uprising, and the *Sonderkommando* at Crematorium II moved into action, killing a *kapo* and several SS men. Several hundred prisoners escaped for a time, but most were recaptured and murdered. Two hundred prisoners who took part in the revolt were executed. The gunpowder theft was traced to the four women, and they were arrested and brutally tortured, but they did not divulge who their coconspirators were. All four were hanged. Roza Robota's final message to her comrades in the underground was "*chazak v'ematz,*" which translates as "be strong and have courage."

Mordechai Tenenbaum

Mordechai Tenenbaum (1916–1943) was a resistance leader in several ghettoes, including Warsaw, Vilna, and Bialystok; he established an underground archive that contained substantial and irrefutable evidence of the Jews' sufferings and their struggle against the Nazi murderers.[16] He was born in Warsaw and went to a secular school in which Hebrew was the language of instruction. In 1936 he was accepted as a student at Warsaw Oriental Institute, where he studied the Semitic languages. His skill with languages would help him later in moving around in occupied Poland posing as a tatar—an ethnic person from Russia, a descendant of the Mongolian conqueror Genghis Khan, perhaps. For a time he was a member of a pro-Israel social movement called Ha-Shomer ha-Leummi (National Guard), and in 1938 he joined the Har Chalutz movement.

Israel Gutman, who has chronicled much of the Jewish rescue and resistance during the Holocaust, relates, "In September 1939, before the fall of
Warsaw, Tenenbaum and his comrades left the city and made their way to
Kovel and Vilna. Their purpose was to evade the Germans and reach Palestine. Tenenbaum then provided his comrades with forged immigration documents, while he chose to stay in Vilna."[17]

In June 1941 the Germans lost no time in launching *Aktionen*—the mass
killing of Jews and the conquering of Vilna. Historian Gutman explains:

> Tenenbaum tried to help his fellow members by providing them
> with forged work permits, but many were caught. During the lull
> in the *Aktionen*, Tenenbaum sent his girlfriend, Tamara Schnei-
> derman, on a mission to Warsaw. In accordance with a joint deci-
> sion made by [the leadership of his group], he moved the
> survivors [of his group] from Vilna to the Bialystok ghetto, which
> was still relatively quiet. He accomplished this thanks to the help
> he received from Anton Shmid, an anti-Nazi Austrian sergeant.[18]

Tenenbaum took part in a meeting of the Har Chalutz youth in the
Vilna ghetto and called for Jews not to permit themselves "to be led like
sheep to the slaughter," to refuse to cooperate with the Nazis, and to resist
deportation by all available means. Then he left Vilna with forged documents identifying him as a tatar named Yussuf Tamaroff. He went to the
Grodno and Bialystok ghettoes, where he again arranged resistance movements. In March he returned to Warsaw and joined his colleagues from the
Har Chalutz head office. At a meeting attended by representatives of all political parties, he gave a firsthand report of the situation in Vilna and other
ghettoes. He assured them all that it was definitely the policy of the Germans to exterminate all Jews under their control. Though some questioned
his assertion, he was too soon proven right. The gassing of prisoners started
in the extermination camps of Poland. The various underground operations
united, and Tenenbaum visited several branches of the underground, including those in Krakow and Czestochowa. Together with Yitzhak Zuckerman,
Tenenbaum edited an underground publication titled *Yediot*, which helped
to reinforce the fighting spirit of youth and their determination to resist the
Nazis. He was also one of the major founders of the Jewish Fighting Organization (ZOB) in July 1942. He was active in acquiring arms outside of ghettoes and training the movement's members in their use. In November 1942

he was wounded while trying to enter the Grodno ghetto, which had been sealed by the Germans.

In January 1943 Tenenbaum sent Tamara Schneiderman to the Warsaw ghetto again and sent Bronka Winicki, a young girl from Grodno, to the Aryan part of Bialystok. Schneiderman took money and reports with her to deliver to the ZOB. However, she failed to return and disappeared during the first Warsaw ghetto uprising. In February 1943 the Germans began the deportation of Jews from Bialystok.

> Because of the scarcity of weapons in [their] possession, Tenen-
> baum decided to keep his forces intact and hold back, but to in-
> tensify efforts to obtain more arms and train his men. He also
> sent emissaries into the forest to make contact with the partisans
> to search for arms. The Jews employed in German factories were
> instructed to sabotage the products on which they were working.
> Weapons were stolen from the Germans, food was stockpiled,
> and, in the large bunker that [the resistance movement] had
> built. . . , its members listened to foreign broadcasts. Tenenbaum
> drew up a call for resistance: "Let us fall as heroes, and though we
> die, yet we shall live."[19]

In July 1943 Tenenbaum displayed superb self-control and leadership, managing to unify the fighting commandos in the Bialystok ghetto. In August 1943, anticipating the liquidation of the ghetto, he gave the signal for uprising. His plan was to break the German force surrounding the ghetto, but it was too strong, and the plan to break the blockade was not successful.

We know many of the details of the last battle.[20] In November 1942 men who had former military training under Tenenbaum had left the ghetto for the forest, where they established the Bialystok Partisan Outpost. In December they experienced their first armed encounter with Germans. In January 1943 another small group of the Bialystok underground left the ghetto and joined them. In the Bialystok ghetto, between January and August, there had been several examples of resistance to the German attempt to force the deportation of Bialystok's 15,000 Jews to the Treblinka death camp. In one rebellion many Germans were killed, but 2,000 Jews died as well. On the night of May 24, 1943, they confronted German police at the border of the ghetto and miracu-lously escaped. Early in June, after this show of force, there was a unified armed self-defense of the ghetto. The underground distributed leaflets encouraging Jews to join its ranks and to prepare to stand up to the Germans in future actions and roundups. It also sought out and executed informants and collaborators during the first *Aktionen*. However, the tactics of armed self-defense proved inadequate to cope with the surprising invasion of the ghetto on the morning of August 16. Tenenbaum attempted to prevent the ghetto population from assembling for deportation and tried to get as many people as possible to follow the underground members and join the partisans at the hideout in the woods, but they were overwhelmed. There were some 300 ghetto fighters, armed with a few machine guns and homemade hand grenades, against 3,000 heavily armed Germans with tank support. For several weeks the fighters persevered in sporadic outbursts of fighting, but most were apprehended and executed. Some retreated into bunkers, but only a few were able to break out and reach the partisans. Except for one or two survivors, all the Jews who assembled for deportation—or who were cornered by the Germans the first days of fighting—perished in Majdanek, another major extermination camp in Poland. Tenenbaum and his assistant, Moskowicz, committed suicide as the ghetto uprising came to an end. After the war the Polish government posthumously awarded a military heroes medal to Tenenbaum.

Outside Ghettoes and Camps

Individuals outside of ghettos, camps, organized groups in the forests, and elsewhere played a crucial role in the rescues. Ellen Land-Weber, once an interviewer of gentile rescuers for the Altruistic Personality Institute, wrote a book entitled *To Save a Life: Stories of Holocaust Rescue.* In it she focuses on the stories of six rescuers, one of whom was Mirjam Pinkhof, who grew up in a loving family, one that believed cruelty and injustice should not be tolerated. Under the leadership of the charismatic Dutch resistance leader Westerweel Joop, Pinkhof successfully rescued a number of German-Jewish children who had come to Holland after *Kristallnacht* in 1938. Among the children was a young woman named Sophie Yaari, who tells the story of her rescue by Pinkhof. Pinkhof's actions are an excellent illustration of how several Jews, at great risk to themselves, performed heroically to save others.[21]

Ernst Papanek

Dr. Ernst Papanek was an educator and psychologist who, with the aid of an organization called the Oeuvre du Secours aux Enfants (the Relief Organization for Children), bought castles in southern France to serve as shelters for children orphaned and made refugees when their parents were slaughtered or shipped to extermination camps. Papanek directed these shelters, and he and his staff attempted to give the children a "normal" life, despite the brutality they had experienced. When the Nazis occupied Vichy France, Papanek took desperate measures to ship children to safety, but his persistent attempts to get the United States to accept some of them met with failure. Not all the children survived; but those who did have recognized Dr. Papanek as their savior.[22]

Marianne Cohn

One heroic young Jewish woman named Marianne Cohn was instrumental in rescuing children from the Vichy government and Nazi occupation in France.[23] In 1934, when she was ten, she and her parents fled to Spain, but during the civil war they moved back to the safety of France. That haven did not last long, because within six weeks the Nazis invaded France and defeated the French army. Her parents were interned, and she and her sister found safe haven at a Jewish children's shelter in Vichy France.

During the "accommodation," Marshal Philippe Pétain negotiated an armistice with Hitler to administer the southern part of France, establishing his government in Vichy. Obeying Nazi dictates, he revoked the citizenship of a number of naturalized Jews, and in 1940 his police helped organize a mass transportation of Jews to their deaths in the camps. Marianne Cohn was a member of the Elcaireurs Israelites de France (French Jewish Scouts), a youth organization deeply involved in all forms of resistance, including saving Jewish children by getting them to Switzerland. The group had to be constantly vigilant because the SS, the Gestapo, and the fascist Vichy police units were on constant lookout trying to capture children for extermination.

On various occasions Marianne Cohn was directly involved in saving the lives of children, arranging false passports for them and accompanying them to the Swiss border. Tragically in May 1944, Marianne was caught near the Swiss border with a convoy of small children, was arrested, and was savagely beaten. Eventually the Nazis removed her from prison, murdered her, and disposed of her body in a shallow grave in the nearby woods.

Bela Elak

The Nazis and the Hungarian Arrow Cross were still rounding up Jews to exterminate them as late as 1944. In Budapest, the Swedish diplomat Raoul Wallenberg succeeded at what couldn't have been accomplished without the assistance of a number of heroic Jews.[24] One such individual was Dr. Bela Elak, one of Wallenberg's right-hand men. Even though Elak's life was often threatened, hundreds owe their lives to him. Elak was working with an organization called Schutzling-Protokoll, a department section of the Swedish embassy, which dealt with persons who had disappeared. He also visited many places such as the forced labor camps from which Jews were taken to the railroad station to be shipped to Auschwitz and death.

Wallenberg established Swedish neutral houses where Jews were given false Swedish passports or Swedish identification papers and then, under Wallenberg's forceful supervision, were extricated from cattle cars on the way to Auschwitz and other camps. Elak performed feats of courage, spending several weeks on the Hungarian border using his own initiative to save Jews. By bribing guards, he was able to drive a car along marching lines of desperate Jews, grabbing people who were barely able to walk from the ranks of the marchers, put them in the car, and take them back to safe houses. His regular method for saving children was to drive very slowly past a column of deportees; when he saw a mother staggering while carrying a child in her arms, he would take the child with her permission and speed off in his car to a safe place. In his rescue efforts he received enormous help from Baron Bilmos Apor, the Catholic bishop of Gayor, who provided refuge for a number of the Jewish deportees Elak brought to him.

Fortunately for Dr. Elak's rescue operations, there were also some police superintendents such as Nador Batizfaly, regular collaborators with Wallenberg's Swedish rescue operations. One day Batizfaly arranged for eight people who possessed Swedish *Schutzpasses* (protection pass) to be brought out from the Olbrect barracks, together with six persons who had Spanish protective papers, and took them all to safety. Labor service workers were escorted from the railroad station at Jozsef Baros to the building of the Swedish embassy at 6 Tatra-Utca, and those who were in the institute of Katalin Boldog were taken to the brick factory for safety.

It sometimes appeared hopeless to get persons with protective passes released, although some foreign countries had issued passes that let the Nazis know who their citizens were. On numerous occasions Wallenberg instructed Police Superintendent Batizfaly and Elak to visit the Hungarian town of Budaors, where they tried to persuade SS commanders to release Jews. They succeeded only in obtaining promises that the commanders would ask their superiors for further instructions. Wallenberg and his assistants pressed the issue, obtaining the release of prisoners holding protective passes from among the deportees waiting at the Budaors station. They succeeded, and a large number of Jews were not sent to Auschwitz.

Hannah Senesz, Haviva Reik, and Sara Braverman

The British cooperated with Palestinian Jews to parachute rescuers into the Nazi-occupied territories of Hungary, Slovakia, and Romania, not only to help save Jews but also to help the Allies in their defeat of the Germans.[25] These were people who had immigrated to Israel several years before but knew the language and the terrain of their native countries. In part, the British chose them because they were European-born and had relatives living in Europe; these people were dedicated to liberation and to fighting tyranny.

Among those who volunteered and were trained by the British were three women: Hannah Senesz of Hungary, Haviva Reik, who was parachuted to Slovakia, and Sara Braverman, who parachuted into Romania. Of the three dozen or more who dropped into Nazi-occupied Europe, Senesz and Reik were among those who lost their lives at the hands of the Nazis and Nazi collaborators. Braverman returned to Palestine, where she played an important role in the kibbutz movement until her retirement after the war.

Hannah Senesz was a twenty-three-year-old poet when she parachuted into Hungary. Tragically, she was caught by the Hungarian police and tortured. The Germans charged her with being a spy, which she denied, saying that she had come to see her family. To torment her further, her mother was brought to the jail. When Hannah saw her mother, she cried out—"Forgive me mother!"—believing that had she not shown up her mother would not have been compromised. Both women were subsequently imprisoned; although her mother Katarina was released in September 1944, Hannah was tried for espionage and executed in November of that year.

Hannah wrote the following poem:

> *Blessed is the match*
> *that is consumed in kindling flame.*
> *Blessed is the flame that burns*
> *in the secret fastness of the heart.*
> *Blessed is the heart with strength*
> *to stop its beating for honor's sake.*
> *Blessed is the match*
> *that is consumed in kindling flame.*[26]

This heroic yet tragic episode underscores how the role of women in wars has been underemphasized, including those in World War II. Women performed heroic acts just as men did during that war. This heroism was recognized in a 1973 film portraying the life of Haviva Reik.[27]

Marcel Rayman

A young man named Marcel Rayman, a Polish member of the French underground in Paris, was one of a group of foreign Yiddish-speaking Jews who, operating in small bands of partisans, bombed restaurants, hotels, cafes, and cinemas frequented mostly by the German military and police; they threw grenades at German soldiers as well. Following a series of mass arrests in 1943, the unit was disbanded, its members reassigned to other resistance units. Marcel joined the Manouchian group, "an underground detachment led by the young Armenian poet Missak Manouchian."[28] On September 28, 1943, Marcel and several others shot and killed Julius von Ritter, the German official in charge of conscripting French labor for work in Germany. In retribution for the shooting of von Ritter, German and French police arrested many members of the resistance. In February 1944, after several months of brutal interrogation, Rayman and twenty-two fellow partisans—many of them Jews—were placed on trial. German propagandists tried to use the proceedings to convince the French populace that the resistance was made up of criminals led by foreigners and Jews. Rayman was sentenced to death and, on February 21, 1944, was executed along with twenty-one others. On the day of his execution he wrote to his family: "When you read this I'll no longer be alive. I'm going to be shot today at three o'clock. I regret nothing that I've done. I'm completely tranquil and calm. I love you all and I hope that you'll live happily."[29]

George Mantello

In the early 1930s, when George Mantello was a successful businessman in Bucharest, Romania, he befriended an El Salvadoran consul member named Paul Castellanos. Castellanos later appointed Mantello honorary consul for Czechoslovakia, Yugoslavia, and Romania, to be based in Bucharest.[30] When the United States got involved in the war, all Latin American countries declared themselves with the Allies and broke diplomatic relations with the Nazis. Mantello, working as El Salvadoran consul, issued documents making people eligible to immigrate to El Salvador. Although passports cost a lot of money, Mantello offered them at no cost, as he was a wealthy man.

One of his most important accomplishments was to gather information about Nazi atrocities and deportations, as well as obtain support from eminent people such as Dr. Florian Manoliu, the Romanian commissioner attaché, Pastor Paul Vogt, Carl Barth, Emile Bruner, and Vissert Hooft. He publicized the atrocities happening in Europe, especially Auschwitz and the massive executions. This resulted in a publicity blitz in various Swiss newspapers with headlines such as "GASSED AND BURNED: THE HORROR AND DISGUST OF THE ENTIRE WORLD," "BUTCHERY OF MAN," "ASSASSINATION OF JEWS," "SILENCE AND COMPLICITY," and "MANKIND, HOW LOW HAVE YOU FALLEN?" Mantello found out that when the Nazis invaded and occupied Hungary in March 1944, their determined intention was to eliminate the 800,000 Jews still alive in that country. Even though the Nazis were losing the war and the Russians were advancing into Hungary, the German mission was to destroy the Jews. Adolf Eichmann and his collaborators had come to expedite the deportation of Jews to death camps. Headlines aroused people around the world. Rabbi Michael Ber Weissmandl and others understood the Nazi program and had already heard reports about the mass murder of Jews in Auschwitz. It seems that the Allies' standard response to the many requests for help—especially to Weissmandl's plea that the Allies bomb the railroads leading to Auschwitz—was that the best way to save Jewish lives was to win the war as quickly as possible.[31] The sad part about this is that the Allies and their diplomats were dragging their feet, and even the Jewish community was not doing its utmost to save the lives of the remaining Jews still alive in Europe. But because of the heroic push and publicity by Mantello, some action was possible, and a number of victims got Swiss and Salvadoran papers, thereby saving their lives.

George Mantello—this man who tried to do so much—would have been better known but for informants who accused Mantello of profiting from the distribution of Salvadoran passports; he was held in detention by Swiss authorities for sixteen days in May 1944. Even though the Swiss government fully exonerated him of the charge, it marked his reputation. Information later provided by one of Mantello's assistants verified this Jewish hero's deeds.

Partisan Groups

The participation of Zionist youth movements such as the Jewish Resistance and Rescue of Children in establishing underground networks kept Jewish spirit alive until liberation. There were a variety of resistance groups consisting of young people: the Representative Counsel of French Jews, the Children Rescue Network, the Jewish Scout Movement (under leader Frederic Hammél), the Jewish Army, and Ha-Shmoer-ha-Zair (Young Guards). All these organizations were involved in resistance, sabotage, and rescue, sending children to Switzerland and/or Palestine, even though it was considered illegal by the Vichy government as well as the British, who were in charge of Palestine at that time.[32]

There were three types of partisan resistance groups in the forests: (1) individuals hidden together in forests linked by friendship or family, without any central leadership or any means of defending themselves; (2) family camps allied with a group of armed men and women under the leadership of a single charismatic personality (which "in some cases . . . went beyond agendas of food, shelter, and self-protection, to rescue and revenge operations, and even to aggressive action against the enemy"); and (3) fully armed partisan fighting battalions, known as *otriads* (which were organized on military lines; some were composed of all Jews, and some were Russian partisan brigades that reported to Moscow and received substantial support in the form of training, troops, ammunition, and medical supplies).[33] Occasionally, it was possible to have Russian partisans flown out of the forests for emergency medical treatment.

Jewish Resistance in Eastern Europe

Jews were involved in a variety of resistance activities under the Nazi occupation of Eastern Europe and the Soviet region. During World War II, 7–8 percent of the total population of the worldwide antifascist coalition was called to the armed services. There were 16–17 million Jews in the world; about 1.5 million Jews (9 percent) were in the military or were partisan members in various underground movements who collaborated in fighting Hitler's armies. In addition, Jews fought valiantly in the Soviet army, and although it was not easy for Jews to get recognized as heroes, 150 received the highest medal awarded.[34]

Jews also participated in Allied armed forces. There were more than a half-million Jews from the United States who were in the military and just as many in the Red Army. A contingent known as the Jewish Brigade from Palestine volunteered to serve in the British army to fight the Nazis. In every country Jews fought against Nazis, they distinguished themselves and won a variety of medals for heroism. It has been concluded that about 1.5 million

Jews fought in the various Allied armies.[35] Through a long, hard struggle and at a heavy cost in lives, Jewish fighters made a significant contribution to victory. Theirs was a fight of the Jewish people for their own future and for the future of mankind.

There were many Jewish partisans who resisted the Nazis between 1941 and 1945 in the vicinity of Minsk, Gomel, Pinsk, Vitbsk, and other places in the Soviet Union.[36] When the Nazis occupied Minsk and surrounding cities, murder, mayhem, and rape began. A group of young men—B. Chaimovich, S. Zorin, H. Smoliar, C. Feigelman, W. Kravchinski, N. Feldman, P. Shedletski, A. Relkin, G. Gordon, and others—started the resistance in the region. Once they realized that the terrible destruction of the Jewish people was beginning, they took up arms to fight the enemy. The Russian government encouraged them to go into the forests to sabotage and resist the Nazi occupation of Ukraine. They tore up railroad beds and tracks, destroyed ammunition dumps, and participated in battles.

When Germany invaded Russia on June 21, 1941, many of the forests in Lithuania, Byelorussia, Ukraine, and Poland became safe places for refugees being hunted by the Nazis. A number of refugees hid there and formed an effective partisan organization. The Russian government recognized their valor.

Even after the German defeat at Stalingrad in 1943, Soviet dictator Joseph Stalin made concerted efforts to enable the partisans to sabotage German forces behind the lines and parachuted Soviet personnel into the forests to train men in sabotage. The 1941 German invasion had caught the Soviet forces by surprise, and they were routed—so much so that when the Russian army hastily retreated, thousands of Russian soldiers were left scattered all over Eastern Europe. Many were captured, and countless numbers were exterminated along with the Jews. Aside from the regular soldiers who had been stranded, there were many criminal prisoners who had been released from prison by the Russians to provide labor for the war effort. Eventually these criminals joined various Russian partisans groups, but

> they became roving bandits who threatened . . . nearby farmers [and] sustained themselves by theft and thuggery. These heavily armed criminals constituted a serious menace [to other groups looking to the forest for refuge]. . . . Though they could be tough, aggressive fighters against the mutual enemy, the number of drinkers, anti-Semites, and rapists within their ranks made

them a continuing source of danger to fellow partisans and especially women.[37]

In addition, there was an overwhelming amount of difficulty caused by
the ultranationalist, rightist Polish partisans called the Armia Krajowa (AK;
Home Army). The AK did not like Jews and continuously tried to harm
them in their hiding places in the forests. Jewish partisans thus had two enemies—the Nazis and the AK. Yet it should be mentioned that some of the
rescuers, survivors, and resisters in the forests were aided by a number of
compassionate farmers in these regions, especially those who were on adjacent land.

Established in 1942, the Nacha forest camp contained a well-known
partisan unit led by Elke Ariowitch, popularly known as Todras, a man with
natural leadership qualities. This brave fighter also conducted heroic acts of
rescue. This group drew a number of people from Eishyshok, the hometown
of the ancient Jewish community in Lithuania, and contained a substantial
number of Jewish fighters, many of whom would lose their lives in raids, by
sabotage, or through betrayal. But Todras's men were armed with the best
weapons available, and their group was well supplied with food, having its
own herd of cows to provide meat and milk; additional supplies came from
local farmers. Todras was greatly respected by some of the local farmers—
but feared by others. Yaffa Eliach tells us that when Todras came across a
Polish policeman who actively participated in the destruction of the Radom
ghetto, Todras accosted him, marched him into the forest, and shot him to
death. When members of resistance groups in the forest were killed, other
members of the camps frequently avenged them, and the killers were sum-
marily executed.

Jewish groups in the forests formed partisan detachments. Unlike the
Russian partisan groups, which were mainly interested in fighting Germans,
these detachments were interested in fighting Germans, rescuing Jews, and
avenging Jewish deaths. Among these heroic rescuers/resisters were Tuvia
Bielski and his brothers in Byelorussia, as described by Nechama Tec.[38] During the summer of 1941, friends warned the Bielski brothers that they were
going to be arrested for their past ties to the Soviets. At about the same time,
the brothers also learned that their families had been exterminated; they
knew that they must resist the Nazis. One of the brothers, Tuvia, set out to
neutralize the danger by cooperating with partisan groups. They formed an
organization deep in the Nalibocka forest, where they eventually established

an entire community and saved more than 1,200 people. They went on missions to fight the Nazis, smuggled Jews out of ghettos, and scoured the area for fugitives from the Nazis. At other times they would go to villages to take revenge on a peasant who had betrayed and delivered a Jew to the Nazis.

This community in the forest had a substantial number of women, children, and elderly people. Other partisan groups did not accept women with children or the elderly because they could not fight. Those who were young and had weapons would be accepted among any partisan groups, but this particular group accepted everyone who was Jewish, providing them with sustenance. This camp was a little town inside the forest and had an assortment of different workshops for repairing guns, carpentry, and locksmithing. They manufactured all kinds of implements, including weapons and barrels. A makeshift hospital and a school were also set up. The cows provided material for the production of leather. They even made sausages for other partisan groups, but the price for getting sausages was delivering cows.

The community lasted until the Soviet army liberated it in the summer of 1944. At the time of liberation, most of the survivors were older women and children, precisely those who no one had wanted. The Bielski *otriad* camp represented the largest armed rescue of Jews by Jews in Nazi-occupied Europe, and their story helps to correct the false image of Jews walking silently to their destruction.

Defense of Lives and Human Dignity

Wilhelm Bachner

The story of Wilhelm Bachner is an example of the fourth type of Jewish resistance: the defense of lives and human dignity.[39] Bachner saved more than fifty people from the Jewish ghettos of Poland, and many of them survived the war. He did this while armed only with skill, courage, and intelligence.

In 1982 I interviewed Wilhelm Bachner in Moraga, California. He was born on September 17, 1912, in the Polish town of Bielsko (German Bielitz). Long a part of the Austro-Hungarian Empire, Bielsko was culturally German, joining Poland only after World War I. Bachner's surname and the fact that he grew up speaking German reflected this German heritage. He studied engineering in Brno, Czechoslovakia, graduating in 1938. After a short stay in his native city, he went to work in Warsaw in the spring of 1939 and soon married. By then the Warsaw ghetto had been established.

Hungry and afraid, Bachner slipped out of the ghetto and applied for a position as an engineer with a local German architectural firm that had recently opened an office in Warsaw. He impressed the firm's owner, Johannes Kellner, and before long Bachner was supervising more than 800 people. The Kellner firm was under contract with the German railroad Deutsche Reichsbahn and was provided with a *Bauzug* (a construction shop on rails that carried its own tools, supplies, food, and sleeping quarters for railroad work crews). Their task was to rebuild destroyed bridges, rail lines, barracks, and railroad stations. Bachner helped more than fifty Jews escape from various ghettos and hired them for the firm. These included his wife—who he passed off as his mistress—and other members of his family. Soon after the Nazi invasion of the Soviet Union, Bachner convinced Kellner to open branches in different parts of newly conquered Eastern Europe, most importantly in Kiev. There he obtained a house with the help of a trusted non-Jewish friend and converted it into a safe house for Jews he rescued from the Warsaw and Krakow ghettos.

With careful planning and anticipatory action, he deflected suspicion from himself and the Jews he hired. All were given false identity papers and worked alongside the 750 Poles and Ukrainians under Bachner's supervision. In this manner fifty Jews survived the war on the Eastern Front until Bachner surrendered himself and his crew to U.S. forces in Germany in 1945.

How and why was this modest man and several of his rescued survivors able to accomplish this feat? Wilhelm Bachner's success in eluding discovery was due to a complex combination of innate and acquired qualities. For Jews in Nazi-occupied Europe, survival was as much a matter of luck as of skill and environment. Recounting the story of his many brushes with death, Bachner admitted, "If I go through my whole story, it looks like God in heaven had nothing else to do, only to look after Willi Bachner with all his family and with all the Jewish friends he saved."[40] But growing up in Bielsko meant that he had absorbed German culture. Bachner's socialization into German culture also gave him a German outlook: "I was used to organizing everything in a perfect, German way," he said, "which was very appreciated by the Germans who were guarding or supervising us."[41] Appearance also helped. Though slight in stature, the photo on Bachner's work permit shows a handsome, dark-haired man with a neat mustache. Had Bachner been born with obvious Jewish features, speaking German like Goethe could not have saved him. Dressed in a black leather jacket and boots, discussing construction plans in elegant German, Bachner's Jewish identity was never suspected.

Fast thinking and sheer luck also played a role. In September 1942, shortly after Bachner had brought the last of his people from the Warsaw ghetto to Kiev, he found himself facing the Gestapo, which had been alerted by an informer. Gestapo officials showed up at his office with guns drawn and accused him of hiding Jews. Hania Shane, whom he had saved, recalled the incident at our interview with him: "Willi, very calm, was yelling back at them, 'How dare you say this; if you are so sure, why don't you go find them yourselves.' While he was arguing with them and prolonging the heated discussion, my friend Heniek left the office and went to the train station where his crew was working and quietly dispersed the Jewish workers, just in case."

These were some of the factors that made him effective, but it was his character, courage, and values that motivated Bachner to act. When asked what induced him to risk his life to rescue others beyond his immediate family, Bachner said, "I did it to show—if you are nice to people, God maybe will be nice to you."

We interviewed Bachner's cousin in Israel, and he described their grandmother telling them how they had the responsibility to do good and that they would receive their reward in heaven. Bachner himself demonstrated caring for others even after the war. He continued to be deeply involved with those he had rescued, even with his German boss, Kellner, who only then learned that Bachner and many members of his crew were Jewish.

In this chapter I have recounted a variety of stories of Jewish resistance to Nazi tyranny. Rubin Ainsztein informs us that there are four types of Jewish resistance possible, ranging from violence to resistance in defense of human life and dignity. Obviously not all resistance incorporated the use of arms; other forms of resistance were moral and spiritual. The myth of Jewish passivity does not bear out because there was a disproportionate number of Jewish resisters against the Nazi oppressors in all of Nazi-occupied Europe. Resistance was more difficult in some countries than in others. For instance, in countries where anti-Semitism was more prevalent—especially the Eastern European countries—resistance and rescue were more difficult because the general populations were more indifferent to Jewish citizens and more fearful of Nazis. It was understood that the Nazis were more punitive if they discovered a non-Jewish citizen helping a Jew. Additionally, the Nazi onslaught was totally unexpected by the Jews because they had reasoned that there wasn't a good explanation to include them for destruction; after all, Jews were neither saboteurs nor resisters nor were they disobeyers of Nazi rules at the inception of Nazi occupation.

In the past, Jews had frequently experienced various forms of degradation by crusaders—pogroms, lynchings, and other humiliations; thus, they did not expect anything different or worse—certainly not gas chambers and concentration camps. Also, resistance grew increasingly difficult because of persistent discouragement, fear, physical weakness, and psychological debilitation. Nazi euphemisms, deceptions, and secretiveness about the Holocaust made any report unexpected and unbelievable to Jews living in Nazi-occupied Europe. It was only after irrefutable evidence had been brought to the Jewish population by sources such as Jan Karski, Rudolf Vrba, and Joseph Lanik, who escaped from Auschwitz and reported the atrocities occurring in concentration and extermination camps, that they could even begin to protect themselves. It was at this stage that young people began to take on the enemy. From my interviews with Wilhelm Bachner and Jack Werber and statements by Luba Tryszynska, Lucien Lazare, Israel Gutman, and many others (see Appendix C), it is clear that the Jews were motivated by their sense of honor that they would not perish without defending themselves—and by their own courage, as we see in the stories of Mordekhai Anielewicz, Abba Kovner, Roza Robota, the Bielski brothers, and others. All show an overwhelming quality of caring, compassion, and social responsibility toward their brothers and sisters. What did these caring heroes have in common with the Carnegie heroes described in Chapter 5? Clearly both exhibited courage and compassion for those in dire need. I agree with Dr. Peter Gibbon, who has said, "A world without heroes gives free rein to apathy and envy and cultivates cynicism."[42]

5

"Those Who Save One Life Are as if They Saved the Entire Universe"

Andrew Carnegie's Heroes

The world has, unfortunately, too many bystanders and "bad Samaritans." David Cash was one such bystander. In 1997 Cash and his best friend, Jeremey Strohmeyer, both eighteen years old, strolled into a casino at the California-Nevada border. Cash idly stood by while his friend struggled with seven-year-old African-American Sherrice Iverson on the floor of the women's bathroom. Instead of helping the girl or notifying security, Cash chose to ignore the situation and go for a walk. A half-hour later Strohmeyer emerges and relays to Cash that he had just molested and murdered the girl. Fifteen months later Strohmeyer appeared in court for the murder of Sherrice. It turned out that these two young men were students at the University of California–Berkeley, but only Cash would return to school, dubbed a "bad Samaritan." Cash stated that he was "not going to lose sleep over somebody else's problems." Strohmeyer received three life sentences without the opportunity of parole.

In the summer of 1996 witnesses again stood silently watching as a New York City cab driver was beaten to death and locked in the trunk of his cab. No one stepped forward to disclose the murder to police, and the cab driver's body was not discovered until two days after the incident occurred.

David Cash's action is reminiscent of the Kitty Genovese case in New York City. On March 13, 1964, Kitty was walking to her car when an assailant approached her and stabbed her once, left, returned a few minutes later, and stabbed her again. She screamed "Oh, my God, he stabbed me! Please help me! Please help me!" The assailant returned a third time and stabbed her, this time fatally. During these events thirty-eight people witnessed the repeated stabbing and cries for help but stood by doing nothing. It was another half-hour after her death before anyone called the police—the reason being "I didn't want to get involved."[1]

Yet we human beings can and often do extend ourselves with unfathomable degrees of caring and compassion. There are many people—ordinary folks, just going about their business of living who risk their own lives in order to rescue others—oftentimes complete strangers—in emergency situations.

In the fall of 1995 a man named Boyd Gavin rescued a two-year-old boy from a house engulfed in flames. Gavin entered the home, crawled along the hallway floor, located the child, and carried him outside to safety as the fire completely destroyed the house. Gavin and the child suffered smoke inhalation and were hospitalized for treatment of burns, but ultimately they both recovered.

In the summer of 1993 a woman named Raemonda Freeman rescued a young man in Pittsburgh who had been shot repeatedly by members of a rival gang. Seeing that he was injured, Freeman shielded him with her own body as the assault continued, and he survived.

On March 2, 1991, Rodney King was driving along Highway 210 in Los Angeles singing to the radio. He was speeding, and officers had signaled for him to pull over. Refusing, King led police on a high-speed pursuit, and he was finally forced to stop. One officer pulled King out of the car, and three others joined in beating him fifty-six times with their batons. The action was caught on videotape, which was delivered to Los Angeles–area news channels and CNN. A year later the police officers went on trial, and on Wednesday, April 2, 1992, three were acquitted, one partially acquitted. It immediately sparked powerful riots among many African Americans in the Watts neighborhood of Los Angeles. Five black men went into a Korean liquor store, hit the store owner's son on the head when he tried to stop them, and shattered the storefront window, yelling "This is for Rodney King!" Soon thereafter a white truck driver, Reginald Denny, drove into the violence; a black man named Damon Williams waylaid Denny's truck, pulled him out of the cab, and beat him severely. A good Samaritan, Bobby Green, was Denny's hero. Black himself, Green, who lived only a mile away, saw what was happening live on television and ran down the street to help Denny. He pulled him back into the truck and drove him to the hospital.

Not all of the people described above have been recognized as Carnegie heroes, but they do take action in extraordinary ways. In this chapter my primary purpose is to illustrate the goodness and heroism of some of the more than 8,500 accounts of heroic acts recognized by the Carnegie Hero Fund Commission.

After a massive coal mine explosion in 1904, Andrew Carnegie was inspired to create the Carnegie Hero Fund Commission for civilian heroism. Since that time the commission has awarded 8,500 medals—20 percent posthumously—and more than $25 million in grants of scholarship aid or continuing assistance to people who risked their lives for the benefit of others. With these funds the commission also offers financial support to people who have been injured as a result of their heroic activity and to the families of individuals who died as a result of their attempts to rescue others. Carnegie did not expect to motivate future acts of heroism with this fund; rather it was his desire that if a hero is killed or injured attempting to save another, he and those dependent upon him should not suffer monetarily. Ten hero funds in Europe, including Carnegie's native Scotland, carry out similar missions. Those heroes who are awarded have performed acts of rescue in a multitude of situations, including saving people from drowning, burning, assault, animal attack, electrocution, and suffocation.[2]

Carnegie's Definition of a Hero

Since the Carnegie Commission was founded, its definition of a "hero" has gone largely unchanged from Andrew Carnegie's original conception; it is the same operational definition used in this study: "A civilian who knowingly risks his or her own life to an extraordinary degree while saving or attempting to save the life of another person."[3] This definition is reflected in the New Testament verse that appears on each medal: "Greater love has no man than this, that a man lay down his life for his friends" (John 15:13).

There are innumerable instances of people attempting to aid others. In fact, since the inception of the medal, the commission has examined more than 75,000 cases of heroism and has chosen 8,500 that fit their criteria.

Any individual who voluntarily risks his or her life to an extraordinary degree is eligible for recognition, but to be awarded the Carnegie Medal one must first be nominated. Nominations can be made by anyone and are frequently made by police or fire departments, members of the victim's family, the press, or bystanders.[4] An investigation is conducted by the commission in order to establish "conclusive evidence to support the threat to the victim's life, the risk undertaken by the rescuer, the rescuer's degree of responsibility, and the act's occurrence."[5] The act must be voluntary, and there must be factual evidence of threat to the life of the victim. The responsibility of the rescuer is based on two constraints: First, was the rescuer responsible for causing the threat through negligence, carelessness, or intent? And second, was the rescuer responsible for the safety of the victim by means of vocation, such as a firefighter, a lifeguard, a police officer, and so on? Beyond this, the heroic act must have been performed in the United States, Canada, or the waters thereof, and the act must be brought to the attention of the commission within two years of the date of its occurrence.

Excluded from the commission's consideration are rescue acts where there exists a full measure of responsibility between the rescuer and the rescued. For example, because parental roles may suggest heroic behavior when one's children are in danger, the commission excludes from consideration persons who rescue family members, "except in cases of outstanding heroism where the rescuer loses his or her life or is severely injured."[6] In addition, the commission does not bestow awards upon persons such as firefighters and police officers whose regular duties require them to perform such acts, unless the behavior performed exceeds the reasonable expectations of the job. Members of the armed forces are excluded from consideration, as are children, who are considered to be too young to comprehend the risk involved.

What Makes a Carnegie Hero?

Upon conclusion of my 214 interviews with Carnegie heroes, my overall impression is that they were motivated by a variety of different factors, including compassion for the victim, and they felt a sense of social responsibility toward fellow human beings (see Appendix D). Though the situations were dangerous, they somehow felt that they could accomplish their mission. Whereas some were triggered into action by a sense of efficacy and self-confidence, others felt that they could not live with themselves if they walked away from a tragedy. Yet others did it for religious reasons, and one rescuer said, "I am certain that God wanted me to walk by this river with my girl-friend so that I would save a couple of people drowning."[7]

Of course, there is no single explanation for heroic rescue or helping others. But from the narratives of the Carnegie heroes, we were able to discern several explanations, which I have categorized as the following motivating factors: *normocentric motives*—those moral values and norms learned from parents and the wider community; *social responsibility; empathy; efficacy*—in which helping comes from a sense that one has the ability to accomplish the mission, to do the thing to effect an improvement in things; *impulse*—an instinctive reaction to other people's troubles; *religious beliefs; reciprocity*—where one helps because one expects someone might help them in the future; *principled motivation*—that is, an internalized universal moral belief in justice and fairness; and *self-esteem, sensation-seeking* (people who are more likely to be risk-takers), and *having something in common with all humanity.*

It is my impression, from reviewing these transcripts, that these were ordinary people whose lives demonstrated the ethic of caring; when the risky situation presented itself, they were able to act to save lives. This further indicates that many people are capable of getting involved in dangerous situations without regard for the risk to themselves, as we shall see in the following stories of heroic behavior.

Normocentrism

In my discussion with the Carnegie heroes, *normocentric* behavior—or the beliefs and values learned from parents and the community—was by far the most significant motivating factor driving helping behavior. In 78 percent of our interviews, rescuers mentioned the importance of parental guidance and development of moral beliefs. Many talked about how they had been taught at some point in their lives that people are supposed to care for one another and felt that being a helper is intimately connected with their own sense of who they are. This included learned values of caring and social responsibility acquired from the moral community in which they lived and from their parents during their upbringing—they modeled moral-spiritual values conducive to forming close, caring attachments to other people. Also included in normocentric behavior is guidance by professional codes or norms and a sense of feeling that it was their responsibility to take action. For example, a forty-seven-year-old male truck driver who rescued a woman from her burning vehicle following an accident stated, "I kept thinking that the car could blow up at any second [and] she was on fire also. I was raised to help people, and that's the first thing that came to mind."[8]

A thirty-five-year-old construction worker who rescued two children from a burning building further illustrates the importance of parental values on his act:

> It felt like I was trying to walk through black, greasy Jell-O; it was just thick. I couldn't see anything, couldn't feel anything, and my hand landed in what I thought was an air duct. . . . I stuck my foot in that duct so I would know where the window was, use that as my focal point, felt around the room. And I felt one kid's leg and I just grabbed the leg and just chucked him out of the window; didn't wait for anyone to catch him or anything. And I had to leave the duct work then . . . crawled around the room . . . found the second kid, who was unconscious, and I threw him out, and then I dove out the window.

In discussing the importance of his childhood socialization—representative of the type of responses offered by other Carnegie heroes—he commented on the strong sense of duty imparted by his adopted father, a U.S. Marine, whom he knew only for a few years while still quite young: "I was only five at the time, but he instilled in me a sense of duty and a sense of responsibility to other people. It's just something that was in my heart."[9]

Another Carnegie hero, a graduate student, risked his life to disarm a mentally unbalanced female sniper on a college campus who injured one student and killed another. He was walking home from class when he heard loud noises, sounding like cannon shots, but at a higher pitch. They might have been fireworks, but he did not think a firecracker could be that loud. He approached the scene not knowing what was going on, and the sounds were echoing off the buildings, confusing the direction of the reports from the weapon. Then he noticed smoke coming from the bushes, which made him think maybe somebody was setting off some huge fireworks. He told us:

> I looked toward the bushes and there's a woman on her knees there. She looks at me, I look at her and kinda nod, and she nods back. Then I notice . . . she's got a rifle in her hands. . . .

> So at that instant I run forward, and as I'm running toward her she stands up and levels the gun toward me, [but] I get there in time, grab the gun by the barrel, yank it out of her hand. . . . Then she pulls a knife from her belt with the right hand and takes a couple of quick stabs, and I step back. Then she takes a big stab at me. I step out of the way; she follows through and hits her own left leg with it. But she's going so quick she immediately pulls it right out. And I thought she had just scratched herself . . . she just kind of collapses to the ground and just drops the knife.

He picked up the knife and gun and yelled for someone to call 911, to get the police and ambulance there quick. Then he noticed that the woman was bleeding badly from the knife wound, so he took the cloth belt off of his trench coat and wrapped up her wound: "Just simple direct pressure, first aid."

In our interview with this young man, he related a childhood experience that had a profound impact on him then and, later, his decisions to help the woman above. He had been waiting in line for a ride at Disneyland, and it was a particularly hot day.

> About two people in front of us, this woman who was in her teens or twenties kind of fainted from heat exhaustion. So my dad, first thing, immediately gets out of line, helps her up, takes her to some shade, and gets her something to drink. Of course, my mom and the kids followed to help out. And I remember the looks on all the other people's faces in the line, like "We'd like to do [something], but we're too concerned about being in line and not losing our place." And my dad has a kind of disdain for that. But he wasn't really focusing on that, he was focusing on helping the girl . . . that's one of the major defining points that I remember. . . . They lived what they told me to do.[10]

A fifty-year-old teacher, a survivor of a school shooting, attributed his rescue of students to the helping norms inherent in his teaching role. He entered a classroom where a fourteen-year-old boy had killed a fellow teacher and shot three of his classmates. The shooter had walked into the classroom and shot one student point-blank, then another sitting behind the first, and then a third—all of them in the same row.

I looked around the room, and there were kids in various states with obvious shock on their faces. As soon as I was there, the student—the shooter—asked me to stand up. I told him I couldn't stand up; I was too afraid. . . . Eventually he told me I had to stand up or he would start shooting kids. And so in my mind I knew what I had to do. I stood up and faced him and we kind of talked for a little bit.

The third wounded student had been shot through the chest and the arm; she was in a great deal of pain, and the teacher knew he needed to do something. Eventually, he got the boy to agree that the girl be taken from the room for medical treatment. Then he was allowed to take out a girl who was diabetic and also in great need of help. Then the boy started organizing the kids and moving them one by one to the back of the classroom and sitting them down. He said he was going to take a hostage.

And I guess I volunteered; I don't remember doing it. So he motioned me to come toward him and he said, "I'm going to put this gun in your mouth." . . . And at that time I was about five or six feet away, and I knew it was probably my best chance to end the situation. So I charged him and pinned him with my body against the wall and also grabbed the gun with his hands on it and pinned it against the wall. And at that time the police came in and the kids went out. It happened all at once.

In reflecting on the reasons behind his brave act, he told us:

I'm a teacher. And I was the adult and I needed to make it better. And that's how I knew. I knew I needed to do it. I don't know if I thought about it then, but I don't know how anybody could live with themselves if they would have left. . . . It had to be me. If anyone was going to make it better, it was gonna be me. And, as I say, I care about kids and I'm a teacher. I needed to do that.[11]

Another Carnegie hero we spoke to, a forty-eight-year-old surfer and seafarer, told us how he rescued a woman from drowning in the Pacific Ocean:

> The moment I saw her . . . the first thought was *somebody's in trouble*. There's no second thought to it. And then once I got my board and launched, it's kind of like what surfers call "total commitment," you know, total involvement. Once you take off, you paddle into a very large wave, there's no other way around it other than to go straight down and give it your full [commitment]. You can't turn around and back off. . . . So once I was going in the water there was no sense of my own peril. I'm going to get her out of here. One way or another, "I'm going to do it." And that's all there is to it.

When asked why he did it, he continued: It is "my knowledge and experience with the ocean. In some ways . . . it's a bred-in thing because fishermen—and this is something about all seafaring people—you see somebody in trouble, you do what you can. . . . It's kind of that unwritten code.[12]

These five Carnegie heroes, it appears to me, have internalized the ethic of caring, the norms and values of their environment in which they were raised, and especially the influence of their parents. Social responsibility, which is also internalized from moral role models, was the next most important motivating factor among Carnegie heroes.

Social Responsibility

Sixty-six percent of rescuers identified *social responsibility* as a motivating factor that influenced their decision to help a fellow human being. The stories of the following people provide good examples of the impact of social responsibility on helping others.

A forty-nine-year-old man risked his life to save a paralyzed woman from being hit by an oncoming train—the spokes of her wheelchair had become stuck between the tracks. He told us he was heading south alongside the tracks when he noticed the woman crossing the tracks while the gates were lowering, signaling the approaching train. She was shaking the wheelchair and crying out for help. So he just stopped his car right there and jumped out. He saw the train was coming; it was about fifty yards away and fast approaching:

> The train was about twenty yards away, and I just grabbed her by the collar in the front and pulled her out onto me, and then she kind of fell on top of me because she was paralyzed from the

waist down. Then the train was there and hit her wheelchair and
drove it into my leg. And what I thought, the train had caught
my leg and cut my leg off, but it was the wheelchair just hitting
my leg.

When asked why many others might not risk their lives in a similar life-
threatening situation, he offered the following: "I think there might be some
liability they're afraid of; something might happen. . . . Well, I don't think
that's right. I think you have a certain degree of responsibility, if you see
something happen like that, to try and offer some kind of help."[13]

In another case of a rescue motivated by social responsibility, a seventy-
three-year-old Alaskan airplane pilot risked his life by landing his plane in
dangerous, freezing waters to rescue three men from drowning, as well as the
crew of a rescue helicopter who crashed while making a rescue attempt
themselves.

In spite of my determination not to land, why, it seemed like we
were the only thing between these people and drowning. The
only thing that was keeping them up was a float. We were landing into the wind, hitting the waves head on. And we hit pretty
hard. We overshot where the people were on the float and everything was drifting at about the same speed. We had to shut the
engine down.

The pilot attempted to get out of the plane, but as soon as he let go of
the controls, the plane veered out of control in the wind; yet he was able to
steady it and kept it from going cross-wise and tipping. One of the chopper crew had seven broken ribs and a punctured lung. They were able to
get the others and him, screaming with pain, into the plane; but taking off
would have torn the plane up, so they taxied two treacherously turbulent
miles to shore, where they beached the plane. A U.S. National Guard helicopter that had been dispatched to help them showed up with a medical
team and flew out the injured. When asked why he dared a rescue attempt
in such volatile weather, he told us, "I think you do what any caring person would do. If somebody's life is on the line, or you feel it is, you just do
what you've got to do."[14]

In another selfless rescue by a Carnegie hero, a man who attempted
several times to rescue a woman from drowning in a culvert expressed his

motivation in terms of an overarching feeling of responsibility for her welfare: "I just felt like it was my duty as a person . . . a matter of being a human. You've got to help somebody if they need help, if they are in trouble."[15]

The story of a forty-one-year-old man who rescued another man from drowning highlights the responsibility that goes along with being the only person available to help: "Seeing [him] out there . . . and there was no one else there. I think in some situations, people . . . count on the people around them . . . but, in fact, when I was there, it was either me or nobody."[16]

Lastly, one man demonstrated the essence of social responsibility when he explained why he risked his life to save another man from being electrocuted: "It's like something in your mind says 'Go help.'. . . It's like another person in me. . . . You know that that person is going to die or that that person needs help, and you know you've got to help them."[17]

Empathy: "I Just Didn't Want to See Him Burn Up"

Empathy is a salient motivating factor centered on the needs of another—on that individual's possible fate. It emerges out of a direct connection with the distressed other, or one's feeling another's pain and not being able to live with that. Thus, 42 percent of the Carnegie heroes reported empathy as their motivating factor. We often use this interchangeably with "compassion," "sympathy," and "pity"—which are, in fact, its characteristic expressions. Reactions may be emotional or cognitive; frequently they contain elements of both. The following stories illustrate both the cognitive and the affective traits (from our hearts *and* our heads).

A tractor-trailer driver told us of his very harrowing yet ultimately successful rescue of another driver. His is a story marked by a great sense of empathy for others.

> [The other driver] went across all three lanes, up on two wheels on one side and then two wheels on the right side, and you could tell he was out of control. . . . So I told my boss, who was behind about a mile or so, on the radio, I says, "Run back there, Davey, and grab the fire extinguisher." And I said, "I can see the guy hanging upside down inside the van, and it's on fire. Nobody's helping him." I said, "I'm going back man. I'm going back to help him."

Running to the van, it seemed like his legs were not moving fast enough: "I was running as fast as I possibly could, but it seemed like I was in slow motion, am I gonna make it, can I make it to get to this guy?" Then he noticed that the front of the vehicle had started dripping and melting:

> Now the truck, mind you, was upside-down, or up on its side, and that would be onto the right side. That meant that the driver was up in the air in his seat and kind of suspended. . . . And I really don't know how the harness even works, the safety belt system works on that, but he was doubled over and I remember he had a big gash in his neck and I was concerned about that— bleeding, and he [seemed to be] unconscious.

Once inside, this hero relates that it didn't seem that bad, other than the smoke billowing out the windows and the victim taking fumes in. The van driver put his hand on the rescuer's shoulder and squeezed. The hero continues his story:

> He [the victim] said, "Please don't let me burn alive in here alone. Don't leave me to burn alive in here. I have a family." At that time I saw my whole life as a young man, even through my tour in the service. I saw my family. I could see my parents [and] I said, "Listen, if I can't get you out of here, I'm going to sit right here with you and I'll hold your hand, and we'll go together." . . . I didn't want to lose hope, and I guess the old boy upstairs said, "Hey, there's the button. I hit it and he fell over my shoulder . . . like a bag of potatoes, perfect. . . . I said, "Just keep your head down, we're goin' through this thing." . . . But the second we got outside, there were all kinds of people just dragging us, pulling us away from it.

He later went on to describe the motivation for his actions:

> We made it. We had just enough time and as far as me doin' it, I just couldn't see this guy burn alive. I just didn't want to see him burn up, because he had no reason to die, and I thought, *Hey, I'm gonna mess somebody's plans up. You're not getting him today. You get him, you get me. You're gonna take us both.* But I'll never forget

him putting his hand on my shoulder and when I looked at him and I could see blood on his face and I could see tears when I said, "I won't leave you. I'll sit here with you." I wasn't sure if he was going to let me go or not. I knew I could get away from him and save my own self, but at that time I just said, "Hey, you know what? You've got to die [eventually]. If it's a cause, it might as well be a damned good cause." And it was a good call, I think, trying to help this man out. . . . What an amazing man.[18]

Similarly, a thirty-five-year-old mother and nurse was motivated by a strong sense of empathy when she saved the life of a drowning child in an ice–covered concrete swimming pool. On approaching the pool, all she could see was a crack in the ice. Not wanting to get stuck under the ice, she knew she had to crack it up, and so she cannon-balled through into the icy water. The second time down, she had to come up for air and still hadn't found anything. But when she went back down again, and felt something brush along her leg, she grabbed it—and it was the child's coat, and he was still in it.

When asked why she dove in after this young boy, she said,

It is a motherly instinct. . . . I knew, when my son said he [the victim] fell in the pool . . . I think the only thing I could keep in my head was, *God, I have got to get him out of that pool.* . . . I remember distinctly I kept telling him in his ear, even though he might have been gone, I kept saying, "JC I have you, you are not going anywhere and I am not letting go."[19]

Another rescuer expressed having similar feelings of empathy when he was attempting to rescue a young woman from her burning car:

My arms were getting all torn up, my face was getting burned, my eyebrows were catching on fire. So I almost had her out. It was to the point where I was completely exhausted and I was about ready to give up. But I wouldn't have left her. I would have died there with her, I think . . . I know. I have a very vivid memory, and I know that seeing her that way, begging for my help, and just knowing that she was relying on me for her life, and then if I [had] failed, I never would have been able to live with it. I would have stayed right there. I couldn't have left.[20]

A forty-eight-year-old male nurse in a nursing home was stabbed while attempting to prevent another nurse—his own wife—from being killed. One evening when they were both working at the nursing home, he saw a man forcibly dragging his wife, who was on duty upstairs, out of the elevator and toward a door leading outside. He described to us what happened:

> I stepped in front of him to prevent him from dragging her down the hall any further . . . and he started punching her and kicking at her, and in the meantime I was trying to free his hands off of her to keep him from dragging her out of the door. And at some point during the struggle, a knife appeared, and the next thing I knew he just started stabbing her . . . at which point I tried all the more to get his grasp off of her. . . . I didn't know at the time that I had been stabbed too. . . . But he renewed the attack . . . with such a vengeance . . . and stabbing her and kicking her . . . and I managed to pin him to the floor . . . and he still had the knife in his hand. And I was able to reach down and get the knife. . . . And I just kept him pinned to the floor until the police came.

When asked why he became involved in an incident that caused him to get stabbed, his reply is rich with empathy: "But she just had that fear on her face, you know, of helplessness, and the fear in her eyes that something terrible was going to happen. It was just etched in my mind. And I knew that if I didn't do something, something terribly worse would happen. So I just tried all I could."[21]

Finally, an empathetic thirty-six-year-old secretary who used her own body to shield a young man from rival gang gunfire explained her motivation: "When I turned and looked at him, it was like we looked eye to eye, and I could see how scared he was. And that captured me. I didn't want to leave him there, you know. I didn't want to leave him there on the ground scared like that."[22]

Efficacy: Belief in Yourself to Do Good

Efficacy, which some scholars see as related to self-esteem, is the sense that one has the power to produce effects or achieve intended results. Throughout my research for this book I discerned the importance of efficacy and courage, which do make a difference and can be taught at a young age. This category was the next most common motivational factor for Carnegie heroes, at 38.8 percent, when the rescuers said that they took action because they felt confident that they would be able to help. Many times this sense of confidence was the result of prior life experience or training, which is why it's so important to impart this to our children and remember it ourselves.

A belief in his abilities coupled with a strong sense of self-reliance caused a forty-three-year-old Carnegie hero to crawl into a burning house to rescue an elderly woman. When we asked him why he thought some people help in these situations and others don't, he replied,

> I probably thought I could do something, I thought I could physically go in there and get her. Had I been on crutches or disabled, I probably wouldn't have even considered it. But me, the age I was, I probably thought I could do something, I guess. Some people wouldn't dream, the house is on fire, and a common term that always bugs me is "let the authorities do it." Like, oh, that is what the fire department is for. But you know . . . I look at it as we have to take care of ourselves . . . that is my theory on this fire department stuff. I mean the fire department is going to come, but if you can pull someone out of a car or help stabilize the situation or something . . . people have to help each other.[23]

Another rescuer, an off-duty police officer and strong swimmer, was similarly driven by a strong sense of efficacy in his rescue of a sixteen-year-old boy drowning in a raging river. He said:

> I had been in the river in that exact same spot a few months before—I went after a Marine who was trying to kill himself. What I wasn't really thinking about is that it was April now, and in Maine we have the snowmelt, and the water was going quite a bit faster. But that didn't faze me at all, there was something that I needed to do and I went and did it. . . . There was absolutely no hesitation, that was something that I had to do and figured with my background and what a strong swimmer I was, if anyone was going to have a chance at doing this, I would.[24]

Another man, a thirty-eight-year-old industrial maintenance worker with Red Cross training, heroically rescued two people from death by pulling them out of burning automobiles following a late-night accident. Driving along, he came around a bend and saw two vehicles on fire. He quickly slowed down and then noticed a fellow in the midst of the wreckage—part of him was underneath a car and there was a small pickup on top of the car.

> I piled out of the car and yelled for someone to give me a hand; there is some people hurt here. Well, no one wanted to get near, so I went to the first fellow . . . and started pulling, and at that time I noticed he had a broken leg. . . . So I dragged him to what I thought would be a safe distance from the wreckage. . . . I go back and I could see a fellow inside [the other vehicle], reached in, and got a hold of him, started pulling him out, and he was super limber and there was blood flying everywhere. . . . I yelled for some people to give me a hand so we could get this man out of here. Well, no one decided they wanted to go anywhere near this, so I got a hold of him, took him out of the driver's-side door, held him as you would hold a kid, started running to where I had the other fellow [and] the gas tank went.

His sense of efficacy seemed to have come from earlier training he'd received from the American Red Cross. He told us:

> The American Red Cross, they were nice enough to teach me years back some rather involved life saving skills, and I volunteered and taught for the Red Cross after they taught me those skills. . . . This was maybe like an extreme example of it, but there were two people needing help, and I possessed a bit of knowledge in first aid. No one else was moving, so someone had to do something or there would be two people dying a rather horrible death.[25]

A forty-nine-year-old teacher pulled two people out of a burning automobile that had exploded as a result of being rear-ended at a traffic stop by another car moving at 65–70 miles per hour. The teacher's eyebrows and all the hair on his arms was burned off by the heat of the blaze. When asked why he responded to this emergency situation and how his previous experiences had prepared him for it, he said:

> I certainly pulled out plenty of people as a lifeguard. When you work at a busy beach, it's an everyday, well not every day, but you

know. I teach at a community college and I teach physical education, so I teach a lot of outdoor recreation, outdoor education,
kayaking, canoeing, backpacking, rock climbing, that sort of
thing. I pulled a few kids out from canoeing accidents on white-
water and that sort of thing. Again, I think it's preparation . . .
just like practicing for a game.[26]

The Instinct and Impulsive Response: No Time to Waste

We also found that an immediate *impulsive* response was the motivating factor more than 27 percent of the time in our interviews with the Carnegie heroes. Frank Farley, an educational psychologist at Temple University who has
been studying heroes for the past fifteen years, has stated that the actions of
situational heroes are frequently impulsive and that oftentimes people sometimes just act before they think.[27] Correspondingly, some of the rescuers we
spoke to could not find another reason for their behavior other than stating
that they just reacted to the situation without thinking. Impulsive behavior
is thought to be found universally by a number of observers.

For example, a thirty-four-year-old woman wrestled to the ground a
prisoner who was going to shoot a police officer. While she was standing just
outside of a hospital emergency room, a female officer was escorting a prisoner out, and the restraint on the prisoner slipped down below her hip.
When the officer went to pull it up, the prisoner tried to run, and as the officer tried to grab her, she hit the officer in the chest and knocked her back-
ward and came down on top of her. The officer hit her head on the
pavement. The rescuer explains:

> I could hear her hit, and so I was just going to pull the girl off the
> officer, and when I got over there and started pulling on the girl,
> the officer starts yelling, "My gun! My gun!" . . . so, I am just try-
> ing to reach down there and trying to find the gun, and the girl
> already had it out of the holster. . . . So then I still couldn't feel
> the gun, and I am thinking, *Oh, my God, she is going to blow my
> head off.* . . . Then somehow I had grabbed her wrist, and the gun
> sort of pointed away from us because I was still trying to bring
> her hand out and away from the officer so she wouldn't shoot the
> officer, and she fired a shot [which did not hit anyone]. Then she
> pointed the gun at me and ran. . . . I was running, but the offi-
> cer's eyes caught mine and . . . I couldn't leave her. It was like her

eyes were screaming for help. So then I ran back and jumped on the girl again and knocked the gun loose . . . and I was able to get the gun, and the officer was able to get up to her radio and [several officers responded].

When asked why she did what she did and why she didn't run when she had the opportunity to, she explained it as a "natural instinct. I knew she was going to shoot the officer. I couldn't let this happen."[28]

Another man explained how he got out of his car to rescue a woman being attacked at knifepoint, eventually knocking the assailant to the ground. He explained his actions as a gut reaction: "When I did get involved, I mean, it was just a reaction. I can't explain it, it was just response."[29]

Another man, a forty-eight-year-old mechanic, rescued a four-year-old boy from a burning trailer. While others looked on, this rescuer responded without thought to his own safety to a mother's shrieks that her babies were inside. He smashed the door open and rushed into the smoke and flames. Three children were in the trailer, and he was able to pull only one of them out before the roof collapsed, killing the two other children still inside. He barely escaped with his own life in attempting to rescue these children, and acted on impulse alone.: "I had to go in there and get them, or at least try to . . . I didn't even think about it. That's all . . . it was just a natural reaction. I guess I would have done it for anyone if I saw somebody in trouble like that."[30]

The Importance of Religious and Spiritual Beliefs: Guidance from a Higher Power

More than 16 percent of rescuers cited the importance of religion and spirituality and the belief in a divine being as a source of motivation for their compassionate acts. Most rescuers who fall into this category spoke of their faith as what propelled them to action in their particular rescue. Some said that God told them what they needed to do, and a few said that God or some higher power completely took over their bodies and that they essentially had no control in the matter.[31] Balwina, my rescuer, was a religious and spiritual person, which promoted her to take a heroic stand on my behalf. Sometimes religious people are spurred to action, as in the following rescues.

A twenty-nine-year-old man was driving down the street when he saw a burning house. He grabbed a blanket from his van and first tried to go in through the garage and then tried through the front door, but in both places there were too many flames. He jumped the fence to the backyard. The patio door was locked, so he grabbed the first thing he saw—a barbecue grill. Swinging it by the legs, he broke the sliding glass door and told the people to get out. But they couldn't.

> I don't know where I got the strength from, but I did and thank God that he gave me strength and the wisdom and the courage to go in there in the first place. And he gave me the wisdom to think and the strength and courage to lead them to safety. . . . I was going to go back into the house, but [moments later] it collapsed.[32]

Another rescuer, a thirty-five-year-old sheetmetal worker who identified himself as a "very religious and spiritual" person, revealed that his motivation was guided by a Christian ethic and a belief in God that provided the norms and values to which he adhered in his daily life. In his interview he talked about a strong belief in God as his guiding force: "We are supposed to be as Christians, Christlike. We're supposed to be willing. And the thought that went through my head, and it hit just as I was going through that window, just in a flash, and, call it a prayer, *God, either I'm coming out with those kids, or I'm not coming out.*[33]

Reciprocity: Helping Each Other in Times of Need

Rescuers, like other people, have multiple values that overlap—such as caring, empathy, and others—and any one of them might assume supremacy at any given moment. For some of the Carnegie heroes, norms and expectations dictate that people help others because they expect others to reciprocate when they are in need. Approximately 10 percent of those interviewed gave the reason for rescue as *reciprocity.*

A twenty-one-year-old male student who rescued another man from his fiery automobile following a crash related this story: He and a friend were just about to cross the street when they heard the noise of somebody's accelerator from down the road. The car proceeded extremely fast and slammed into the rear end of a car that was waiting for them to cross. After it hit this car, the speeder kept going and jumped a curb and hit a tree at the bottom of a ditch. The car that had been rear-ended spun around into the opposite traffic lane and left in its wake a gas trail twenty feet long. The gas sparked; the rescuer's friend froze and urged him away from the scene. "I just kept thinking, *What if it was me? What if I got smashed?* And if nobody helped me, I would just sit there and burn. I just hope and pray that if that ever happened to me, somebody would do the same thing for me."[34]

Morality and Principled Rescues

For some Carnegie heroes, standing by would violate their *moral principles*. Four percent of the rescuers felt that not helping would violate their moral precepts and that rescue reaffirms each rescuer's own autonomously derived moral principles of justice, respect, equality, and caring for the helpless. As implied above, none of the motivating factors are exclusive of each other; rather, many of these factors work together in various degrees for many rescuers, as told by the following rescuer, who's triggering mechanism was moral principles.

An example of a principled rescuer is a thirty-one-year-old man who rescued a woman from a brutal assault. He was driving on a rainy night when he saw two people sort of wrestling around at a street corner. The only light came from his headlights. At first he thought it was just two people messing around, but when he got closer he could tell they weren't playing around—one of them was a woman, and the man was hitting her. He thought he should just call the police and let them deal with it, but as he got even closer, he could see that she was being struck forcefully with a small hatchet.

When asked what motivated him to risk his life on her behalf, he said: "In hindsight, I think it's more that I have this contempt for people taking advantage of other people. That's probably the number-one reason. I mean, whether it's a guy kicking a dog or a corporate type sticking it to the small worker, I just don't like it when people take advantage of others."[35]

In October 1994, another Carnegie hero, a thirty-eight-year-old man, was visiting Washington, D.C., for work and a brief vacation. As he was walking past the White House, he heard a series of popping noises. His first thought was that somebody had thrown a string of firecrackers over the fence. He said,

> I saw the shooter [with] an assault rifle, and he was shooting at the White House. . . . He was kind of trotting, and he had a trench coat on, and as he started to pass me I noticed that he looked down at his weapon, and [he had] his hands on the middle of the stock. . . . I figured that was probably a good opportu-

nity to do something, and so I let him pass a little further, figuring I would hit him in the blind spot . . . and my only thought was . . . getting there as quickly as I could because I knew he could turn around and blast me. . . . Right before I got to him I jumped and just kind of tackled him at the chest level . . . and then my only thought at that point was to hold on to him as tight as I could because I didn't want [him to be able] to access a pistol or knife . . . and I remember watching out of the corner of my eye and seeing a secret service guy jump the fence . . . and then I saw one of the white-uniformed officers had pinned his hands behind his back and they were putting cuffs on him.

When asked why he became involved in the situation, he replied: "I thought, *He shouldn't be doing that.* . . . I would think that I was probably concerned about him hurting people. But really it wasn't a matter of him hurting people. It was a matter that he was doing something wrong and I was going to stop him."[36]

Our interviews with the Carnegie heroes further corroborates that these people are not larger-than-life individuals; rather, they are ordinary people who, through their socialization, have internalized a sense of responsibility and empathy for fellow human beings. They have acquired caring norms in their lives and developed skills that both prompt and enable them to respond in emergency situations. Their sense of self and the moral values they have acquired would not let them be bystanders. Each of us needs to learn more about compassion and caring ourselves—and to teach these values to children and young people. Every person has the potential to be a rescuer, but the transformation is not one that occurs overnight. Parents and institutions have to take part in teaching and empowering young people to care. It is through a continual process of learning and practicing caring norms—internalizing the skills and values that we identified as the salient motivational factors of Carnegie Medal recipients—that one is able to respond heroically in emergency situations. It is also through this internalization that military heroes such as Hugh Thompson and Larry Colburn (whom I address in Chapter 6) would not stand by while innocent civilians in My Lai were being massacred.

6

So Others May Live

The Courage of Military Heroes

> But if for any reason war becomes inevitable, courage is not just desirable, it is essential. Without courage whole armies disintegrate and flee in confusion, and lonely men die an ugly death for want of anyone brave enough to rescue them. Without courage there is no power on earth to deter an aggressor, nothing to oppose the principle that might is right.
>
> **—John Percival—***For Valour*

I arrived in New York Harbor as a legal immigrant on December 12, 1950. After a short time working with my uncle, I was drafted into the U.S. Army. My introduction to military culture began the day I arrived at Fort Dix, New Jersey, for basic training. Our heads were shaved—a first step in the degradation ceremony—and we were led to the barracks where we would live for the next sixteen weeks of training. Every day during that time efforts were made to break us down, to turn us into "real fighting men."

Drill Sergeant Gene Gillespie was our nemesis for those sixteen weeks. He insulted us constantly and generally made our lives miserable. The slightest disobedience was punishable by an immediate twenty push-ups, and I did my share of push-ups. Sergeant Gillespie had a regulation crew cut, a red face frozen in a constant grin, a black belt in judo, and a build like a professional wrestler. For any comments that he interpreted to be a "wise guy" crack—which were most—he made me carry my backpack full of rocks around the barracks for an hour. One time he punished me by making me dig a foxhole. He came by later, dropped a cigarette into the hole, and said, "Oliner, now bury it."

Now, as then, military culture must focus on *patriotism* and its evil but necessary twin, *indoctrination against the enemy*. These were two ideas that I had grown familiar with as a child. Later, during my military service in the Korean War, we were reminded daily about the communist threat and our duty as Americans to battle it.

In November 1951 we boarded a ship in Seattle and sailed to Korea. A group of us were told that we would be made into provisional police escort guards and that our job would be to guard prisoners of war. By the time we arrived, many North Korean prisoners had been brought to South Korea and placed in POW camps on islands near Pusan, at the southeastern tip of the Korean Peninsula. The camp at Koje-Do, where I was assigned, held thousands of North Koreans. Riots and attempts to take U.S. soldiers hostage were common. Wisely, the United Nations (UN) command decided to move some of the POWs to another camp, so I and a few hundred U.S. soldiers went as guards to the island of Pongan-Do. Life went on uneventfully for a while. I was promoted to corporal and was in charge of supervising some of the GIs guarding the prisoners.

The cease-fire negotiations at Panmun-Jam in 1952–1953 were not progressing because the North Koreans and Chinese demanded total return of their prisoners. In the meantime, North Koreans, through spies and other methods of communication, told the POWs to make trouble for us—to organize riots, sing anti-American songs, shout out anti-American slogans, and in general be as disorderly as possible. On December 14, 1952, the 3,600 POWs locked arms and started singing in both compounds. A leader would stand on a soapbox and instruct the thousands of prisoners to yell and sing loudly and hurl rocks at the UN guards—so much so that they made the perimeter guards nervous. Our officers instructed us to announce over loudspeakers for the prisoners to cease their now-deafening yelling and protest and to return peacefully to their huts. Instead, the noise intensified, and many began to push toward the barbed-wire fences surrounding the compound. One of my commanding officers, a colonel, decided that we had to stop the escalating riot by any means necessary for fear that the POWs would soon take over the camp; after all, there were thousands of them and a only a few hundred of us.

As we faced the screaming prisoners, now pushing closer toward the barbed-wire fences with tremendous force and aggression, the first order came to fire above their heads, which didn't make any difference. Next came the order to aim and fire on the prisoners leading the riot. They fell down dead. This was followed by an order to shoot right into the prisoners, who were maybe fifty feet away—basically point-blank range. It all happened very fast and in a blur of shouting and confusion. But I knew it was wrong. Though the prisoners were rioting, they didn't have any weapons and could have been subdued by other means—with tear gas, for example. I didn't fear for my life. Instead of firing point-blank, I fired above their heads. The commanding officer saw this and kicked me hard in the butt and yelled, "Oliner, what are ya, a yellow-belly?!" I couldn't and didn't follow the order to kill—and haven't regretted it to this day. It was so inhumane and terrible and against every moral belief I had, even at such a young age.

When it was all over, the prisoners were rushed back into their barracks while the wounded were carried out for medical treatment. As punishment for disobeying orders, I was assigned the grim task of supervising prisoners who were to carry their dead comrades down to the beach to await transport. In the dark, another soldier and I kept watch over the dead bodies piled on the beach; the only sound was the hissing of air through the bullet holes in the dead bodies.

The armed forces newspaper *Stars and Stripes* wrote that on December 23, 1952, brave soldiers controlled a group of "reds" trying to take over the camp: "In one section of the camp, enclosure number two, compound F, a revolt there this week took the lives of 87 inmates and injured 118."[1]

I experienced a sense of moral dilemma, having to tackle my own sense of right and wrong—to shoot unarmed prisoners or follow orders. Some U.S. military personnel in the Vietnam War, such as Bob Kerrey and Hugh Thompson, also wrestled morally with what to do at the time, weighing the efficacy of orders to kill versus moral courage.

The Moral Dilemma of Military Heroism

There is a moral dilemma inherent in this discussion, because to be a hero in the military, it would seem, one has to become a killer. Heretofore, our definition of "heroism" has involved saving lives, rescuing fellow humans, risking everything to save another. So what is a "military hero"? Can there be such a thing as a hero in an institution that teaches—indeed *requires* in the name of love and protection of country—its members to excel in the killing of other human beings? Are we so accustomed to the incongruity of this idea that we no longer even *see* its incongruity? There are certainly many men and women in the military whose brave deeds can only be defined as heroic, and some of them will be discussed later in this chapter. But we need to remember that we're navigating murky territory, moralistically speaking. Often it's the soldier who wrestles with his own conscience *against* the indoctrination of the military who best illustrates the difficulty in determining just what makes a military hero.

In war, heroism is born of violence. It is a sad truth that in war the soldier must resort to violence for survival. Logic dictates that because he's taught to defeat the enemy, then the enemy must be villainous. But it is not always that simple. "The enemy" is really merely a social construct—we are the *good guys* and they are the *bad guys*. The circumstances are further muddled when we couch the conflict in terms of who started the war, who wanted to conquer and suppress the other, and who, in turn, brought liberation. Is there an absolute moral high ground? And if there is, then who occupies it?

Trying to understand military heroes who have achieved their distinction under circumstances of violence is difficult, because heroism involves killing the enemy as a necessary element of the courageous deeds that are performed by those we honor—very much the opposite of the rescuers we describe in previous chapters who were heroes precisely because they preserved life while risking their own. Military heroism acknowledges the killing of the enemy, as in the case of Lieutenant Bob Kerrey.

Bob Kerrey, a former U.S. senator from Nebraska, later became president of the New School for Social Research in New York City and has been a serious candidate for U.S. president. He was awarded the Congressional Medal of Honor for his heroism in Vietnam, but his tour of duty was not without moral ambiguity. On February 25, 1969, Kerry led a squad of U.S. Navy SEALs into the village of Thanh Phong, where intelligence had reported high-ranking Vietcong soldiers to be hiding. Kerrey's Raiders, as they were known then, had little experience but a lot of enthusiasm. Despite considerable danger, near midnight on a moonless night the men piled into swift boats and headed for Thanh Phong. Darkness gave cover but also heightened the fear and confusion. As the men headed toward the village, they heard gunfire coming from nearby huts. According to Gerhard Klann, a member of the SEALs on the mission, Kerrey gave the order to shoot.

According to Kerrey's interpretation, he and five other SEALs murdered a number of civilians—women, children, and elderly men—by mistake.

The story of the massacre came to light thirty-two years later when Klann told *Time Magazine* and *60 Minutes* that Kerrey had knowingly ordered this massacre. "Klann said, 'an order was given' to shoot them. 'We lined up, and we opened fire.'"[2] Kerrey received the Congressional Medal of Honor for a later operation in which he lost the lower part of his leg. Kerrey's critics accused him of doing what Lieutenant William Calley had done at My Lai (the most notorious incident in which U.S. soldiers killed Vietnamese), and some thought Kerrey should return his Medal of Honor and other medals he received.

Kerrey was an enthusiastic, gung-ho, middle-class youth when he enlisted in what was considered an elite unit in a dangerous part of the military service. His Congressional Medal of Honor says: "Kerrey's courage and inspiring leadership, valiant fighting skills, and tenacious devotion to duty in the face of almost overwhelming opposition sustained and enhanced the finest tradition of the U.S. naval service."

But February 25, 1969, is a date that became seared into Kerrey's memory, and he grieved for the innocent people killed:

> Standing on the fantail of the destroyer watching the silvery wake recede behind us; I felt a sickness in my heart for what we had done. . . . The young, innocent man who went to Vietnam died that night. After that night, I no longer had illusions or objectivity about the war. I had become someone I did not recognize. I had been in Vietnam for five weeks and this was my first firefight. It had not ended in the heroic way I had expected.[3]

Senator Kerrey sees the dilemma in being indoctrinated to kill or be killed; the faces of the enemy were evil, and so were their intentions.

Hugh Thompson was another soldier who wrestled with his moral dilemma. The courage of this helicopter pilot and his rescue of innocent Vietnamese civilians at My Lai is a particularly compelling example of an unusual kind of military heroism. On March 16, 1968, Thompson, his gunner, Larry Colburn, and crew chief Glen Andreotta were flying over the vicinity of the Vietnamese hamlet of My Lai searching for the enemy and trying to draw enemy fire. They saw only one draft-age male all day. They left the area to refuel and upon returning saw dead bodies everywhere. A 1999 *Newsweek* article details the experience:

> There were infants and toddlers, women and very old men, but no young men. On one pass just outside the village, we saw a teenage girl lying on her back in a rice field. She was flailing back and forth, obviously wounded. I hovered over her and marked her with a smoke flair and got on the radio to call for help. A captain approached. He nudged her with his foot, shot and stood back, then put his weapon on automatic and blew her away. We didn't know what to think of that.[4]

They flew over the scene and came to a ditch filled with living people—women, children, and old men. Thompson put the helicopter down and asked the sergeant on the ground if he could help. But the sergeant replied that the only way was to put them out of their misery. Thompson thought the sergeant was kidding, and the chopper lifted off; he heard gunshots and saw soldiers randomly firing into the ditch. It took Thompson and his crew a moment to comprehend what they witnessed.

Thompson told me that he saw a woman with children hiding behind a bunker as U.S. soldiers led by Lieutenant William Calley were approaching. Thompson realized that time was precious, and he set down the chopper between the civilians and the soldiers and ordered Colburn to aim his guns. He told the officer in charge about civilians in the bunker, who thereafter suggested, "A hand grenade would get them out." Thompson was shocked and decided to get the civilians out alive and to a safe zone.

Thompson then circled back over the ditch and saw bodies moving. He set the helicopter down, and Glenn Andreotta pulled out a little girl covered in blood but without a scratch on her. In my interview, he told me that when they got back into the helicopter Colburn held the child in his lap. They flew her to a nearby hospital and turned her over to a Catholic nun. Then Thompson flew back to the base to confront his superiors.

During my interview with Hugh Thompson, he said that he first experienced a state of disbelief—unable to accept that his comrades in arms would slaughter innocent people. Then came a realization, stating, "I could not live with myself unless I took some action to save the innocent."

Examining Thompson's background and upbringing, I see that he learned the difference between right and wrong from his parents and was disciplined in a manner in which misbehavior toward another person was unacceptable. He told me that as an adult he had internalized the soldiers ethic as described by General Douglas MacArthur in 1946: "The soldier, be he friend or foe, is charged with the protection of the weak and unarmed. It is the very essence and reason for his being."[5]

It would take time, but the horrible killings at My Lai did become public. My Lai was not an accident; it was premeditated murder, one of the most shameful chapters in U.S. military history. The fact that the U.S. government, for a time, considered Thompson to be a traitor and a coward is a horrible affront to such a brave hero.

The army tried to cover up this massacre of innocent civilians.[6] It was a particularly gross miscarriage of justice when House Armed Services Committee chairman L. Mendel Rivers and special subcommittee chairman F. Edward Hebert attempted to convince Congress and the public that Hugh Thompson was not a hero. Rivers attempted to portray Thompson as a traitor because he had turned his weapons on other U.S. soldiers. Understandably, Thompson was humiliated. Alone and unappreciated, he decided to fight back and "spent the better part of a year in and out of Washington, doing his part to help the Army understand what happened . . . and testifying before various boards and committees."[7]

The army finally recognized Thompson, Colburn, and Andreotta as military heroes, and in March 1998 they were awarded the Soldier's Medal in a public ceremony at the Vietnam War Memorial in Washington, D.C. Andreotta's award was given posthumously—he had died in Vietnam after the incident. These men, despite almost thirty years of humiliation and disillusionment at the hands of the U.S. government, were finally vindicated.

Heroes Under Fire

In looking at the deeds of military heroes, I am interested in discovering what motivates those who have been trained in a particular ethos to fight and protect, to risk their lives for the benefit of others. Specifically, I'm interested in three questions: How can heroism under fire be explained? What are the special characteristics of military heroes? Are personality traits or are situational variables more important in determining heroic behavior in war settings?

We need to remember that in most cases military heroes are not like everyday heroes. During the Korean War, I was trained to be brave, courageous, and willing to save others on "my side." But then, one may ask, Why did I shoot over the heads of the prisoners in Korea instead of into them as ordered? What prompted Hugh Thompson to put himself in conflict with his own side in order to save the innocent civilians at My Lai? Were we defying our training? Did we pay our allegiance to a higher ethical code?

Carlos Bertha, a scholar on the psychology of war, discusses the moral psychology of soldiers and argues that there are two questions to ask regarding war heroes: What kind of person makes himself a hero—or, alternatively, a monster of atrocities—during war? And is a war hero the same as a nonwar hero? [8]

First, Bertha concludes that military heroes as well as perpetrators of massacres have similar psychological profiles. They are passive-aggressive, raised in rural rather than urban areas, volunteer as opposed to being drafted, and academically, have lower literacy and aptitude scores.

Second, he asserts heroes in war are not the same as heroes in nonwar for two reasons: first, in war one is protecting the self from other shooters; and second, there is an expectation during war that atrocities and massacres are possible. The conundrum that Bertha ponders is how to decide between moral convictions and military orders. If one follows orders, the unit as a whole will be dependable and strong. But following orders, by definition, deprives an individual any opportunity to exercise moral ideals or judgments. Thus, it is impossible to avoid the question: Is there such a thing as a moral and justified war? There are, of course, many views on this issue. For me, it is clear that some wars have begun for immoral reasons: the destruction of the innocent and the conquest of territories.

Specifically, people on "our side" are awarded heroic distinctions because they have demonstrated extraordinary courage and valor for the good of their brothers and sisters and for our country. For the enemy, these people were not heroes at all.

U.S. Army Sergeant James Logan was awarded the Congressional Medal of Honor for his heroic behavior during World War II. Exposing himself to enemy fire, Sergeant Logan "single-handedly captured a German machine-gun position in the first hours of the landing at Salerno, Italy."[9] Although certainly a hero for his brave and gallant display of courage, Sergeant Logan had to kill five German soldiers in order to accomplish his mission. What might the kin of these soldiers call him?

Questions thus remain: Is killing justified under any circumstances? Should we kill to avoid being killed? Is there such a thing as a just war? Has one a moral obligation to defend the innocent? Is courage a wide-ranging and enduring personality characteristic, or are courageous acts spawned by the demands of prevailing circumstances?

Psychometric, psychiatric, and field-performance measures obtained from a group of British army bomb-disposal operators—all experienced soldiers with a satisfactory standard of proficiency—showed that the most successful operators in this highly competent group possessed some distinctive features. Specifically, those soldiers who had received the George Cross Medal had exceptionally low scores on a scale measuring hypochondria. A low score on this scale indicates healthiness and well-being ("I feel fit and happy," "my mind works quickly and well these days"), a particularly well-adjusted and stable group. This finding appears to support the idea that heroic behavior results from a general personality type. However, to conclude this, it must be determined that this group of decorated soldiers would also behave courageously in a range of situations. Alternatively, there is argument for situational specificity in that these soldiers constituted a highly trained group working in an efficient and supportive unit and did, in fact, express fears of objects or situations unrelated to bombs, such as heights, snakes, dentists, and injections. Based on this finding, the researchers concluded that the determinants of particular acts of courage are a combination of general personality characteristics and of specific situational factors. Whereas individuals may not exhibit heroic behavior in one situation, they may respond quite courageously in another. Or, looking at it the other way, a specific situation may invoke certain personality types toward heroic action while simultaneously inhibiting others with differing personality types.

Other studies examine various aspects of the Arab-Israeli wars, looking at tactics, the quality of battlefield performance of soldiers, and performance of weapons. The Israeli Defense Forces conducted one such study following the 1973 Yom Kippur War, which looked at soldiers who had achieved heroic distinction. This study found that both heroism and psychiatric breakdown became more likely as battle intensity—measured by the number of physical casualties—increased. Heroism was found to be associated with additional situational variables, namely, that high morale—as indicated by strong unit cohesion and good leadership—was the primary factor related to heroic behavior on the battlefield. A later study correlated company morale with personal morale and found that the components of personal morale include "trust in the company commander, confidence in one's own skills as a soldier, one's feelings about the legitimacy of the war, trust in one's weapons, trust in one's self, confidence in one's comrades' readiness to fight, the unit's cohesiveness, and the quality of one's relationship with one's commanders."[10]

In another careful evaluation of battlefield heroism in the Israeli Defense Forces during the Yom Kippur War, Reuven Gal and Richard Gabriel analyzed nearly 300 cases of extraordinary heroism for which the Israeli Medal of Honor was awarded. These heroes were ordinary men—most were reservists—who faced overwhelming numerical odds. All of the medal winners exhibited a high level of leadership, devotion to duty, decisiveness, and perseverance under stress. A large percentage came from the officer corps and had been taught in training that individuals were responsible for one another and for their units, a factor that may also have an important bearing on understanding military heroism.[11] Analyzing specific situational variables, the authors found four situations that influence who will engage in heroic behavior.

- The first consists of troops who find themselves *isolated* and fighting with their backs to the wall, surrounded by the enemy, outnumbered, and *engaged in defending or retreating battle.* In this instance, the act of heroism is most likely to be carried out by commanding officers. However, the act might not happen in isolation—typically, there is some participation by other soldiers.

- The second situation is referred to as *last remnant and savior,* implying *face-to-face combat* during an offensive. An example might be that a commander is injured and another individual spontaneously takes command and assumes leadership. Statistically, this type of individual tends to survive the battle.

- The third is *self-sacrifice.* This involves the situation in which the hero is with his regular unit, the enemy encircles the soldiers, and the act of heroism *saves the lives of the group.* These acts usually result in the death of the hero.

- The fourth and final situation is *fight to the last bullet*. This situation implies that a single soldier or crew remains in an offensive battle. The act of bravery results neither from a direct order nor from a desire to save the lives of others. Rather, it results from an attempt to *complete the mission*. This encounter continues until the hero is killed.

Gal and Gabriel conclude that heroes neither are a distinct species nor are they born heroes nor extraordinary men of courage. Based on this, it is difficult to predict who might become a hero. The study suggests, however, some consistent themes: Men in battle feel attachment for one another and for their leaders, and they feel that their friends would have done the same thing if the situation called for it. Thus, men commit heroic acts on behalf of cohesion and on behalf of their comrades.

In order to fight heroically, the soldier must recognize fear and cope with it. Courage comes about from fortitude, inner strength, and the will to persevere despite fear and the adverse conditions of combat. Winners of the Congressional Medal of Honor speak about fear and how they were able to overcome it. Fortitude—that particular strength of mind that allows one to endure pain and adversity—is made up of inner moral strength, willpower, and resolution. This kind of fortitude, or *battlemind*, is considered a strong motivating factor in combat, causing people to fight and sustain the will to fight despite fear. It is a state of mind that can be developed through training.

Factors such as comradeship, self-reliance, a sense of efficacy, bonding that occurs when soldiers depend on each other, and courage are crucial to motivation. It is very important to build efficacy and self-reliance through training, to develop a sense of self-worth and self-discipline, to practice assertiveness, and to hone skills. Other factors in building efficacy include physical conditioning, a sense of esprit de corps, and an understanding of the reasons for the fight—what ideals one's nation and leaders stand for.

Unlike Bertha, whose research concluded that character traits of heroes are passive-aggressive, Judith Banks's research on a group of Vietnam War heroes indicates that they possessed some sort of internal strength and fortitude. There is a sense that these heroes had come from loving homes and that they felt loved and approved of by their mothers and, occasionally, by their fathers, and their parents had a good relationship. The heroes had had a good education that overlapped with a religious upbringing. It was found that the stringent environments of their early backgrounds reinforced their sense of discipline and responsibility and prepared them for the rigors of their duty.[12]

Heroic Suicide

One of the first Medal of Honor winners of the Vietnam War, Sergeant Daniel Fernandez, was posthumously awarded for saving his squad members by covering an enemy grenade with his body. What went through Fernandez's mind in the split second between deciding to act and acting? Was it reflexive action? There is reason to believe that those soldiers who commit such a heroic suicide are primarily motivated out of loyalty to the group. Rather than see group members perish, they sacrifice their own lives; and it seems that the more cohesive the group, the more likely it will be that an act of sacrifice *for the group* will be made. The sacrifice affirms the worthiness of the group of which one is a member.[13]

Jeffrey Riemer has examined Emile Durkheim's classic statement on heroic suicides to better understand actual cases of combat suicide drawn from Congressional Medal of Honor data. He says that according to Durkheim:

> Altruistic suicide can occur when a person becomes strongly integrated into a social group, and suicide becomes a "duty" for those who are integrated, citing the aged and sick in some societies, women who are expected to commit suicide after a husband's death, and servants on the death of their chief as examples. Under conditions of strong societal bonding to persons or groups, an individual may be punished, ridiculed, or ostracized for not committing suicide: the expected conduct for the person is not to please himself or herself but to please the group to which he or she belongs.[14]

Jeffrey Reimer concludes that, indeed, Emile Durkheim's work on suicide—although now a century old—is still useful in analyzing heroism in the military, especially the kind of heroism that results in the voluntary death of the hero in order to save the group.

Military heroes from many countries, both men and women, have been recognized and decorated for their gallantry. In tracing these heroes through centuries of recorded history, I find many individual leaders and commanders who have achieved legendary distinction through their heroic feats. Military heroes in Britain are recognized by receiving the George Cross and Victoria Cross, and in the United States by the Congressional Medal of Honor, the Soldier's Medal—to those who have shown exceptional valor in the face of extreme danger—and the Purple Heart. Below I describe each of these medals and some of the individuals who received them.

The Victoria Cross

The Victoria Cross is given for most conspicuous bravery, daring, or outstanding act of valor or self-sacrifice and for extreme devotion to duty in the presence of the enemy. It was introduced in 1856 at the end of the Crimean War by Queen Victoria, who had a hand in designing the medal. The Victoria Cross has been awarded not only to British citizens but also to the soldiers of the British Empire, with some 1,350 Victoria Crosses presented to individuals, 300 of them posthumously.

John Percival has traced the history of the Victoria Cross from its 1856 inception through the Falklands War in 1982. He explored the nature of courage and asked what it is that makes people act courageously and show extreme heroism. He asks if it is possible to see "courage as altruism as a quality which enables one individual to triumph over his own fear and risk his life for others."[15] Attempting to explain the motivational characteristics of the recipients of the Victoria Cross, he found that many exhibited stubbornness, cool-headedness, a strong sense of social responsibility, courage, caring, a moral responsibility for taking action to enable others to press on in battle, risk-taking, determination to overcome difficulties, a sense of chivalry, and philanthropy.

Percival also cites examples of Victoria Cross winners, such as Lieutenant Arthur Roden Cutler of the Australian military, who served under the British flag and ultimately lost a limb as a result of his outstanding acts of valor. At Merdjayoun, Syria, on June 19, 1941, the Vichy French enemy forces counterattacked with machine guns and tanks, killing many of Cutler's soldiers. He manned rifles and Bren guns and fought back, driving the enemy infantry away. The tanks continued to attack, but, under the constant fire, they eventually withdrew. Lieutenant Cutler then personally supervised the evacuation of wounded members of his party.

> Undaunted, he pressed for a further advance. He had been ordered to establish an outpost from which he could register the

only road by which the enemy transport could enter the town. With a small party of volunteers he pressed on until finally with one other he succeeded in establishing an outpost right in the town, which was occupied by the Foreign Legion, despite enemy machine gun fire which prevented [the British] infantry from advancing.[16]

During the Falkland Campaign of 1982, there were two Victoria Crosses awarded; both illustrate characteristics. Percival states:

> Both of the actions. . . involved extreme risk—indeed they involved the ultimate risk, since both men died winning it—and both materially affected the outcome of the battle in the areas where they were won. Both actions were also undertaken in the hope of saving the lives of others. There was that element of self-sacrifice.[17]

Lieutenant-Colonel H. Jones commanded a paratroop battalion with fewer than 500 men and was credited with directly aiding in the collapse of the Argentine resistance. He and his men took on a much larger force of well-armed men defending a critical position. Jones was killed leading the charge. As with so many others, he had acted with total disregard for his own safety.

In the closing phase of the Falklands Campaign, platoon Sergeant Ian McKay took over when the company commander was wounded. McKay realized that the position the platoon occupied was untenable and that hiding or retreating was impossible, so he mounted an attack, and when the men with him fell, he "charged on alone, reached the bunker and hurled a grenade into it before he too dropped dead. The rest of the platoon was able to follow up his lead" and succeed in the assault.[18]

Another review of Victoria Cross winners by Vidya Anand showed that the heroism of Indian soldiers fighting for the British Empire in various wars had been underreported. There were many who should have received the Victoria Cross, but only about thirty did.[19]

An example of one who acted heroically is the recently deceased Ganju Lama, who risked his life for his country and comrades during World War II. In June 1944 the Japanese were advancing on two strongholds in Burma. They had three tanks and were firing on precise targets. The Gurkha Ganju

Lama encouraged his fellow soldiers to keep up their momentum for a counterattack; though seriously wounded, he single-handedly took out two of the three tanks approaching the line. He did not withdraw to have his wounds dressed until all were killed or wounded. Lord Wavell, the viceroy of India, awarded Ganju the Victoria Cross in 1944.[20]

The George Cross

King George VI established the George Cross and George Medal in 1940 to recognize the fortitude and courage shown by civilians and those engaged in bomb and mine disposal during the London Blitz. The George Cross is awarded for acts of great heroism and courage in circumstances of extreme danger. It was intended primarily for civilian bravery, but its scope has been broadened to recognize the many heroic feats for which military honors aren't awarded because the acts were not carried out in the face of the enemy. In order to recognize that contribution, the George Cross is appropriately given to civilians and to military personnel, and many of the recipients have been members of the armed forces. Several other awards already existed that could be given to civilians and to military personnel for heroism in circumstances other than battle, but none of them were equal to the distinction of the George Cross.

Since the medal's inception, approximately 400 George Crosses have been awarded in Britain and Canada. One recipient, Princess Noor Inayat Khan of the Hyderbad royal family, was an undercover agent with the French resistance and the first female agent to be parachuted into France. For more than a year she evaded the Gestapo and sent vital information to British military intelligence for D-Day landings. She was betrayed, captured by the Germans, and executed in 1944 at the infamous Dachau concentration camp. The French posthumously decorated her, and three years later the British awarded her the George Cross Medal.

The Congressional Medal of Honor

The Congressional Medal of Honor is the highest award for valor in action that can be bestowed upon an individual serving in the U.S. armed services. This decoration dates back to the Civil War and is awarded to those distinguished by their gallantry in action. Since it was established in 1863, the medal has been awarded to 3,410 servicemen, 574 of them posthumously.[21] The inspirational stories of three Medal of Honor winners are featured here.[22]

In October 1942 Mitchell Paige, a Marine Corps platoon sergeant on Guadalcanal, was outnumbered by an advancing Japanese force intent on capturing Henderson Field, a crucial airfield in the Solomon Islands. During the night, Paige and his platoon, down to thirty-two men, kept firing their machine guns until all except Paige were dead or seriously wounded. Even though he had been hit with shrapnel and had a Japanese bayonet plunged through his hand, Paige—completely alone by now—fired back at the Japanese until his gun was destroyed; he then moved from machine gun to machine gun, never ceasing his withering fire against the advancing hordes until reinforcements finally arrived.[23] He then "led a bayonet charge, driving the enemy back and preventing a breakthrough in our lines. When the smoke cleared, there were 920 dead Japanese soldiers."[24] Paige was commissioned as a lieutenant and stayed in the Marine Corps until he retired as a colonel in 1964.

In March 1968 near Phuoc Vinh, Vietnam, U.S. Army Captain Paul W. Bucha led his infantry company on a reconnaissance-in-force mission against enemy troops. "Seeing that his men were pinned down by heavy machine-gun fire from a concealed bunker located some 40 meters from the front of the positions, Captain Bucha crawled through the hail of fire to single-handedly destroy the bunker with grenades."[25] It became apparent that his men could not hold their position, so they moved to a spot where they could direct more firepower on the advancing North Vietnamese.

> When night fell, Bucha kept moving from squad to squad, encouraging his men, distributing ammunition and directing "artillery, helicopter gunship and Air Force gunship fire on the enemy strong points and attacking forces. . . ." Then in "complete view of enemy snipers," he stood up in the landing zone and directed the melee of Medevac helicopters coming in and out to rescue the wounded.[26]

Bucha subsequently attained the rank of captain and left the army in 1972.

Harold A. Fritz was an army first lieutenant leading a platoon of the 11th Armored Cavalry Regiment in Binh Long Province, Vietnam. The platoon was on its way to meet a truck convoy when they came under fire from the enemy. Fritz was seriously wounded, and his platoon was vastly outnumbered. Nonetheless, he leaped to the top of his burning vehicle and directed the positioning of his remaining vehicles and men. With complete disregard for his wounds and safety, he ran from vehicle to vehicle in complete view of the enemy gunners in order to reposition his men.[27] While Fritz fired at the enemy, a second force advanced against his platoon, threatening to overwhelm it. "Lieutenant Fritz, armed only with a pistol and bayonet, led a small group of his men in a fierce and daring charge which routed the attackers and inflicted heavy casualties."[28] Fritz retired from the army in 1993 as a lieutenant-colonel.

Subsequent to receiving the Medal of Honor, these three men have had important roles in finding and exposing "false heroes"—imposters who hold fake medals and fraudulently claim to have been recipients. As legitimate medal-holders upset by false claims, they have organized in order to track down and expose such imposters. The indignation of the true Congressional Medal of Honor winners is quite marked. Paige has made the search for imposters his life's mission. There are only 157 living medal holders, and they all know each other, so most of the time it is easy to identify the fakes. Fritz, referring to an incident where he exposed a very flagrant violation, said that he thought it was despicable that somebody would dishonor veterans. Paige claims that he and others have exposed 500 phonies and states that he is pushing for tougher legislation to punish them and that the U.S. government has been taking the problem more seriously. After a recent investigation, a firm that was the official government contractor for the medal admitted to having sold 300 unauthorized medals. These medals retailed at military collectible shows for about $500. The firm was fined and is barred from any future government medal contracts.

The Congressional Medal of Honor Society reports that in 1998 two Congressional Medals of Honor were awarded—one to James L. Day for his heroism on Okinawa during World War II, and the other to Robert R. Ingram for heroism in Vietnam. As stated by the society, the medals were for "conspicuous gallantry and intrepidity at the risk of life above and beyond the call of duty."

James L. Day was a squad leader serving with the 2nd Battalion, 2nd Marines, 6th Marine Division on Okinawa during World War II.[29] On the first day of the combat operation, Corporal Day led his squad and the remnants of another unit to the front lines of Sugar Loaf Hill. Japanese soldiers attacked with intense mortar and artillery, quickly followed by a ground attack. Although Day lost half his men, he remained at the front and shouted encouragement while throwing hand grenades and repelling enemy fire. He then led his squad in defending against three nighttime attacks; although five Marines were killed, he escorted four wounded soldiers to safety—one at a time. After this feat,

> Corporal Day then manned a light machine gun assisted by a wounded Marine, and halted another night attack. In the ferocious action, his machine gun was destroyed and he suffered multiple white phosphorous and fragmentation wounds. He reorganized his defensive position in time to halt a fifth enemy attack with devastating small arms fire. On three separate occasions, Japanese soldiers closed to within a few feet of his foxhole, but were killed by Corporal Day.[30]

The second day of attacks proved as difficult as the first. When the attacks subsided, more than seventy enemy soldiers were sprawled dead around Day's position. And on the final day of the attacks, an exhausted and wounded Corporal Day continued to defend the position, killing nearly a dozen enemy soldiers. The citation reads that for "his extraordinary heroism, repeated acts of valor, and quintessential battlefield leadership, Corporal Day inspired the efforts of his outnumbered marines to defeat a much larger enemy force, reflecting great credit upon himself and upholding the highest traditions of the Marine Corps and the United States Naval Service."

Petty Officer Robert R. Ingram was serving as a medical corpsman accompanying the point platoon as it aggressively dispatched an outpost of a North Vietnam battalion.[31] The attack originated from a ridgeline, beyond which was a small paddy village. Suddenly, the village tree line exploded with an intense hail of automatic rifle fire from approximately one hundred North Vietnamese regulars. In mere moments, the platoon ranks were decimated. Oblivious to the danger, Ingram crawled across the bullet-spattered terrain to reach a downed Marine. As he administered aid, a bullet went through the palm of his hand. Calls for "corpsman!" echoed across the ridge. Bleeding, he edged across the fire-swept landscape, collecting ammunition from the dead and administering aid to the wounded.[32]

Ingram received two more wounds; looking for a way off the ridge, he kept hearing the call for a corpsman, and he responded. When he finally reached his platoon and was dressing the head wound of another corpsman, he sustained his fourth wound. Disregarding his own wounds, Ingram came to the aid of his comrades, saving the lives of many that day. The citation for his medal reads, "by his indomitable fighting spirit, daring initiative, and unfaltering dedication to duty, Petty Officer Ingram reflected great credit upon himself and upheld the highest traditions of the United States Naval Service."

During World War II, Lieutenant John Fox "was killed after ordering his own men to fire on his position to stem an enemy attack."[33] He made the order when his position was about to be overtaken by German and Austrian soldiers. Military historians suggest that this selfless act may have bought the Americans time to retreat, thereby saving lives. In 1997, more than fifty years after the fact, Fox, a veteran of the segregated Black 92nd Infantry Division, received his Medal of Honor.

Of the numerous Congressional Medals of Honor awarded, William Carney was the first African American, Mitchell Red Cloud was one of the few Native Americans, and Sadao Munemori was one of several Japanese Americans to receive it. To date, Dr. Mary E. Walker is the only woman to receive the medal.

According to Paul Bucha, president of the Congressional Medal of Honor Society in 1999, Dr. Mary E. Walker received her medal for service during the Civil War caring for the sick and wounded, risking her own health and life. Interestingly, Dr. Walker's medal was revoked in 1916 because she was a noncombatant, and it was not until 1977 that it was restored.

William Carney was born in 1840 in Norfolk, Virginia. His mother had been a slave freed by her master at his death, and his freeman father was a sailor. Carney's boyhood was hard, but at the age of fourteen he attended a secret school in Norfolk (in most places in the South before the Civil War, African-American children generally did not attend school). At the age of fifteen, he and his family moved to New Bedford, Massachusetts, where he worked for a time as a handyman. He considered becoming a minister, but at the start of the Civil War that plan came to an end. He wanted to join the Union Army, but President Abraham Lincoln had a problem in forming a black fighting unit. Lincoln knew that creating all-black units would be a difficult undertaking, complicated by the enormous social, political, and military implications (in both the North and the South) that would entail. However, after the Emancipation Proclamation was issued, the formation of all-black units occurred.

The first black regiment was the 54th Massachusetts Infantry formed by John Andrews, the abolitionist governor of Massachusetts. Blacks could not rise to the rank of lieutenant, so they were commanded by white officers. On February 17, 1862, Carney enlisted in the new regiment. He was made a sergeant and assigned to Company C, known as the Massachusetts Company. On May 28th the unit was shipped south and ordered to capture Charleston, South Carolina—a tough assignment because it was guarded by two forts: Fort Sumter, built on an island in the Charleston Harbor, and Fort Wagner, built at the end of Morris Island. Fort Wagner was known to be the greatest earthwork fort ever built, constructed of double walls of sand and logs and defended by some 1,700 Confederate troops.

As the 54th approached Fort Wagner, the rebels started shooting from the parapets. Carney, while saving a number of white soldiers, was wounded in several places and taken to the hospital. "As Carney entered the hospital, still clutching the Stars and Stripes, wounded men cheered him. Exhausted and bleeding, he collapsed. 'Boys, the old flag never touched the ground,' he exclaimed as he fell."[34] The attack resulted in 256 soldiers of the 54th being killed, wounded, or missing in action.

Carney survived the battle and was discharged because of his wounds. He was considered a hero and received the Medal of Honor for his bravery. The flag he saved is enshrined today in the Massachusetts State House. After some time in California, he returned to Massachusetts, where he worked for the postal service for thirty years. He died in December 1908. There are, of course, a number of African–American Congressional Medal of Honor recipients today, but Carney was the first to be recognized as an American hero.

Mitchell Red Cloud Jr. was born on July 2, 1924, near Hatfield in central Wisconsin. He and his family were members of the Ho-Chunk tribe. He attended Neillsville Indian School and Black River Falls High School. He enlisted in the U.S. Marines at seventeen and was sent to fight in the Pacific with Carlson's Raiders, trained to wage war behind enemy lines. He and his comrades landed on Guadalcanal, where they hacked their way through thick jungle and engaged in at least a dozen battles. Later that year he caught malaria and in January 1943 was sent home for treatment. Although eligible for medical discharge, he wanted to stay with the Marines, and in December 1944 he was sent to Okinawa. He was discharged in 1945, having been awarded two Purple Hearts.

In 1950 the Korean War broke out and Red Cloud joined the U.S. Army and fought with Company E, 19th Regiment, 24th Infantry Division. This division was fighting against overwhelming odds, facing the enemy on both flanks. On November 4, 1950, Red Cloud was assigned to duty about a hundred yards from company headquarters on Hill 123. The enemy rushed his position, but Red Cloud jumped to his feet and shot many of them. Thanks to Red Cloud's alertness, his company was able to mount a hasty defense and even carry some of the wounded away. Although his company was ultimately driven from Hill 123, Red Cloud saved many lives, one of those being Kenneth Bradshaws, who said Red Cloud "was a true warrior . . . and I owe him my life."

Red Cloud was killed in battle in Korea and on April 3, 1951, was posthumously awarded the Congressional Medal of Honor by General Omar Bradley in a special ceremony at the Pentagon. In 1967 the ceremonial grounds in Wisconsin where he is buried were named in his honor by the Ho-Chunk tribe.

Private First-Class Sadao Munemori was a member of Company A, 100th Infantry Battalion, assigned to take a hill near Seravazza, Italy. After the squad leader was wounded, Munemori led Company A through minefields toward the German trenches. He gathered hand grenades from his men and attacked and blew up a German machine-gun turret. The squad was attacked by another, so he took that one out as well. Returning to a shell hole where two of his men waited, he saw a German hand grenade land in it. "Without hesitation he fell onto the grenade, smothering the explosion with his body to save his men."[35] He was awarded the Congressional Medal of Honor posthumously.

In June 2001 Carlos C. Ogden died at the age of eighty-three in San Jose, California, and, on the fifty-seventh anniversary of the day he became a hero, was buried in Arlington National Cemetery.[36] In 1941 Ogden went to Officer Candidate School in California and earned the rank of first lieutenant. He was in Company K, 140th Infantry Regiment, 79th Division, a unit mostly of inexperienced soldiers who landed in Normandy on D-Day. The port city of Cherbourg was being defended by several forts occupied by the German army. The German guns pinned down Company K at Fort du Roule, a key station. Ogden's commanding officer was wounded by German fire. Lieutenant Ogden said, "I might as well get killed going forward as back." He grabbed an M1 rifle, grenade launcher, hand grenades, and several other rifles and went uphill toward the fort. He was hit in the hand by two glancing bullets and had blood streaming down his face from a head wound, but he continued up the hill. Ogden hit a German 88mm antitank gun with a rifle grenade and was wounded again, this time in the arm. With courage and perseverance, he kept using grenades to knock out two German machine guns. He was wounded a third time but still managed to kill a German soldier. Finally other troops followed, and the mission was accomplished. On June 25, 1944, Carlos Ogden was awarded the Congressional Medal of Honor for his actions during World War II, and it says on his citation that he exhibited heroic leadership and courage.

After the war, Ogden settled in San Jose, where he worked for the Veterans Administration for ten years, and another ten for the San Jose Chamber of Commerce. His son, Bud Ogden, says his father was a modest man and "dedicated himself to his family."

As with other types of heroes, military heroes have medals and citations that honor their heroism consistent with the language of the legislation that brought the citation into being. Every country and culture gives awards for valor and always has. Those discussed here are primarily from the United States and its allies but are suggestive of the scope of such recognition for all people.

James Webb, a Vietnam veteran said, "My heroes are the young men who faced the issues of war and possible death, and then weighed those concerns against obligations to their country."[37] He tells us that two-thirds of the 3 million soldiers who fought in Vietnam were volunteers. Of those who died, 73 percent were volunteers. Their common regret, it seems, is the fact that they were unable to do more for each other or for the people they'd come to help. He concludes, "I am alive today because of their quiet, unaffected heroism. Such valor epitomizes the conduct of Americans at war from the first days of our existence."

The Purple Heart

On August 7, 1782, General George Washington inaugurated the Badge of Military Merit, a citation to recognize "any singularly meritorious action." Three citations were awarded during the Revolutionary War, but this medal—the predecessor to the Purple Heart—was all but neglected by 1832. Although the badge had fallen into disuse, the idea of a decoration for individual gallantry had not.

In December 1861, President Lincoln established the Navy Medal of Valor and signed it into law. The medal was bestowed during the Civil War upon petty officers, seamen, landsmen, and Marines that distinguished themselves by gallantry and like qualities; a similar resolution was introduced in the army and signed into law in 1862. This became the Purple Heart and was subsequently awarded to wounded soldiers. Army regulations were revised to define the following conditions of award: "A wound which necessitates treatment by a medical officer and which is received in action with an enemy, may in the judgment of the commander authorized to make the award to be construed as resulting from a singularly meritorious act of essential service."[38]

Years later the award's scope was expanded to include personnel of the navy, Marine Corps, and Coast Guard. It now includes all the services and "any civilian national" wounded while serving with the armed forces. After 1932, recipients of the Meritorious Service Citation Certificate awarded in World War I could exchange it for a Purple Heart.

More than 800,000 men and women have been recognized with distinction and awarded the Purple Heart. The Civil War saw the largest number of recipients, followed by World War II and then Vietnam. Throughout U.S. history, these medals and citations have recognized acts of bravery and heroism.

Women Military Heroes

Although men primarily are involved in military conflict, thousands of women have joined wartime efforts as nurses and ferry pilots, among many other duties.[39] Florence Nightingale, a British nurse born to an influential family, served in the Crimean War in 1854. She took thirty-eight nurses with her to Turkey, where they tried to save the lives of British soldiers. It was a terrible conflict; it was also the first time in history that the British government had allowed women to serve under such conditions, and many modern nursing techniques can be traced to Nightingale's service. As a legacy of her service, she suffered from post-traumatic stress disorder for the rest of her life.

In subsequent wars, women have taken a heroic part, not usually killing the enemy but rather saving the wounded. One such example is Genevieve Galard, known as the "Angel of Dien Bien Phu." During the First Indochina War in 1954, this well-educated woman from an aristocratic background lifted the morale of the wounded French soldiers and comforted them during a horrible time. She was asked many times to stay away from the battlefield, but she refused. Galard won the French Legion of Honor medal for the heroic and unselfish risk that she took on behalf of wounded troops. She flew more than 149 medical missions to Dien Bien Phu in an older-model C-47. She was shot at and nearly lost her own life a number of times. In 1980 Genevieve Galard became a commander of the Legion of Honor, receiving her decoration under the Arc de Triomphe directly from the president of France. She, and many others, were lucky to have survived the war after the French defeat.

Military heroes are not born; rather, they have been trained in the group, socialized, and internalized the military moral code to "protect our own." Courage, empathy, a sense of efficacy, and valor are salient motivating factors. However, some soldiers face a serious moral dilemma in the act of killing the enemy, for to them, killing another human being is wrong. And to be in a position where one might kill innocent noncombatant civilians— women, children, and elderly men—by accident or purpose is morally painful. The difference between military heroes, in general, and ordinary heroes among us is that ordinary heroes invariably extend themselves to *save* lives, whereas to become a military hero implies *taking* lives. The soldier is praised and honored for killing the enemy and, in that taking of life, fulfills his duty as a soldier.

I hope that the time will come when there will be no need for military heroes, for such heroism must be hard on the soul.

7

Visions of a More Just World

The Acts of Moral Leaders

There's a light in this world: a healing spirit more powerful than any darkness we may encounter. We sometimes lose sight of this force when there is suffering, too much pain. Then suddenly, the spirit will emerge through the lives of ordinary people, who hear a call and answer in extraordinary ways.

— **Richard Attenborough,**
from the 1986 film *Mother Teresa*[1]

T he moral exemplars discussed in this chapter reflect the profundity of this epigraph. They each cast their individual light in a broad and growing circle of healing and helping. They are everywhere, in all walks of life, putting a stop to darkness with their positive light.

In my own home, Northern California's Humboldt County, lives one such moral exemplar. Dr. Wendy Ring, a general practitioner, has established a mobile clinic to serve the county's homeless, poor, and those otherwise lacking medical services, especially those in isolated towns and rural areas.[2] Her attempts to fill this need have been an uphill battle, to say the least.

Humboldt County has a disproportionate number of people who are poor, homeless, or substance abusers in need of medical attention. At first, other medical professionals did not look favorably upon Dr. Ring's work, and she did not get much support or cooperation from the medical establishment.

In 1992, using her own money, Dr. Ring bought a twenty-foot trailer and outfitted it as a mobile medical office complete with basic equipment. She and her volunteer staff travel to specific locations on prearranged days. Unlike other medical practitioners with comfortable offices and clinics, Dr. Ring works in very tight quarters, far from medical support services, all the while providing vital health care for hundreds of outpatients. Most days might include prenatal care and advice, vision screening, and dispensing of medications. In more serious cases, Dr. Ring makes sure the patients see a specialist, frequently delivering them to the specialist's office herself.

Dr. Ring's motivations are both empathic and practical—two vital qualities for a moral leader. She told me that she couldn't stand by and watch members of the community suffer, and she saw that conventional doctors' offices weren't filling this need—including her own. Coming from loving parents who inculcated in her the importance of justice, kindness, and compassion, her desire to help the rural poor caused her to relocate from New York, where she got her medical degree at Columbia University, to Humboldt County. During our interview I observed her interacting with the nurses, taking telephone calls from patients; I saw that this was indeed a compassionate woman. She said, "It is unfortunate the way medicine is practiced in this country. It seems that it helps poor patients fall through the cracks."[3] Prevention is key to her mobile practice:

> It's very important to me to prevent diseases that are preventable,
> like HIV infection and heart disease and things like that where if
> you intervene early, you can do a simple thing and keep people
> from having a terrible problem. I think that for the community it
> is important that there is always a place where people can go
> when they are sick and need to see a doctor.[4]

As with many spiritual and moral leaders, whether at the grass-roots or the national levels, Dr. Ring's spiritual beliefs and transformation are at the heart of her motivation for doing good. Like other moral leaders, including the more famous that we discuss in this chapter, Dr. Ring has internalized a vision of a world that can be better and brighter, and she knows that what is required is to act on that vision rather than merely give it lip service if she is to improve the lot of the less fortunate. Like other leaders who have taken a stand, she acts upon her moral conviction, believing that she can accomplish her mission. A more famous example of this sort of determination in the face of opposition would be Nelson Mandela, who faced overwhelming opposition and hardship yet persisted in his vision and goal of liberating his people from oppression.

Wendy Ring's friends and patients see her as an important moral leader because of her commitment to live her beliefs, to take action that confirms her humanity. As she crisscrosses the roads of Humboldt County in her mobile medical office, Dr. Ring is making a positive difference in the lives of those around her—one of the hallmarks of a moral leader.

Like Wendy Ring, moral leaders can be, and often are, everyday people who work for social change in their own communities. In fact, many of those I profile in this chapter—including Dr. Martin Luther King Jr., Nelson Mandela, and environmental activist Julia Butterfly Hill—became known for their work in their immediate communities, and that recognition brought them to greater prominence. Such moral leaders can be religious, political, or literary figures who bring the world's attention to human plight; they may work for the betterment of all in areas such as science, medicine, human rights, the environment, and community action. Or they may be quiet philanthropists, such as Melissa, who wanted to be someone who "cared about other people. I hope to leave a legacy that I cared. Maybe that I left behind an attitude, a positive attitude, that life can be good, it can be shared, and you can get a lot of pleasure out of that. I guess I look at life as though the glass is always half full."[5]

Moral exemplars are ordinary people of all ages from the very young to the elderly, from all ethnic backgrounds and creeds. Robert Coles, a Harvard scholar, relates a compelling example of ordinary people who extend themselves to help. Don was a student of Dr. Coles who worked as a grocery clerk. He was becoming tired and apathetic and was diagnosed with leukemia and in need of blood transfusions. His coworker, a middle-aged woman who had a son the same age as Don, learned about his illness and went to the hospital to offer her blood. Her blood was not the right type, so she decided to call neighbors and friends and eventually had a "whole army" of people donating blood, some of which was the same type as Don's. Don and his parents called her an angel, "a blood friend," and "general of a blood army."[6]

Moral exemplars need not be perfect people, but they must have an accurate moral compass, fortitude, and a fervent wish to serve their fellow human being. They must provide a moral example to those who follow them. It is vital that we read and hear about moral exemplars as role models, and it is particularly crucial for our children to know such models. And because moral exemplars achieve different degrees of recognition, it is especially vital that we understand and teach our children that there are exemplars all around us who live their daily lives performing service to their communities and who never become famous.

Philosophers and social scientists have wondered if human beings are selfless, or if they are mostly selfish and looking out for number one. What made people such as Mahatma Gandhi—passively resisting and conducting hunger strikes for India's freedom—and Andrei Sakharov—fighting for humanity, truth, and justice during the Soviet nuclear ascension—act for what they believed in rather than ponder the issue and do nothing? There is evidence that cultures and cultural values can produce both selfless and selfish individuals. Pitirim Sorokin, a renowned sociologist, has convinced me that society—through parents, schools, churches, and other institutions—can "manufacture altruistic behavior."

The work of social psychologists Anne Colby and William Damon is especially helpful in understanding what makes a moral leader and what spurs such people to action. These researchers find that such people often share the following characteristics:

- A sustained commitment to moral ideals or principles that include a generalized respect for humanity; or a sustained evidence of moral virtue.

- The position to act in accordance with one's moral ideals or principles, implying also a consistency between one's actions and intentions and between the means and ends of one's actions.

- A willingness to risk one's self-interest for the sake of one's moral values.

- A tendency to be inspiring to others and thereby to move them to moral action.

- A sense of realistic humility about one's own importance relative to the world at large, implying a relative lack of concern for one's own ego.[7]

Although Colby and Damon have found that a leader's individual personality and charisma play an important role in effecting broader moral change, the primary force for such action is social support and communication, allowing feedback and development of the whole, and thus benefiting the group and ultimately the cause. For example, the Danish King Christian X and the Danish Lutheran church created a climate that enabled the rescue of Danish Jews in 1943. Where such a climate did not exist, many more perished.

Colby and Damon mention *positivity*, an attitude that includes optimism, love, and joy, as closely linked with morality and a positive quality evident in the lives of most moral exemplars. The relationship between a positive approach and absence of focus on self is known as *learned optimism*. Moral leaders often share this quality. They would not blame others for their lot in life; instead, they focus on how best to tackle the task at hand. Learned optimism can, as the name suggests, be learned.

Colby and Damon have also found that there is a uniting of self and morality in moral leaders and note that they share the crucial qualities:

> a disregard for risk and a disavowal of courage; certainty of response about matters of principle; unremitting faith in positivity in the face of the most dismal circumstances; a capacity to take direction and support from the followers they inspire; and the presence of a dynamic interplay between continuity and change in their personal life histories.[8]

These characteristics of moral exemplars leads them to interpret that it is possible to have a strong sense of individuality while still being committed to a larger cause. Indeed, there is no conflict between the two attributes. As we'll see later in the example of Martin Luther King, his intensely personal religious beliefs as well as his desire to succeed academically fueled his commitment to achieve social justice for all races.

Moral leaders need not deny themselves life and comfort in order to be sensitive and helpful to others. Thus, they are not necessarily deprived; neither do they need to suffer physical or psychological pain. In fact, it may be their spiritual, physical, and psychological health that contribute to their drive to create a better future and a better world for others. All of us, if we're lucky, have known people who are moved to help others, and certainly we're all familiar with many of those moral leaders whose contributions to the betterment of society and all humanity started in a similar way—as one small act of positivity and kindness. I have chosen to look more closely at a few of these leaders, individuals who were dedicated to loving kindness, justice, and equality for those in need in the community.

Robert Coles describes convincingly the attributes of moral leaders who act unselfishly for the benefit of others and are able to enlist others in their cause. Among those attributes are the need to exhort people to action, to remind them, to criticize them, to reprimand them, to make them reflect on what they are to do, to inspire them, to inform them, to dramatize for them the particular issues that matter most, to invoke for example moral traditions and beliefs in teachings, to reason with them, to warn them of danger, to uplift them, to tell and announce issues, to spell out the plan, to engage with others so that what is proposed is taken to heart and connects with the consciousness of the listener.[9]

Many of our moral leaders have acted within the sphere of human rights, taking their movements for social justice from their local communities to the world stage. Mahatma Gandhi, the Dalai Lama, Martin Luther King Jr., Nelson Mandela, Elie Wiesel, Mother Teresa, Reverend Eric Duff, Craig Kielburger, and others all have worked tirelessly in pursuit of equitable treatment for all people—and not only in their own era and geographical place. Universally, each worked from a moral base, whether political, religious, or both.

Mahatma Gandhi

Mohandas Karamchand (Mahatma) Gandhi was born on October 2, 1869, in western India and in 1891 he got his law degree in London. In 1893 he took a one-year contract to do legal work in South Africa, specifically in defending the poor, many of whom were from his native India. Gandhi dressed in typical European attire and led a good life; then one day he got thrown off a train for sitting in first class, something "coloreds" were not allowed to do. This practice of racial separation was also happening in the United States. Due to this incident and other indignities, Gandhi made the decision to act; but he would not only *not* yield to force, he would not use force himself in order to get his way. Rather, he would use cleverness and correct persistence to win the day. One example of his resistance to injustice took place in 1913, when he led a large army of nonviolent resident Indians across provincial borders—an illegal act—in an attempt to affirm the right of mobility for Indians living in South Africa. Gandhi and his army were quickly arrested; they did not resist arrest and pleaded guilty to all charges. As planned, a second nonviolent army of Indians moved across provincial borders and was in turn arrested as the third army was mobilizing. The government despaired. The jails of South Africa were unable hold 20,000 Indians, and the campaign was victorious. The Indian Relief Bill passed on June 30, 1914, giving the Indians back their rights.

In 1915 Gandhi returned to India, where he began his struggle for Indian independence. From his experiences in South Africa, he began to build a nonviolent movement, marking the beginning of a personal journey that would impact and inspire countless others around the world. Gandhi is often credited as the father of nonviolent resistance. His inspirational messages give hope that justice will triumph in the end: "I can see that in the midst of darkness light persists. Hence I gather that God is Life, Truth, Light. He is Love. He is Supreme Good."[10] Gandhi called this nonviolent action *satyagraha* (truth-force)—acts of nonviolent resistance in the service of moral truth. There were different forms of *satyagraha*: civil disobedience; breaking specific laws and accepting the legal penalties; noncooperation in the face of injustice no matter the personal cost; and fasting, his personal *satyagraha*, used as an individual action.[11] This was a means of political struggle that was powerful enough to rid India of British colonial rule.

Like many moral leaders, Gandhi had to overcome the resistance of friends, relatives, and others who refused to give up what was easy and familiar and join him on his peaceful protest against British rule. He was able to persuade some around him to live a more simple life. Gandhi made intense moral appeals, supported by his personal willingness to suffer, to be jailed, and to fast for long periods of time. Gandhi had a profound influence on the Dalai Lama. When asked what it was about Gandhi that inspired him most, the Dalai Lama said,

> One thing, of course, is his simplicity, his way of life. Also, I think the level of modern education he achieved. At the same time he remained a true Indian. As a citizen of a modern nation

it was necessary for him to have Western education, but he personally remained a typical Indian within the tradition. And that's good.[12]

As a world-famous teacher of love and justice who regarded all people as children of God, Gandhi was an imperfect man who through his actions became a moral role model to many:

> The students were inspired by knowing that one man, whom their studies had shown had many of the same human frailties they possessed, could rise to make such a profound impression on modern history. Gandhi, through his work, became a saint, yet the students, through their investigations, had come in contact with Gandhi the man, and were therefore more easily able to accept their own potential for the saintly within themselves.[13]

Thus, Gandhi was such an effective moral leader in part because of his ability to reach a broad spectrum of people and to spread the messages of nonviolent disobedience, empathy, compassion, inspiration, and love.

Of all the social revolutions that have taken place, Mahatma Gandhi's *satyagraha* was one of the most influential events of the twentieth century. In 1948 India gained its independence largely through nonviolent resistance and Gandhi's strong leadership. Gandhi's ideology of nonviolent resistance on behalf of freedom and human dignity is undoubtedly his most durable legacy. As a result of his teachings, Martin Luther King Jr., Nelson Mandela, and others were able to pursue such a philosophy, save lives, gain freedom for the oppressed, and, perhaps most important, work side-by-side within their communities—the very idea of an exemplar leader.

The following statements by Gandhi offer us insight into the nature of his moral leadership:

> Mankind is one, seeing that all are equally subject to the moral law. All men are equal in God's eyes. There are, of course, differences of race and status and the like, but the higher the status of a man, the greater is his responsibility. I do not believe in the doctrine of the greatest good of the greatest number. The only real, dignified, human doctrine is the greatest good of all.[14]

Dalai Lama

The Dalai Lama was born into a peasant family as Tenzin Gyatso on July 6, 1935—the day that the thirteenth Dalai Lama died—in northeastern Tibet. At the age of two it was determined that he was the reincarnation of Avalokiteshvara, the Lord of Compassion, and at age five he was taken to the holy city of Lhasa and installed as the fourteenth Dalai Lama. At this time it was prophesized that one day he would leave Tibet and not return for many years.

In 1950 the People's Republic of China invaded Tibet, overthrew its Buddhist leadership, and claimed it as Chinese territory. The Dalai Lama struggled to maintain the cultural heritage of his people and to serve as a mediator for peace; however, Chinese domination grew to savage proportions, and the brutality directed against the Buddhist monks and their monasteries was increasing. After a failed uprising by the Tibetan people in 1959, the Dalai Lama was forced to flee to India and was soon followed by 100,000 others. The refugees settled in the beautiful and tranquil Himalayan village of Dharmasala, and since then the Dalai Lama has served as the head of a government-in-exile. He has traveled the world raising global awareness of the plight of the Tibetan people while consistently maintaining strict adherence to his position of nonviolence, tolerance, patience, and compassion as the means for attaining peace.

In the course of his life's work, the Dalai Lama has taught the world a great deal about compassion, happiness, love, and the possibility of becoming a human family, thereby endearing him to the hearts of millions. On a visit to New York in April 1994, he said, "I believe that to meet the challenge of the next century, human beings will have to develop a greater sense of universal responsibility. Each of us must learn to work not just for his or her own self, family or nation, but for the benefit of all mankind."[15] According to Kenneth Liberman, "In Tibetan society lay persons, as well as Buddhist monks, are disposed to submit themselves to a body of time-honored socio-religious practices which are designed to culminate in the total reformation of one's character—the generation of a selfless aspiration to serve only the interests of others, or what is termed (from the Sanskrit *bodhicitta*, in Tibetan. *Byang.chub. sems.pa*), the altruistic mind of enlightenment."[16] Compassion for the Dalai Lama is "a mental attitude based on the wish for others to be free of their suffering and is associated with a sense of commitment, responsibility, and respect towards the other."[17] The type of attitude he is speaking of is a feeling that enables people, when faced with a choice, to choose another's welfare rather than their own.[18] The development of this type of compassion is not an easy task; nevertheless, he understands that there exists various means for its cultivation. He suggests that "one could begin with the wish that oneself be free of suffering, and then take that natural feeling towards oneself and cultivate it, enhance it, and extend it out to include and embrace others."[19] Despite his own plight, he shows the ability to rise above these circumstances and exhorts others to do the same. He succeeds as a moral leader by emphasizing the importance of love and compassion:

> Compassion is what makes our lives meaningful. It is the source of all lasting happiness and joy. And it is the foundation of a good heart, the heart of one who acts out of a desire to help others. Through kindness, through affection, through honesty, through truth and justice toward all others we ensure our own benefit. . . . Nor is there any denying that the more our hearts and minds are afflicted with ill-will, the more miserable we become. Thus we can reject everything else: religion, ideology, all received wisdom. But we cannot escape the necessity of love and compassion.[20]

Empathy—the ability to appreciate another's suffering—is a cornerstone of Buddhism and is another important factor for the development of compassion. The Dalai Lama said: "Once you encourage the thought of compassion in your mind, once that thought becomes active, then your attitude towards others changes automatically. If you approach others with the thought of compassion, that will automatically reduce fear and allow an openness with other people."[21] With this attitude being carried into every social interaction, he sees that "whether it is an old friend or a new friend, there's not much difference anyway, because I always believe we are the same; we are all human beings."[22]

The Dalai Lama's contribution toward global promotion of peace was formally recognized in 1989 when he won the Nobel Prize. According to the Nobel committee, he was selected because in his campaign he "consistently has opposed the use of violence. . . and advocated peaceful solutions based upon tolerance and mutual respect in order to preserve the historical and cultural heritage of his people."[23]

He teaches us that the attitude of loving compassion by which he lives his life is available to us all. He repeatedly declares his belief that every human being has the potential for love, compassion, patience, tolerance, and mutual respect. "Within all human beings there is the seed of perfection."[24] Consistent with this belief, he has claimed that his case is nothing special. He states that he is a simple Buddhist monk, no more, no less. [25]

Despite everything, he does not speak bitterly against the Chinese who oppressed his homeland; rather, he stresses human rights and the struggle to remain human and to preserve Tibetan cultural values. He has a great desire and need not only to hold onto faith and spirituality but also to seek truth. Truth leads to understanding, to inspiration, and to a full liberation from ignorance and the suffering that we impose upon each other. Buddhists believe suffering can cease, and lasting peace can be achieved—both peace of mind and peace in the world. The path to such peace is said to begin with the development of a calm abiding. According to the Dalai Lama, "Developing calm abiding demands that you devote yourself to the process utterly until you master it."[26] He believes people need to have faith that they can achieve a more enlightened state of existence even when the material world seems to deny such a possibility. There must be an ongoing interaction between reason and faith, between analysis and the growing conviction that one can find ways to live for the betterment of all human beings.

The Dalai Lama also maintains that there is a third aspect of spiritual wholeness—and that aspect is found in compassionate action. Just as reason and faith interact to enhance conviction, so, too, do reflection and action interact to determine our spiritual faith. He further believes that all religious thought points toward loving kindness and to compassionate action. We must not believe that we are alone and isolated, independent operators in this world. Rather, we must think that we are interdependent and that we are woven together by spiritual life. If we can maintain faith and conviction that such an understanding is the foundation upon which we build our lives, then it makes perfect sense for us to treat all human beings and all other living things with respect and love. He says, "Whether we succeed or not is a different question. What is important is that we try our best. At least we will have made an attempt to form a better human society on the basis of love—true love—and less selfishness."[27]

Martin Luther King Jr.

Martin Luther King Jr. was born to the middle-class family of an African-American minister in Atlanta, Georgia, at a time when the nation and the world were experiencing a tremendous economic depression. Throughout his early years, King endured the humiliation of "separate but equal" Jim Crow laws—sitting in the back of the bus, using substandard public facilities, attending schools not as well funded or well equipped as those that whites attended—and, worst of all, being denied the human dignity and respect to which all people are entitled.

Dr. King persuaded social and political institutions in the United States that the position of black Americans was both appalling and out of line with the original mission of the Founders of the republic. Africans Americans had suffered deeply from the heritage of slavery, experiencing unequal justice in an oppressive society. Through his marches, speeches, and writings, Dr. King rallied many concerned Americans—black and white—to protest against both the daily indignities and systemic racism he and others had faced all their lives. King protested against American apartheid, but he was also profoundly aware of racism, anti-Semitism, and injustice elsewhere in the world. Like other leaders, he was influenced by Mahatma Gandhi of India, whom he and his wife, Coretta, met in 1959.

Unlike the black Muslim movement, which called for violence to spark anger and contempt against the white majority's cultural and political denigration of black people, King spoke of racial understanding and peaceful negotiation for civil rights. He worked toward the hope that white institutions would recognize the humanity of black people and that all could live together harmoniously.

King believed that African Americans' strongest weapon in the fight for justice and racial equality was nonviolent resistance, and he advocated this belief in all his speeches. He was convinced that what would save humanity is *agape* love, which he understood as creative, redemptive goodwill for all. He also believed in a power in the universe that ultimately works for justice and that God was his moral compass. One of his most dramatic speeches ("I See the Promised Land," delivered on the eve of his assassination) showed him to be a man with a profound sense of calling. God had asked him to engage the country in a nonviolent dialogue to admit and rectify its injustices. King was discouraged because he felt progress in the civil and human rights movement was slowing. In this speech, he said that people must struggle for human rights; they must not give up despite setbacks. Although he was experiencing a setback himself, he was able to push on—a characteristic of a moral leader. He continued to advocate nonviolent protest, saying prophetically:

When I got into Memphis . . . some began to say the threats, or talk about the threats that were out. What would happen to me from some of our sick white brothers?

Well, I don't know what will happen now. We've got some difficult days ahead. But it doesn't matter with me now. Because I've been to the mountaintop. And I don't mind. Like anybody, I would like to live a long life. Longevity has its place. But I'm not concerned about that now. I just want to do God's will. And He's allowed me to go up to the mountain. And I've looked over. And I've seen the Promised Land. I may not get there with you. But I want you to know tonight, that we, as a people, will get to the Promised Land. And I'm happy, tonight. I'm not worried about anything. I'm not fearing any man. Mine eyes have seen the glory of the coming of the Lord.[28]

Like King's voice, the voices of all moral leaders express a clear message: Unless we unite and become part of the human family, we won't survive. Rabbi Abraham Heschel, a philosopher and theologian who marched with Dr. King, has expressed a similar sentiment, warning us that peoples will either care for each other or will perish together. Even though King was arrested fourteen times, he exhorted blacks to remain part of the human family and not separate themselves from the oppressors; he warned black Americans that they should resist the urge to depart the path of brotherhood. Like Gandhi, he urged blacks to stay the course with their peaceful protests:

There is something that I must say to my people who stand on the warm threshold that leads into the palace of justice. Through the process of gaining our rightful place, we must not be guilty of wrongful deeds.

Let us not seek to satisfy our thirst for freedom by drinking from the cup of bitterness and hatred. We must forever conduct our struggle on the high plane of dignity and discipline. We must not allow our creative protest to degenerate into physical violence. Again and again we must rise to the majestic heights of meeting physical force with soul force.

The marvelous new militancy which has engulfed the Negro
community must not lead us to a distrust of all white people, for
many of our white brothers, as evidenced by their presence here
today, have come to realize that their destiny is tied up with our
destiny and they have come to realize that their freedom is inex-
tricably bound to our freedom. We cannot walk alone.[29]

Gandhi's message of nonviolent protest for his people to end British rule
in India is echoed in King's words. Both believed there must be a bridge between the oppressor and the oppressed, impossible though it may seem. In
1963 King was jailed for leading a peaceful protest on behalf of black voters
in Birmingham, Alabama. In his famous letter from the Birmingham jail, he
asserts his place in America:

We will reach the goal of freedom in Birmingham and all over
the nation, because the goal of America is freedom. Abused and
scorned though we may be, our destiny is tied up with the destiny of America. Before the Pilgrims landed at Plymouth we were
here. Before the pen of Jefferson etched across the pages of history the majestic words of the Declaration of Independence we
were here. . . If the inexpressible cruelties of slavery could not
stop us, the opposition we now face will surely fail. We will win
our freedom because the sacred heritage of our nation and the
eternal will of God are embodied in our echoing demands.[30]

Later that same year, King pursued his quest for freedom and justice,
demonstrating Coles's characteristic of persistence on focus of moral goals.
On the occasion of the March on Washington he made his famous "I Have a
Dream" speech:

I say to you today, my friends, that even though we face the difficulties of today and tomorrow, I still have a dream. . . . I have a
dream that one day this nation will rise up and live out the true
meaning of its creed. . . that all men are created equal. . . . I have
a dream that one day even the state of Mississippi, a state swelter-
ing with the heat of oppression, will be transformed into an oasis
of freedom and justice. I have a dream my four little children will
one day live in a nation where they will not be judged by the

color of their skin but by the content of their character. I have a dream today. . . . And if America is to be a great nation, this must become true. So let freedom ring.[31]

On April 4, 1968, Martin Luther King Jr. was assassinated in Memphis, Tennessee, where he had traveled to support and speak out on behalf of sanitation workers. Dr. King's writings, sermons, and speeches encapsulate his vision, wisdom, and ideology and offer an important profile of how a great prophet thinks in the midst of a whirlwind of social change. King provided a sense of calm, reason, and hope in the face of death threats and ominous signs of disillusionment within the African-American community. Toward the end of his life, King was seen as a communist threat by the Federal Bureau of Investigation and faced power struggles within his own movement.

King, a Nobel Prize winner, has the attributes and character to be considered one of the great moral leaders of the twentieth century. He founded a social movement advocating justice for all, including blacks and other poor people who suffer from racism and other forms of oppression. His message of love, forgiveness, and reconciliation continues to inspire people. His dream is a dream of all moral leaders—that the world can become more caring and just for everyone.

Nelson Mandela

On the other side of the globe, but near in spirit to the struggle for civil rights in this country, Nelson Mandela inspired generations of South Africans to work against centuries of racism, terrorism, and oppression against all non-whites in that country and on that continent. He was born in 1918 in a tiny village in Transkei, a tribal region established by the South African apartheid government and located in South Africa near the Indian Ocean. Although his father belonged to the Thembu tribal group, his parents were Methodist. He was sent by his mother to a Christian school and was given an English name by the teacher on the first day of school. He was taught that English culture and civilization were superior and that there was no such thing as African culture. His father, Gadla Henry Mphakanyiswa, was of royal blood and an adviser to Thembu chiefs. As a result of that association, Mandela had some privileges that enabled him to go to English schools. He saw the injustices of white domination and superiority throughout his childhood.

In 1939 Mandela was admitted to University College of Fort Hare, where he met other South African blacks. Oliver Tambo became his partner in the struggle for South African liberation. Throughout his young life, Mandela could not stand by and witness humiliation and the indignities suffered by blacks. He studied law and became a friend of Walter Sisula, who would have great influence on his life. Sisula's father was white and his mother African, and both were nationalists looking for justice for South Africa. Sisulu introduced Mandela to a friend, a Jewish lawyer named Lazar Sidelsky, who was a member of a large law firm in Johannesburg. Sidelsky gave Mandela a job as a law clerk in 1932, enabling him to continue his studies and also learn the law.

In 1942 Mandela met two people who would influence him throughout his life: Gaur Radebe, a black, was a member of the African National Congress (ANC) and the South African Communist Party. He was a true radical who spoke openly against oppression. Nat Bregman, a white, was a dedicated Communist, a fact that put Mandela off because of his Christian upbringing acquired in Methodist schools. But he continued to know Bregman and later became more sympathetic to the Communists because they seemed to be antiracist. These two friends introduced Mandela to the ANC, established in 1912 to fight discrimination against blacks and coloreds; it was the major organizing group opposing discrimination and apartheid.

Mandela was also influenced by Anton Lembede, one of only a few black African lawyers in South Africa and a powerful spokesman for the new militant antiwhite Africanism. A powerful member of the ANC, Lembede was among the first to raise black consciousness and black empowerment in his writings and speeches. In 1948 white nationalists officially gained political power and established apartheid, the legal separation and segregation of people of color into special tribal areas, known as Bantustans. Mandela became more active in local ANC rallies and other political activities, so much so that he was frequently threatened with arrest and violence. When asked when he started to become devoted to the liberation of other oppressed people, he said, " I cannot pinpoint a moment when I became politicized." He wrote,

> When I knew that I would spend my life in the liberation struggle, I felt no epiphany, no singular revelation, no moment of truth, but a steady accumulation of a thousand slights, a thou-

sand indignities, a thousand unremembered moments, produced in me an anger, a rebelliousness, a desire to fight the system that imprisoned my people. There was no particular day on which I said, From henceforth I will devote myself to the liberation of my people; instead, I simply found myself doing so, and could not do otherwise.[32]

After years of activism Mandela was caught and arrested in 1962—he says because he got careless, although he may have been betrayed. He was transported to the infamous Robben Island prison off Cape Town, where he would spend twenty-seven years. Although incarcerated, he was still considered the leader of South African blacks and the ANC. In prison he was brutalized by the guards, but even then he stood up, saying to a guard, "If you so much as lay a hand on me, I will take you to the highest court in the land and when I am finished with you, you will be as poor as a church mouse."[33] Mandela also fought against the smaller daily indignity all blacks in the prison faced—of wearing short pants while whites wore long pants. And he protested against the practice of giving black prisoners less and substandard food. He eventually won out for equal treatment in both cases and, in the process, won the respect of some of his captors. His courage and his belief in the dignity of every human being contributed to his lifelong friendship with a warden named James Gregory, who guarded him from 1966 until his release in 1990. Once Mandela was freed, one of the first people he wrote to was Gregory, praising him for his humanity.

Mounting international pressure against apartheid forced the white South African government, led by its new president, F. W. de Klerk, to release Mandela. In February 1990 de Klerk informed a stunned South African parliament that the time had come to negotiate with the black opposition. He announced that all legal restrictions on the ANC, the South African Communist Party, and some thirty-one other parties that had been outlawed would cease and that those groups would now be constituted as legal. On February 11 Nelson Mandela was freed.

Many, including the Nobel committee, consider Nelson Mandela as one of the outstanding souls of the twentieth century. He was labeled such for good reason. He embodies great courage and a strong sense of justice, empathy, forgiveness, and social responsibility. He views all humanity as family rather than separate races and ethnicities. What makes Mandela such an outstanding moral exemplar is that rather than taking revenge on white oppressors when he gained power in South Africa, he established the Truth and Reconciliation Commission, whose function was to forgive all those who came and told the truth about their inhumanity toward others—both blacks and whites. He relates, "From the moment the results were in and it was apparent that the ANC was to form the government, I saw my mission as one of preaching and reconciliation, of binding the wounds of the country, of engendering trust and confidence."[34]

F. W. de Klerk and Nelson Mandela together won the Nobel Prize in 1993, and on May 14, 1994, the newly elected President Mandela made his inaugural speech to hundreds of millions of people, saying:

> We, the people of South Africa, feel fulfilled that humanity has taken us back into it's bosom, that we, who were outlaws not so long ago, have today been given the rare privilege to be host to the nations of the world on our own soil. . . . We have triumphed in the effort to implant hope in the breasts of the millions of our people. We enter into a covenant that we shall build the society in which all South Africans, both black and white, will be able to walk tall, without any fear in their hearts, assured of their inalienable right to human dignity—a rainbow nation at peace with itself and the world.[35]

Mandela—then and now—exemplifies courage, efficacy, sympathy, statesmanship, honor, healing, compassion, and forgiveness. These are, I believe, some of the dominant traits of any great moral leader and any truly altruistic person; but forgiveness looms large particularly in the case of Mandela and South Africa, for the healing process is necessary if the people and the country are to move forward.

Most moral leaders have internalized a universal ethic of caring. The more famous have gone through a period of personal suffering. Some suffered because of who they were, some for what they believed in, and some suffered for both. For example, King, Mandela, and Gandhi suffered because of who they were—oppressed minorities. The Dalai Lama still suffers because his belief in freedom for the Tibetan people has not been realized. By "suffering," I do not necessarily mean *physical* suffering from brutality; it can also be moral and psychological pain experienced through injustice and oppression against humankind.

Elie Wiesel

Like Gandhi, Mandela, and King, Elie Wiesel has become a modern-day prophet, traveling to places where there is injustice, brutality, and genocide. Wiesel, a moral leader, a Nobel Prize recipient, and a peacemaker, goes directly to the leaders—often the perpetrators of the injustice—and pleads with them to stop the cruelty. He went to Slobodan Milosevic to try to convince him to stop the genocide in Bosnia and to provide blankets to the freezing Muslim prisoners in the concentration camps. He has pleaded for involvement:

> I think the greatest source of infinite danger in this world is indifference. I have always believed that the opposite of love is not hate, but indifference. The opposite of life is not death, but indifference. The opposite of peace is not war, but indifference to peace and indifference to war. The opposite of culture, the opposite of beauty, and the opposite of generosity is indifference. Indifference is the enemy, and the context is memory. As long as we remember, there is a chance; if we forget that, all that really matters is forgotten.[36]

Wiesel was born in 1928 in Sighet, Romania, a small, predominantly Jewish town in Transylvania. His parents were devout Jews. In 1940, with the help of Hitler, fascist Hungary annexed that part of Romania. Jews lived under the systematic cloud of anti-Semitism, being first identified—required to wear the yellow star; then, as the Germans crossed the Romanian frontier ahead of the advancing Soviet armies, the Jews were rounded up into ghettos, and it was not until 1944 that they were shipped out to extermination camps. The extermination of Jews began in 1940 in Eastern Europe; the Jewish people of Hungary and Romania suffered but were not sent to extermination camps, even though their countries were allied with Germany.

When the Jews were being marched to the trains that took them to the camps, one of the Wiesel family's Christian maids, Maria, came to their home, imploring them to run and hide with her. They refused, wanting to keep their family together. At this point, in 1944, the Wiesels and most other Jews did not yet believe that a tragedy was awaiting. Even when a Jewish friend came and reported to them about the crematoria and Auschwitz, they refused to believe him. They refused to believe that such inhumanity was possible against people who had done nothing, did not disobey any laws, did not steal, and did not murder. Why, then, should they be murdered en masse? It was incomprehensible.

No one has been able to express the diabolical aspects of Auschwitz more graphically than did Elie Wiesel in his book *Night*.[37] Early in May 1944, two high-ranking German officers came into town. One of them, Wiesel believes, was Adolf Eichmann himself, the notorious administrator of the Final Solution. Wiesel claims that Eichmann personally came to arrange the evacuation of the Jews from Sighet. In 1962 Wiesel—at the time a journalist in Jerusalem attending the trial of Adolf Eichmann—became convinced that he recognized Eichmann from some previous encounter; it could only have been in Sighet or in Auschwitz itself. At the age of fourteen, Wiesel, his family, and many other Hungarian Jews were shipped to Auschwitz, where he and his father were separated from his mother and eight-year-old sister, who were immediately exterminated. An SS soldier addressed them saying, "Remember it forever. Engrave it into your minds. You are at Auschwitz. And Auschwitz is not a convalescent home. It's a concentration camp. Here you have got to work. If not, you will go straight to the furnace. To the crematory. Work or the crematory—the choice is in your hands."[38]

Wiesel says,

> Never shall I forget that night, the first night in camp, which has turned my life into one long night, seven times cursed and seven times sealed. Never shall I forget that smoke. Never shall I forget the little faces of the children whose bodies I saw turned into wreaths of smoke beneath a silent blue sky. Never shall I forget those flames which consumed my faith forever. Never shall I forget that nocturnal silence which deprived me, for all eternity, of the desire to live. Never shall I forget those moments which murdered my God and my soul and turned my dreams to dust. Never shall I forget these things, even if I am condemned to live as long as God Himself. Never.[39]

In April 1945, when he was sixteen, Wiesel was liberated from Buchenwald (to which he had been moved that January). After liberation he went to school in France and became a journalist. Subsequently, he moved to the United States, but he did not begin to speak out about his experiences in the concentration camps until after he had an unfortunate brush with death when a taxi hit him. It was after he recovered, in 1956, that he began work on *Night*, his first book. Although rejected by many publishers as too upsetting, *Night* went on to sell millions of copies worldwide.

Some people have called Wiesel a modern-day biblical prophet because he so vividly recalls for us the consequences of acts of immorality and cruelty. For him, no matter where injustice takes place in the world, that place then becomes the center of the universe, and all attention must be focused there to alleviate suffering and restore justice. As a philosopher, historian, playwright, novelist, and world citizen, he raises his voice against injustice and urges us to do the same. In 1985, when U.S. President Ronald Reagan announced that he would travel to Bitburg, Germany—a military cemetery where Nazi Waffen SS officers are buried—Wiesel protested, pleading with Reagan not to go. The president went anyway, and Wiesel's appeal to Reagan not to honor these killing units of the German army was publicized on international television.

Above all, Wiesel believes that we must learn from the past. As a single outstanding voice on behalf of Holocaust victims, he has organized conferences on resolving hate through dialogue, inviting other Nobel Prize winners such as the president of the Czech Republic, Vaclav Havel, and South Africa's Nelson Mandela to participate. A world with hate cannot survive—what is desperately needed is to purge ourselves of hate, bigotry, violence, and genocide. He appealed on several occasions to President Bill Clinton to do something about the murder of Islamic people in Bosnia during the conflict in Yugoslavia, where people were dying on all sides.

At the request of President Clinton, Wiesel spent three days in June 1999 touring camps in Macedonia, where he interviewed refugees who had fled Kosovo. He spoke to children and parents, asking how they deal with the trauma. He encouraged them to think about a brighter future. He also encouraged them never to forget—to remember what happened to them, because someday they, too, may want to write about this experience—to bear witness to what occurred.

Though Wiesel is understandably upset by the violence in the Middle East, he does not automatically side with the Israelis because he is Jewish; rather, he is very conscious of the great complexity of the issues that divide the Israelis and the Palestinians. Wiesel's biographer, Robert McAfee Brown, considered him someone who kept his conscience finely tuned. Brown warns Wiesel's readers of the danger of reading his works, because he opens our eyes to things we choose to avoid seeing. Yet Brown reminds us of the importance of reading Wiesel and other reports of the witnesses.

Although Wiesel has always had a hard time understanding the killers and their collaborators, he is continuously troubled by the role of the bystander. He often questions where the good people were when horrific events were occurring. And even now wonders how the world can stand by and do nothing when innocent people are being tortured and murdered— often by state-sanctioned regimes. He is joined in this by a number of other authors, including Gordon J. Horwitz, in asking how people can live with themselves when they've witnessed such evil right outside their windows. In Horwitz's book *In the Shadows of Death: Living Outside the Gates of Mauthausen*, Horwitz ponders how ordinary Austrian civilians could witness tragedy on a daily basis and still deny its existence.[40] At the end of the war, when the Americans arrived, the Austrian citizens greeted them as if nothing had happened. The civilians saw no Nazis, they saw nothing, and they knew nothing. Wiesel says:

> This, this was the thing I had wanted to understand ever since the war. Nothing else. How a human being can remain indifferent. The executioners I understood; also the victims, though with more difficulty. For the others, all the others, those who were neither for nor against, those who sprawled in passive patience, those who told themselves, "The storm will blow over and everything will be normal again," those who thought themselves above the battle, those who were permanently and merely spectators— all those were closed to me, incomprehensible.[41]

To this day he travels around the world bearing witness to violence and genocidal massacre in an attempt to sensitize people to tragedies and to bring about peace. Whether in Bosnia, the former Soviet Union, Cambodia, or Kosovo, he asks the same question: How can the world stand by? Like Gandhi, Mandela, and King, Wiesel pleads for a just world and bears witness and teaches kindness and compassion—peaceful dialogue instead of thoughtless brutality.

In 1986 Wiesel won the Nobel Prize for his efforts to sensitize all of us to our collective moral failings and shortsightedness. The chairman of the Nobel committee, Egil Aarvik, introduced him as a fighter for freedom and human dignity all over the world, saying: "I doubt whether any other individual, through the use of such quiet speech, has achieved more or been more widely heard. The words are not big and the voice which speaks them is low. It is a voice of peace we hear. . . .Truly, prisoner A-7713 has become a human being once again, a human being dedicated to humanity."[42] In his acceptance speech, Wiesel said: "Sometimes we must interfere. When human lives are endangered, when human dignity is in jeopardy, national borders and sensitivities become irrelevant. Whenever men or women are persecuted because of their race, religion, or political views, that place must—at that moment—become the center of the universe."[43]

Wiesel used his prize money to create the Elie Wiesel Foundation for Humanity, its mission being to create awareness around the world to decency, compassion, and altruism. Through his work, Wiesel has kept alive the names and the spirits of innocent victims, those that hatred had destroyed. "I've tried to do something with my life to help others do something with theirs. Helping others, that's the main thing. The only way for us to help ourselves is to help others and to listen to each others' stories." [44] His foundation has provided people with truckloads of medicines and blankets. Wherever there is evil, Elie Wiesel is there to speak out.

David Aikman, in his book *Great Souls,* said,

> Elie Wiesel is the youngest of the Great Souls, and perhaps the most sobering of them all. Billy Graham has pointed us towards salvation. Nelson Mandela has challenged us to forgive. Aleksandr Solzhenitsyn has required of us truth. Mother Teresa has epitomized love. Pope John Paul II has reminded us of the God-given gift of human dignity. Elie Wiesel is a great soul because of another reminder, the terrible truth about the human capacity for evil and our need never to forget it. All have been gifts to our century, indeed to our millennium. As we face the next one, they are bright lights to all of us, illuminating the uncertain pathway ahead.[45]

Mother Teresa

In yet another part of the globe, Mother Teresa brought world attention to the misery of the poor and neglected. Like Wiesel, she lamented the indifference of the rich and bystanders. Mother Teresa of Calcutta was born Agnes

Gonxha Bojaxhiu on August 26, 1910, in Skopje, Macedonia, the second child of Albanian parents, loving and pious Roman Catholics. While she was growing up, statues and shrines of the Madonna and child impressed her, and she became increasingly involved with the activities of the local Sacred Heart church. One of the most influential priests in her life was Franjo Jambernkovic, a Croatian who encouraged her to become involved in missionary work. It was he who pushed her toward doing missionary work in India, where the need was great.

In 1928, at the age of eighteen, she traveled to Ireland, where she entered the Order of the Sisters of Our Lady of Loreto; she was later sent to Darjeeling, India, for her training. She then studied for a teaching certificate at Loreto Entally in Calcutta, taking her final religious vows in 1937. Every time she left the convent and ventured out into the city streets, she was moved by the presence of the sick and the dying she saw there.

One day in 1946, Mother Teresa heard the call from God that transformed her life, thus beginning her quest to minister to the sick and dying. She later described the incident as follows: "While I was going by train from Calcutta to Darjeeling to participate in spiritual exercises I was quietly praying when I clearly felt a call within my calling. The message was very clear. I had to leave the convent and consecrate myself to helping the poor by living among them. It was a command."[46]

In 1948 she was granted permission by the Vatican to leave her post at the convent. She founded the Missionaries of Charity in 1950, and a number of nuns came to be trained and work with her. Initially, she believed that the nuns should eat as meager rations as the poor on the streets but was soon convinced that they needed a more balanced diet to keep up their strength so they could effectively help and feed the poor. During the day the nuns taught, and in the evening they cared for the poor in the slums of Calcutta. Their creed and purpose, as established by Mother Teresa, was as follows:

> To fulfill our mission of compassion and love to the poorest of the poor we go: seeking out in towns and villages all over the world even amid squalid surroundings the poorest, the abandoned, the sick, the infirm, the leprosy patients, the dying, the desperate, the lost, the outcasts; taking care of them; rendering help to them; visiting them assiduously; living Christ's love for them; and awakening their response to His great love.[47]

Their order was recognized as a pontifical congregation under the juris-diction of Rome, which allowed them to preach, serve, and do conversion. Upon acceptance by the religious community, members of this congregation took four vows. In addition to the three basic vows of poverty, chastity, and obedience, the fourth was a pledge of service to the poor, who Mother Teresa described as the embodiment of Christ. In 1952 she opened the Nirmal Hriday (Pure Heart) Home for Dying Destitutes in Calcutta and subse-quently extended her work to five continents. She was awarded the Nobel Prize in 1979. In 1990 she became ill and was forced to scale down her ac-tivities. After a long and selfless life, she died in 1997.

Malcolm Muggeridge was a British journalist who wrote the book *Something Beautiful for God*, initially making Mother Teresa famous by de-scribing her as being "completely dedicated to God."[48] He wrote of his en-counter with Mother Teresa as she boarded a train at the Calcutta station in 1968: "When the train began to move and I walked away, I felt as though I were leaving behind me all the joy of the universe. Something of God's uni-versal love has rubbed off on Mother Teresa, giving her homely features a noticeable luminosity; a shining quality."[49] Prince Michael of Greece, who met Mother Teresa in 1996, wrote his impression: "A tiny figure, bent al-most double; her hands, as tiny and wrinkled as her face. She took our hands between hers and electrified us with her smile—the smile of a young girl. An extraordinary warmth seemed to surround her—and immediately enveloped us too. With all the love in the world, without a trace of judge-ment, she seemed to understand each one of us."[50]

Others think of Mother Teresa as the Virgin Mary. When she received the Nobel Prize, chairperson John Sanness said:

> Can any political, social, or intellectual feat of engineering, on the international or on the national plane, however effective and rational, however idealistic and principled its protagonists may be, give us anything but a house built on a foundation of sand, unless the spirit of Mother Teresa inspires the builders and takes its dwelling in their building?[51]

Although it is clear that moral leaders accomplish much on behalf of others, they are human beings, and one could dig into their background and find frailties. Mother Teresa is no exception, and there have been criti-cisms—some might say potshots—portraying her as self-aggrandizing, publicity-seeking, antiabortionist, a user of other people, and a great exaggerator of her accomplishments. It has been said that she did not take the proper stands on various political issues and that when dictators were pressing their people, she went with the winning side as long as they supported her mission and her religion. One such accusation was that during her visit to Haiti in 1981, she sang the praises of Michele Duvalier, wife of Jean-Claude "Baby Doc" Duvalier, son of the ruthless dictator "Papa Doc" Duvalier. Another criticism was that Charles Keating, who defrauded a number of people in the United States, was a great admirer of hers and gave her a substantial amount of money. During the Indian-Pakistani wars, she took a stand against the women who had been raped by soldiers, saying they should not commit further murder by aborting the children they had conceived.

Of course, it is not necessary, or even possible, to look at a moral exemplar—that is, a human being who has done extraordinary things for the benefit of others—and expect them to be perfect in every instance.[52] For instance, criticisms of Mandela, King, and Gandhi included womanizing, among other misdeeds. There is no doubt that Mother Teresa and the others dedicated their lives to easing the burdens of others. And it is also not in doubt that Mother Teresa did it for primarily human reasons, namely internal satisfaction. Like most other moral leaders, her acts of altruism were voluntary, and she was not coerced by anyone to be helpful and to care for others. Her deeds were those of a human being who actively tried to ease the burden and pain of diverse others.

India's Prime Minister K. R. Naryanan has said, "Such a one as she rarely walks upon this earth."[53] She was a small woman, who may have appeared fragile, but she carried an enormous power. Even with her death, the light her spirit emanates cannot be extinguished. She has been hailed by the famous and the poor as a "living saint," "the hero of the poor," and an "angel of mercy." Very few people in the twentieth century have had such an influence and developed such a reputation for caring, compassion, and selfless love.

Jonas Salk and Albert Sabin

Moral leaders are engaged in helping humanity, whether in the private arena, medical field, or for the cause of the environment. Both Jonas Salk and Albert Sabin—"the science heroes"—contributed much toward eliminating the scourge of polio from the world. Both doctors won many awards, and each respected the other's work.

Jonas Salk, born in 1914 in New York City to Russian-Jewish immigrant parents, was a gifted student and a humanist. His first wife said of him, "Jonas . . . from the time he was quite young . . . wanted to do something that would make a difference to humanity. . . . He was fueled by idealism that was sincere, backed by all the scientific knowledge, and his personality, and his ability to follow through."[54] This desire strengthened him as he worked his way through college and medical school, ultimately leading him into the field of virology. Upon receiving his medical degree in New York, he began to do research to fight influenza and eventually went to the University of Michigan, where he developed a vaccine for polio. At the time, polio was crippling and often deadly; the epidemic peaked in 1952, with some 58,000 cases and 3,000 deaths across the United States. Salk's research resulted in a vaccine method that used dead viruses and required multiple injections, which led many scientists to doubt it would work. However, it *did* work, and he had created the world's largest vaccine trials to date; more than 1 million children participated in the testing, some receiving the vaccine and some receiving placebos. It proved to be so effective that by 1962 there were fewer than 1,000 cases of polio in the United States.[55] He was a healer and an optimist. He said, "It is always with excitement that I wake up in the morning wondering what my intuition will toss up to me, like gifts from the sea. I work with and rely on it. It's my partner."[56]

During and after his scientific work, Salk also contributed much to world peace—or, as he put it, "finding a cure for the cancer of the world." He devoted most of his energy to "traveling to international conferences and speaking to world leaders about the imminence of peace."[57] For his work on peace and his medical accomplishments he won the Nehru Award for International Understanding and the Presidential Medal of Freedom. Prior to his death in 1995, he began to do research on the AIDS virus. He compared the research on AIDS to Michelangelo's statue of David, saying, "To be unveiled and revealed, little by little. . . . It is just a matter of time and it is just a matter of strategy."[58] Until his death, he found joy in helping others. He said, "I feel that the greatest reward for doing is the opportunity to do more."[59]

A colleague and contemporary of Salk's, Albert Sabin, was born in 1906 in Russia and arrived in the United States unable to speak English. Sabin barely passed primary school but ultimately worked his way through college and medical school. His area of interest was biomedical research, which during World War II led him to find cures for dengue fever in Japan and a Japanese type of polio. For two more decades he dedicated his life to fighting polio. Unlike Salk, Sabin used live viruses that would actively fight the disease (they were taken orally in a lump of sugar). This method was first introduced in the Soviet Union and Eastern bloc countries and, eventually, in the United States. The oral method was ultimately preferred because it provided longer-term immunity and needed only one inoculation. Sabin also refused to hold a patent on the vaccine, thus freeing up the vaccine and its administration. This was truly a moral act—valuing people's lives as priceless. Both Salk and Sabin felt a moral imperative to work on this crippling disease. Some estimates place the number of the vaccinated children in Europe and the United States at some 100 million on each continent.[60] Beyond his work on polio, Sabin, until his death in 1993, continued to work for humanity by fighting poverty and by conducting research on cancer, for which he has won numerous awards.

It is estimated that the polio vaccine has prevented 5 million cases of polio and 500,000 deaths. Since the polio epidemic, there have been fewer than ten cases per year in the United States. Dr. John R. Paul, emeritus professor of preventive medicine and epidemiology at Yale University, wrote about Sabin's contribution to the cure of polio: "No man has ever contributed so much effective information and so continuously over so many years to so many aspects of poliomyelitis as Sabin."[61]

Salk and Sabin were pioneer researchers who devoted their lives to finding cures; they worked to save lives in the way they knew how—through intense scientific research and medical knowledge. These are just two of many lights in the medical research field—men and women who work tirelessly for the good of us all.

Rachel Carson

In the area of environmental issues, Rachel Carson was an outstanding moral leader, and she is often considered to be the founder of the environmental movement in the United States. As a girl, she aspired to be a writer and often entered contests in such magazines as the *New Yorker*, *St. Nicholas*, and *Reader's Digest*. After taking a required college biology course, she switched her major from English to science, and although she feared doing so would diminish her chances for a writing career, her scientific training and her passion for the natural world provided her with meaningful content for her writing. This passion for writing on the subject of the natural world led her to receive a number of literary awards and write best-selling books such as *Under the Sea Wind*, *The Sea Around Us*, and her famous *Silent Spring*—a title she chose because the use of such chemicals would "still the song of birds, and the leaping of fish in the streams"—resulting in silent springs.[62] After Carson received her master's degree in biology, she gained experience working for the U.S. Fish and Wildlife Service, where she became concerned about the hazards of DDT and other pesticides used in agriculture. *Silent Spring* was published in 1962 despite attempts by the chemical industry to block it. Some companies attempted to sue her for slander; others would spend millions in advertisements trying to discredit Carson. However, their efforts failed because the book struck a nerve with the public at a time of increased interest in environmental issues.

She wrote to a friend, "The beauty of the living world I was trying to save has always been uppermost in my mind—that, and anger at the senseless, brutish things that were being done. . . . Now I can believe I have at least helped a little."[63] Helped a little, indeed! She died six years before Earth Day was first celebrated, but she is credited with having spawned many grass-roots movements for saving Mother Earth and its creatures—human and nonhuman; endangered species and water and air pollution issues were raised by her call for awareness. Former Vice President Al Gore has said that had it not been for her book and her desire to understand what humans were doing to humankind and the environment, the environmental movement may have been delayed or not occurred at all.[64]

Chico Mendes

Brazilian activist Chico Mendes had a similar environmental consciousness and dedicated himself to saving the Amazon rainforests. Mendes was fighting for the rainforest and its vitality—not only as the vast source of carbon dioxide for the planet but also as the shelter for many diverse species and indigenous tribes, including his own. Mendes was the leader of rubber-tapping *seringueiros*, an indigenous group that had lived in the rainforest for more than 100 years, sustaining themselves by tapping rubber trees, collecting Brazil nuts, and pursuing other activities that provided the people with a healthy life. Mendes had organized a union—the Xapuri Rural Workers

Union, consisting of rubber-tappers and small farmers—"against encroaching cattle ranchers who were incinerating the rain forest to create pasture and to profit from tax breaks and booming real estate prices."[65] As part of his efforts, Mendes convinced the Brazilian government to preserve 61,000 acres of rubber trees as an "extractive reserve," an area designated only for the purpose of sustainable harvesting of resources native to the area.

As union president, Mendes had made trouble for many powerful stakeholders and businessmen, cattle ranchers, and the owner of Brazil's largest meatpacking corporation, Darly Alves da Silva, a rancher, headed a notoriously dangerous family who usually got its way; if somebody bothered them, they might die at their hands. Many attempts had been made on Mendes's life, and when he prevented Alves da Silva from taking certain tracts of property and converting it into pasture for cattle, unknown men assassinated him. Thousands attended his funeral on Christmas Day 1989.

Chico Mendes's life and work are reflective of great leaders of revolutions and reform for the workers. It has been said, "He was to the ranchers of the Amazon what César Chavez was to the citrus kings of California, what Lech Walesa was to the shipyard managers of Gdansk."[66] Mendes's inspirational leadership in Amazonia is desperately needed again, because the Brazilian government has done little to save the forests. Money continues to be the driving force behind the plundering. Brazil is pressured into repaying its debt to the International Monetary Fund, and repayment comes from its primary resource—the rainforest. "We cannot let Chico Mendes be forgotten. His struggle is everyone's struggle, because justice for the people of the Amazon can benefit everyone's future."[67]

Julia Hill

Another environmental activist gave two years of her life to save one tree. These were the words of Julia "Butterfly" Hill when her feet touched the ground after living for two years at the top of a redwood tree she named Luna, located in Stafford in Northern California on land owned by the Pacific Lumber Company: "I understand all of us are governed by different values. I understand that to some people I'm just a dirty tree-hugging hippie. But I can't imagine being able to take a chainsaw to something like this. . . . I think before anyone could be allowed to cut down [a tree] like this they should be mandated to live in it for two years."[68]

By making Luna her symbol and gaining an agreement with the lumber company that it would never be cut down, she brought to the world's attention the plight of U.S. forests. Her fight was to make the world aware of the clear-cutting of old-growth redwood forests. Trees that had existed for a thousand years—sometimes even two or three thousand years—were being cut down in minutes. Clear-cutting practices demolish thousands of acres of trees to profit the timber industry. For Hill, a young woman of twenty-five years, not only was the clear-cutting itself a concern, it also caused the devastation of the environment around the clear-cut area. When rain falls, the slopes cannot absorb it if all the trees have stopped growing and the roots have died. This results in landslides and more disasters. Such was the fate of the little town of Stafford—which was demolished after the hillside above was clear-cut and mudslides followed heavy rains.

To Hill, these trees were God's creations, and there is a need for preserving them. When we interviewed her, she said:

> I took [the project] on because I had to make a stand against the raping of the forest unnecessarily. The human species can survive without having to cut down ancient forests. We should be recycling, reusing, less wasteful, and while I am not against cutting down old trees, it should be done with an ecological plan in mind so as not to destroy everything around.[69]

The daughter of an itinerant minister, she considered herself a very spiritual person and was taught to take care not only of herself but also others. This meant caring and seeing the connection between all living things. In her book *The Legacy of Luna*, she expresses, "I've always felt that as long as I was able, I was supposed to give all I've got to ensure a healthy and loving legacy for those still to come, and especially for those with no voice. That is what I've done in this tree."[70]

I asked if she was afraid during those two years in the tree. She said she had felt fear, anger, and disappointment. She cried and screamed. Initially, she was afraid to be on the top of the tree, and she questioned whether she was doing the right thing. She was afraid of the lumber company's security guards, the lumberjacks who harassed her by cutting down nearby trees that grazed hers, by noises in the night (including horns that kept her awake), and being buzzed by company helicopters. But she added, "I had to conquer my fears. . . through prayer and the support of many, many people, I was able to prevail. . . . I was able to carry on there. . . . Besides praying, I did a lot of singing, so much so that even some lumberjacks would sometimes stop and listen. That is how I conquered my fears."[71]

Since her tree-sitting experience, she has continued her fight for more sustainable cutting and planned cutting of second- and third-growth trees—those trees that are replanted or sprouted from seeds after an area is cut. Hill also helped found the Circle of Life Foundation, which was created to promote sustainability and the preservation of life. Her hope for the future is to sensitize people to what is happening in the environment, particularly with old-growth forests and logging practices. She believes that each person who becomes sensitive can make a difference—by speaking out, recycling, and "taking on corporations who are involved in the unnecessary destruction of the environment."[72] Julia is concerned about the destruction of the environment and continues to educate groups about the dangers of allowing this destruction to go unchecked. When describing how she felt when she came down from Luna after spending 738 days in the tree, she said:

> I began to sob once again. How would I be able to keep the focus, grounding, and truth that I had found in Luna? How would I be able to keep going when it felt like I was dying, having to leave this incredible living being? I prayed, and for the last time in her branches, Luna spoke to me and reminded me of something I had received in prayer nearly a year before: "Julia, all you have to do when you are afraid, lonely, worn out, or overwhelmed is touch your heart. Because it is there that I truly am, and it is there I will always be."[73]

Julia Hill became famous because her situation invited national publicity, but there are other local moral leaders who make a difference in less public ways.

Eric Duff

One such moral exemplar is the Reverend Eric Duff. Duff, an Episcopal minister in my town of Arcata, California, told me that he learned social consciousness and inclusiveness of others from his parents. He praises his mother's community involvement—working on school integration and inclusion of diverse others in Cincinnati, where he grew up—with molding his sense of tolerance, norms, and values. He also credits books such as *Anne Frank's Diary* and Richard Wright's *Black Boy*, as well as moral exemplars such as Gandhi, King, Mandela, and Desmond Tutu, as having influenced him. As a young minister, Duff lived in Newark, New Jersey, where he had a largely African-American audience; there he established the Apostle House to help and shelter drug addicts and others. The center is still in existence, and other centers modeled it. Duff is a moral activist who doesn't simply speak about what needs to be done—he actually does it. Currently he is trying to involve the community in establishing a campground for the homeless and traveling poor as an alternative to the streets and city parks in Humboldt County. During our interview in January 2000, I asked him a number of questions regarding his moral vision and goals. He said he wanted to guide his parish and his community to reach and attain a moral essence. "My vision is that we in this community and perhaps by virtue of what we do here, helping other communities to better model what it is to be God's people, I guess would be how I would put it, to be God's people in the world."[74]

Duff has strong moral beliefs and goals that guide his work, much like other moral leaders.

> As far as my goals to help to create community and to try to help us to be the people of God, that is a moral goal and that's living a moral life. "Moral" is a big word. . . . I like to think of the ancient tradition of justice and righteousness as the bottom-line of morality. The things that our churches and synagogues and so on, we have gotten so caught up in sexual morality and things that to me are red herrings that distract us from I think the heart of the issue. Certainly you can be immoral in many, many ways, but [we] focus so much on personal morality as opposed to the much more important social morality.[75]

Craig Kielburger

Moral thinking is not only the province of adults like those described above. In April 1995 Craig Kielburger, a twelve-year-old boy from Thornhill, Ontario, read a newspaper article about the death of another twelve-year-old boy, Iqbal Masih. Iqbal was a Pakistani child who had been sold into slavery when he was four; for six years he worked twelve-hour days, six days a week, shackled to a loom making carpets that were to be exported to the Western world. Craig's response was,

> I just compared our two lives—we were the same age. . . and the difference between us was so overwhelming. At that point I decided that I wanted to do some further research into it, and then I wanted to do something about it. I made a small presentation to my class, and before I knew it, "Free the Children" was founded.[76]

Free the Children, a nonprofit organization that works against child labor, is composed of more than 100,000 children organizers in twenty-seven countries around the world. Kielburger and the other organizers educate the public and write letters to world leaders, politicians, educators, and various funds to create alternatives for child laborers who are being abused and exploited. He has traveled to more than thirty countries to meet with working children and other human rights workers. The ultimate purpose for Craig's involvement was to raise the issue of child labor. He stated, "No one has a good excuse for ignoring this problem. . . I believe that society has taught them (young children) they don't have the power to change things, that they have to wait until they are adults to achieve results."[77]

The prime minister of Canada, Jean Chrétien, turned down the opportunity to meet with Craig and the exploited street children due to his busy schedule. Craig's reply was direct and true to heart: "Forget being the Prime Minister . . . it's his moral responsibility to do this."[78] Oftentimes it is easy to dismiss children as being nonactive in social causes, to think that adults must be the ones to change the world because children need to be children or because children don't think about such issues. But for Craig, that is precisely the issue. Children can think outside of their protected and innocent worlds; but more important, they are the future, and a change in attitude toward all children is in order if we are to have a better future.

For his cause and his efforts in addressing inhumanity and child labor issues, and for founding Free the Children, Craig has been awarded the Roosevelt Freedom Medal (with Free the Children) and the State of the World Forum Award. He has been named a Global Leader of Tomorrow and an Ambassador of the First Children's Embassy. He has also appeared on major TV networks in North America, South America, and Europe, gaining international recognition and awareness for the cause of children.[79] He continues his work to bring attention to the world about the exploitation and brutalization of children.

Conclusion

Moral heroes are judged by the truth of their principles and the strength of their ideology of justice, caring, compassion, and the kind of moral community/ society they're able to influence. Moral leaders have profoundly innovative ideas about how to better this world and improve the lives of people and the environment. Their work requires them to be open to moral change and social influences. Evil triumphed during the Holocaust because large groups of people were bystanders—because they did not have strong moral character and found excuses to do nothing.[80] People with strong moral character and the virtue of caring were much less likely to be among the bystanders or to blame the victims for their own victimization because they will have developed a sense of personal identity and integrity based largely on their moral commitments and values. Such people found it psychologically impossible to act against their own principles even if doing the right thing meant risking death.[81]

Studies on the great variety of rescuers of Jews and resistance in different parts of Nazi-occupied Europe have shown that genocide and murder were less likely to occur in democratic societies that foster the importance of tolerance, the ethical self, and universal benevolence than in authoritarian or dictatorial societies. Three factors are necessary to prevent them: (1) a high level of the individual virtues of universal benevolence and conscientiousness; (2) a set of liberal political institutions characteristic of constitutional democracy; and (3) a good political culture, including the civic virtues of respect for the rule of law, support for and loyalty to the other institutions of constitutional democracy, and mutual respect and tolerance among citizens.[82]

Cynics say that there is no such thing as altruism, compassion, and goodness. I feel that goodness, caring, and love exist and are teachable, just as bigotry, racism, sexism, homophobia, and other hatreds are taught by one person to another. All the individuals that we have named as moral exemplars possess traits of caring and putting the welfare of others alongside their own. A quote from the famous Polish Queen Jadwiga (1374–1399) encapsulates the message from the moral exemplars:

Nor can that endure which has not its foundations upon love. For love alone diminishes not, but shines with its own light; makes an end of discord, softens the fires of hate, restores peace in the world, brings together the sundered, redresses wrong, aids all and injures none. And who so invokes its aid will find peace and safety, and have no fear of future ill.[83]

8

"When I Give, I Give Myself"

The Acts of Philanthropy

W e are naturally fascinated by philanthropists—individuals who have the means, the will, and the commitment to take on large social problems and, through their wealth and will, effect change. Yet philanthropists aren't always super-rich. Certain people, regardless of income, are compelled to undertake philanthropy in the community in many ways (e.g., wealth, public influence, time, energy, or expertise). Like moral exemplars (see chapter 7), they lead by example. Like other helpers, philanthropists have a sense of their efficacy and ability to do good, in the rightness of their vision; for the most part, they have the financial means to indulge those beliefs. And like all helpers and rescuers, they have a deep motivation that propels them. This chapter explores those motives, as well as the manner in which philanthropy is practiced in human societies.

Today there appears to be a hands-on philosophy toward philanthropy. This reflects the old Carnegie adage encouraging "getting engaged while you are alive." Carnegie believed in participating in his philanthropy, but he also believed that the act of philanthropy was, for one such as him, essential. He said, "He who dies rich dies thus disgraced." Perhaps the nascence of philanthropy for some is a rich person's guilt, but what keeps it going is the satisfaction it gives the giver.

Bill Gates expresses his philanthropic vision this way: "We give to projects we think can improve the lives of people. Our goal is that millions of people will receive the benefits of new medicines and the empowerment of access to information."[1] This kind of gratifying power, this effective clout, is easily understood, and we of modest means relish knowing just how the rich are giving away their wealth. But also qualifying for the title of philanthropist are many among us who are not necessarily wealthy or can easily spare a million or two but who nonetheless feel compelled to help wherever they can.

Matel Dawson

Matel "Mat" Dawson is a man who devoted much of his working life to helping the community through monetary support. Dawson has spent his career (about six decades) at Ford Motor Company building wealth to share. This octogenarian forklift operator followed his parents' advice and worked overtime and invested his money, allowing him "to give away more than $1 million over the past eight years."[2] A generous portion of Dawson's donations go toward helping students at Wayne State University in Detroit through the Mat Dawson Jr. Endowed Scholarship. His goal through the scholarship is to ensure that deserving students, regardless of race, gender, or religion, have the opportunity to complete an education, an opportunity not available to Dawson. Dawson personally hands out the scholarship so that he may "meet the kids, follow their progress and know who they are."[3] Dawson states the reasons for his philanthropic actions much as Gates did above: "I've owned big homes and big cars and that don't excite me. I just want people to say that I tried to help somebody."[4]

The word "philanthropy" is rich with positive meanings. It comes to us from *philanthropia*, a Greek word that describes man's love for his near ones, his affection and active concern not only for his kin and friends but also for his fellow man in general. *Philanthropia* is closely related to *agape*— the divinely inspired love for fellow human beings. Agape love underlies an active benevolence toward any person, independent of that person's identity or actions. Agape is selfless.

Webster's dictionary defines philanthropy as "a desire to help humankind, especially as shown by gifts to charitable or humanitarian institutions and to individuals." This desire to help, combined with the ability to indulge it, makes a philanthropist. Philanthropists need not be rich; they do need to have an awareness of a need in the community and knowledge that they have to help meet it. In recent times, the word "philanthropy" has replaced "charity," which has a somewhat patronizing connotation to those who either give or receive it. Also, we take "charity" to mean immediate relief for the poor, whereas "philanthropy" in addition encompasses a wider range of private giving for public purposes.

In the early 1880s the Russian philosopher Vladimir Solovyev fostered a notion in which love of God and love of one's fellow human beings are combined into the principle of charity, which, in his treatise *The Spiritual Foundation of Life,* he called "alms." This is a form of altruism based in compassionate *pity.* Altruism based on *compassion* prevents the individual from doing to others what he or she would not like to suffer. Pity and altruism are aimed at transforming society into an integral organism originating in maternal love, extending to others, then out to all humanity and eventually to the entire universe. In this context, then, pity is not patronizing but expresses the principles of altruism that should reign in human relations.

Writers, thinkers, philosophers, poets, and the religious-minded have long been fascinated by goodness and virtue as "things in themselves" and not only as the opposite of evil. But it seems that we as a nation are as preoccupied with evil as with rescue. We confront evil at various places in this book, but I want to be clear that philanthropy is not a reaction to evil. Philanthropy is proactive rather than reactive. Whereas the presence of evil requires that the good act, goodness alone, requires action as well. As a fifteen-year-old boy, I personally experienced an act of kindness. In 1945 a compassionate group of people—the British refugee committee—decided to bring 2,000 orphans from displaced refugee camps in Germany to Britain. I was among the 2,000 orphans who were treated with great kindness and respect. This philanthropic group absorbed the cost of housing, clothing, and education.

Virtue implies patterns of action, but they must be valuable patterns of emotions, attitudes, desires, reasoning, and relationships. According to Mike Martin, in *Virtuous Giving: Philanthropy, Voluntary Service, and Caring,* "kindness is sensitive concern for the well-being of others as manifested in action, words, reasoning, and feelings."[5]

Iris Murdoch, in *The Sovereignty of Good,* says that virtue is an attempt to pierce the evil of selfishness and join the world as it really is. Giving, then, is virtuous only when compassion, generosity, and public-spiritedness accompany it. It must not diminish the respect of the recipient. It requires a morally-based leadership. Martin Luther King Jr., in *Strength in Love,* maintains that "philanthropy often is commendable, but it must not cause the philanthropist to overlook the circumstances of economic injustice which make philanthropy necessary."

Is it possible for philanthropy to lack a moral purpose and be harmful? At its worst, it can be divisive and demeaning to everyone involved. Suppose that philanthropy was in the cause of the Aryan Nation, the Ku Klux Klan, and other hate groups. Giving in support of evil cannot be construed as philanthropy. Giving that demeans the recipient is not philanthropy. One must also be vigilant against calling *coercive giving* philanthropy. True philanthropy thus means voluntarily and willingly donating one's resources and energies for the benefit of others and focusing only on the possible benefit to the recipient.

At each previous step in the web of caring we are constructing, there seems to be a necessary condition for altruism or heroism, one that could occur only at an accidental juncture of history or geography. Some individuals step forward when others step back; it is in their nature. Thus, not every person can be a hero; but every person can embrace philanthropy in one of its many guises and be the better for the act. And many find in philanthropic giving the personal satisfaction that goes beyond a job well done or a task seen to completion; the giving behavior defines them as truly human. Philanthropy expresses some deep and intimate truth of character. Winston Churchill realized the truth of that idea and reminded us that you earn a living with what you get, but you get a life with what you give.

Our intellectual interest in generous giving is not new. Over the centuries scholars and researchers have looked at the nature of giving and quantified it in a variety of ways, defining and analyzing the motives and the methods. Let's look at some of those now.

Moses Maimonides, a twelfth-century Jewish rabbi and philosopher from Spain whose ideas about philosophy, religion, and medicine greatly influenced later thinkers, laid out a hierarchy of giving that is useful in exploring the nature of philanthropy. The lowest rung in Maimonides's "Golden Ladder of Charity" is giving with reluctance or regret. This gift is the gift of the hand, not of the heart. The second is to give cheerfully, but not proportionately, to the distress of the sufferer. The third is to give cheerfully and proportionately, but not until solicited. The fourth is to give cheerfully, proportionately, and even unsolicited and to put it in the poor man's hand, thereby exciting in him the painful emotion of shame. The fifth rung is to give charity in such a way that the needy person knows the benefactor without being known in return. In the sixth, the giver takes special care to remain unknown; even gratitude once removed is unnecessary. The seventh rung is altruistic in that it bestows the gift in such a roundabout way that neither the benefactor nor the distressed person know the name of the other. The eighth and highest rung is the height of altruism—to anticipate charity by preventing poverty.

The compassionate act of philanthropy is universal, and the philanthropic impulse is available to everyone. Examples are found in every culture. At its heart philanthropy is a felt joy in virtuous giving and a morally desirable caring for others as well as for oneself. Caring and giving can fill our days with righteous good feeling. Philanthropy gives life to our daily toils.

There is some overlap between philanthropy and volunteerism—both imply acts of helping. However, voluntarism does not usually involve giving money but giving of one's time to help the other. Righteousness—that quality of just virtue—is one of the many sources of caring, and it fosters valuable caring relationships. In the Western world, the ethical source of this notion comes from Aristotle's and Plato's works about love, as well as from Judeo-Christian teachings. Both encourage us to be good to others as a way of being good to ourselves—thus not only enhancing humanity but also increasing self-understanding.

The eighteenth-century philosopher and historian David Hume said, "The epithets *sociable, good-natured, humane, merciful, grateful, friendly, generous, beneficent*, or their equivalents, are known in all languages, and universally express the highest merit human nature is capable of attaining."[6] Walt Whitman said, "When I give I give myself."[7] Philanthropy unites individuals in caring relationships; it enriches both the giver and the receiver; it requires and speaks to our best selves. It is often heroic and inspiring. But it is just as meaningful for being homely and understated, for coming from John and Jane Doe. Philanthropy is not the private property of the wealthy or the famous; it is the natural home of each of us.

Philanthropy is a seed that exists everywhere and is rooted in every ethnic, cultural, and spiritual tradition. It is one of the core precepts of all world religions, and it is clear that all religions—both literate and preliterate—have practiced traditions of philanthropy, although the practice itself may have taken different forms.

Each culture has its own way of giving to others, but it is a fairly common and universally accepted concept that philanthropic giving and helping should be done with dignity, with no strings attached. Sometimes philanthropy is motivated by reciprocal necessity—community members helping each other in order to survive and prosper. But in some cultures philanthropy stems from the notion of hospitality; and though hospitality often has a reciprocal component, it doesn't have visible strings attached in the contractual sense.

In South Asia, giving is not universally mandated, but it is nevertheless contextualized in Asian society, and each situation calls for some form of selfless giving on behalf of others.[8] Among Native Americans, spiritual forces and ritual lore dictate philanthropy. The belief in the harmony and integrity of the whole—that all are connected—is fundamental to the life philosophy, and the perpetuation of that wholeness requires generous giving from everyone. Native American individuals and institutions appear not to separate philanthropic altruism as a humanitarian act from philanthropy as motivated by cosmological concerns reaching into all realms of life. It is an aspect of cultural life and essential to its perpetuation.

Simon Ortiz, the Acoma poet, places "the intimate connections of an individual to his or her people . . . in the context of a 'collective communal spirit,' 'people and place,' 'people and their religion,' 'the source,' 'wholeness,' and 'the All-Spirit.'"[9] He describes the philosophy best when he says,

> There's no other purpose for which a person lives. Again, I refer
> to what my heritage is. It's a central philosophy; you don't speak,
> you don't live except on behalf of your people. You can't live, you
> are not alone; only because of the people are you in existence. It
> doesn't just mean people as physical beings, but people in terms
> of people and place, people and their religion, people as the
> source of who you are. Without that you are not really anything.
> So your voice is their voice, in terms of a collective communal
> spirit. Obviously, there is a contradiction, as there is in most
> everything. A person as a spokesperson, a person as an artist who
> has an ability, a gift given to him by his creator, by the All-Spirit,
> given to him to utilize, is going to do a lot of his work individu-
> ally, but with the understanding that he doesn't exist without this
> context; without this wholeness and source he is nothing. That is
> essential.[10]

This differs from Western Euro-American context in which the term "philanthropy" emerged as a largely human-centered act of beneficence by individuals, associations, and institutions—an aspect of cultural life but not essential to its perpetuation.

Over the centuries, religion, philosophy, and politics have shaped and colored the nature of philanthropic concepts. In Theraveda Buddhism, *dana*—generosity, service to others, and giving—is a very pervasive phenomenon and is manifested in the context of religion. There are ten virtues that must be perfected if one is to reach enlightenment: generosity, morality, renunciation, wisdom, energy, patience, truth, resolution, loving kindness, and equanimity. This path is considered a way of cultivating and attaining the twin ideals of the religion: love and compassion.

Nothing is possible without first manifesting generosity. If we cannot give, we cannot be moral or wise or resolute. In the give and take, give comes first. In China, there arose a debate between two schools of philosophy. One was developed by Mo Tzu (479–438 B.C.E.) and consisted of universal love for all humankind and a belief that all are deserving of help. This philosophy was bitterly opposed by the Confucians, especially Mencius (371–289 B.C.E.), who argued for the need to have love with distinctions—a philosophy of particularized love. Mencius charged that Mo Tzu's doctrine of universality would diminish people's ability to concentrate their efforts on those close to home. The Confucianists also disagreed with Mo Tzu's notion of mutual benefit because they saw it as too utilitarian, saying that one should be motivated by righteousness and not by personal gain. We should be good for goodness sake, not because we will get presents. In East Asia today, philanthropy is based on Mencius's notion of love with gradation, which has become the dominant Confucian ethic there, as has Mencius's notion of a humane or benevolent government. The reasons for government's existence is to assist people and to help promote agriculture or provide relief efforts when crops fail or when floods occur, as was frequently the case throughout history.

In Japan a similar hierarchy of reciprocal obligation and responsibility has developed under this notion. A complex web of these relationships existed in premodern Japan and continues to influence human relationships today. Obligation to the family is central. It then opens outward to relatives, teachers, neighbors, and business associates. Thus, anonymous philanthropy to strangers and organizations that promote philanthropy are almost unknown in Japan.

In Jewish culture, philanthropy stems from Halachic literature in the Hebrew bible—the explanatory sources for expected levels of charity and philanthropic action. The Hebrew term *tsedakah* (charity) is also part of the ancient Jewish tradition. As with many cultures, Jews faced enormous hardships—violence, robbery, bigotry—so the community had to organize self-help for victims, especially in the Diaspora—those racial groups who live in countries other than their own. This commitment to self-help reflected the teachings of helping, and the community continues to stand out for its philanthropy, not only in its own communities but also in volunteer and charitable organizations for the benefit of everyone.

Robert H. Arnow, a Jew and former chairman of Ben-Gurion University in Israel and a semiretired corporate executive who now lives in Pennsylvania, has been concerned with a number of causes, including the arts and after-school programs, but his main interest has been the Bedouins of the Middle East, whose traditional social and economic lives are destabilized when they make the transition from nomadic ways to a more urban existence. He is working to increase educational opportunities for Bedouin students, setting up the Center for Bedouin Studies and Development at Ben-Gurion and creating an endowment for developing curricula.[11]

In pre-Soviet Russia, the Russian Orthodox church played a major role in helping the poor. Philanthropic traditions were established by members of the ruling families, and the village commune was important at the local level in nurturing an anti-individualistic ideology among the peasantry. The Russian government was concerned about poverty and found its main expression of that concern in state philanthropic agencies and individual charitable institutions under the patronage of the imperial family—in contrast to the poor law reform of Victorian Britain and the social insurance legislation of Bismark's Germany.

In 1918 traditional philanthropy was abolished by the Marxist regime because altruism and philanthropy were considered oppressive. For Karl Marx, altruism was merely a mask for class egoism and the selfishness of capitalism. In his mind, it had nothing to do with loving your neighbor, at best being the fulfillment of the moneyed aristocracy's self-love—serving their pride and their desire for amusement. Marx believed philanthropy should be a function of the state, which would foster the well-being of all peoples. Well-being is a right not a beneficence.

Alms-giving and philanthropy never entirely disappeared under the Soviet system, but with the fall of the Soviet Union churches have again been encouraging the giving of alms. The Russian Orthodox church has taken a major role in helping the poor and has reestablished parish charitable brotherhoods, not seen since the nineteenth century, and the old traditions of compassion and private giving have begun to thrive once again.

I think there are other motivations underlying philanthropy. Perhaps most important among them is the simple desire to help others during hard times. This entails an ethic of caring, sharing, and social responsibility—helping our fellow man or woman as if they are members of our own families. The media has contributed to the outpouring of care since the World Trade Center disaster. In fact, our mechanisms for massive giving have been honed over decades as the global community has mobilized to meet the needs brought about by disaster, both man-made and natural. Musicians, film and TV stars, professional athletes, corporations, and individuals—all have sent money to the Red Cross and the United Way since September 11, with the combined sum given in the first four weeks about $500 million.[12]

There is a long tradition in the United States that fosters motivations for philanthropy, and the cultural and ethnic environment in which individuals are raised may contribute to their spirit of giving. Some philanthropists feel they have an obligation toward stewardship—that it is necessary to consider and help the community and society where they live. Frequently their families introduce and promote the path to philanthropy; inheritors are taught that they ought to give; it is expected of them because they have acquired their wealth in the community and they ought to return some of it. Administering the philanthropic fund can be a full-time job for some members of the family who are heads of philanthropic foundations, such as the Ford Foundation. Also, religious teachings may indoctrinate and encourage giving.[13]

Many philanthropists have expressed that they would prefer to give their wealth to worthy organizations and institutions during their lifetime. They want to do this because they're deeply concerned with what will happen after they die—whether their wealth be squandered or mismanaged. In addition, as many of us do, they have a desire for immortality and wish for a remembrance of their good deeds. "One man, who said that a desire for immortality plays a role in his thinking, spoke of giving 'a wing in a hospital, a gallery in a museum' as a way of leaving 'footprints in the sand of time.'"[14] Thus, many people are planning to bequeath their wealth in their lifetime rather than wait until they die.

Although many philanthropists undoubtedly feel a genuine sense of responsibility, are trying to resolve social ills, or want to express gratitude to the country for the opportunities they were given, there are, not surprisingly, more critical views. Steven Burkeman, a foundation consultant in England, discussed individual motivations for giving of time or money. In a speech he asked: "When was the last time someone dared say to a wealthy philanthropist: I can see what you do with your money, but what do you do with your time? Or, I can see how you spend your money, but how did you come by it? Or, I can see what good you think your money did, but what did you learn from the experience?" [15]

Burkeman defines philanthropy as something that "used to mean love of humankind [but] now means giving money away."[16] Many give because of a desire for immortality combined with a sense of familial and religious responsibility, but desire for immortality may really mean fear of judgment day: "Those with great wealth may be aware that—either because of the way in which it has been gained, or because of the inequities around them, or both—theirs is an uncomfortable position to defend in the great hereafter, and that even very thin camels do not fit through the eye of a needle."[17] Philanthropy can bring a sense of moral superiority to the donors, and it can assuage the guilt some feel simply for being wealthy while others are poor. The intention of a foundation may be to continue the family dynasty. In some cases, foundations establish a policy of funding only specific programs or using their assets to influence government policy. Many very wealthy philanthropists have totally neglected to specify what they want their money to be used for, seemingly just trying to wrap up their fiscal affairs as they reach the end of life without really caring where the money goes.[18]

Should the motivation for philanthropy always be only pure altruism, that is, an unselfish concern for others? Or is it permissible for self-interest to be mixed in with altruism? Although a caring relationship does imply altruism, our own well-being can be a strong stimulus. Therefore, philanthropic giving can spring from a combination of altruism and self-interest. It is reasonable to assume that altruistic motivation must consist of some internal reward for helping, so it should also be assumed that there is a relationship between *justice* and *reciprocity* in virtuous giving. The word "justice" implies both fairness to those who are in need and a reciprocal reward to the giver. It also means treating people as moral equals, especially in situations that involve competition or inequities of power and opportunity.

Kristen Renwick Monroe, a political scientist, examined altruism as existing on a continuum that situated self-interest at one end and pure altruism at the other.[19] She identified archetypal figures representing various points on the continuum, with the rational actor—in this case, the entrepreneur—signifying pure self-interest, the rescuer signifying pure altruism. The philanthropist and the hero were situated at points between. Unlike the entrepreneur, the philanthropist gives away wealth with no apparent strings attached. But unlike the hero or the rescuer, the philanthropist is not put at risk and is certainly keeping enough wealth to maintain a comfortable existence. What is it that motivates the philanthropist to engage in altruistic behavior? Monroe looks at Melissa to illustrate the evolution of a philanthropist.

Melissa was born into a family of modest means in a Missouri farming community in 1926. The family moved around a lot, and she found those transitions difficult. She identified her grandfather as being an important role model, teaching her to value family, hard work, and self-reliance. Melissa's grandfather dealt with adversity on his own, without help from anyone, and was instrumental in the formation of Melissa's views on how people deal with adversity and on the structural problems of poverty.[20] After Melissa married, she and her husband started a family business that thrived, and she began volunteering for local school activities and neighborhood causes. As the business became more lucrative, she did more. Within the five years before Monroe interviewed her, Melissa had donated more than $6 million and who knows how many hours of her time to various causes. The death of her husband prompted her to develop an even stronger commitment to philanthropic pursuits.

Melissa viewed her philanthropy as a way to give back to the people who helped her family prosper. She also viewed it as a social responsibility, a duty to help others. In discussing herself in relation to others, she viewed herself as "someone that cared about other people. I hope to leave a legacy that I cared. Maybe that I left behind an attitude, a positive attitude, that life can be good, it can be shared, and you can get a lot of pleasure out of that. I guess I look at life as though the glass is always half full."[21]

I have found that philanthropists often mention that the act of altruistic behavior made them feel good and that their feeling good was a surprising result of their philanthropy. Often, altruists, including philanthropists, were generally modest about their acts, viewing them as not extraordinary, and they perceive themselves as ordinary people. Also, philanthropy has practical consequences because it enables philanthropists to express their values and their sense of obligation to the community from which they have extracted much of their own wealth—expressing the feeling that they should give back to the community.

One such philanthropist is a building contractor in San Francisco who became financially successful in the 1960s. He perceived that African-American contractors were being discriminated against, and he encouraged them and awarded them subcontracts on his projects and helped break through the prejudices. When I asked him why, he said he was brought up to help his fellow human beings and that his Jewish background and education instilled the idea of *tikkun olam*—the need to help fix the world. He asked, "What are we here on this earth for if not to participate in helping, caring, and being responsible for our fellow human beings?" This man is now retired and has become involved in various community affairs, helping other groups to succeed and founding a Jewish community center, which he helped build by providing funding and volunteering his time and talents.

I also interviewed a lumber businessman living in the redwood forests of Northern California who has given away a substantial amount of funds secretly; he did not want the recipients to disclose how much money they received. When asked why he did this, he said, "Well, I have more than I need to live on and, therefore, I thought I'd make contributions." When I questioned him further, he said, "Well, I just felt that I had to do it for no big reasons. I'm not a 'bleeding heart,' nor am I involved with community affairs. I just thought, 'I have money, and I'll give.'" He added that it made him feel good about himself; also, it was good for his business in terms of public relations.

Thus, we have two examples of those who are driven to give, but for different reasons. The building contractor was prompted by a sense of justice. The lumberman gave no specific reason other than he had money and he wanted to give some away and it was good for business and it made him feel good, indicating both reciprocity and an internal reward.

Who Are the Philanthropists?

In *The Seven Faces of Philanthropy*, Russ Prince and Karen File suggest that there are seven types of philanthropy.[22] The first group is the *communitarians*—local business owners who give back to the community because they believe that it makes sense to support local charities. Second are the *devouts*—people who contribute because it is God's will. They are motivated to support nonprofit organizations for religious reasons, are mostly from local churches, and allocate 96 percent of their giving to religious institutions.

The third group, *investors,* includes donors who establish philanthropic interests because of the tax advantages. They donate to a wide range of nonprofit organizations and are likely to support umbrella nonprofit groups such as community foundations. The fourth group is *socialites*—people who donate and do good works because it is socially rewarding. These donors are members of a local social network within which they interact, and they support and have leverage in fund-raising activities. The fifth group is *altruists*—people who are doing good because it feels good or because they want to help their fellow man. They give out of generosity and empathy, and some remain anonymous. For them it's a moral obligation to help their fellow human beings because their feelings and values have developed into a sense of caring. The altruists usually focus their philanthropy on social causes. The sixth group is *repayers*—donors who feel that they have personally benefited from institutions such as schools and medical centers, and they show their loyalty and obligation by their support. Last are the *dynasts*—those who contribute out of family tradition. Their giving stems from their socialization and upbringing; the family believes in respecting and supporting nonprofit groups.

Whether giving makes people feel they are part of the community, are serving their religious beliefs, are socializing and making friends, are investing their assets to benefit the institutions they feel strongly about, are repaying the community out of obligation or loyalty, or are giving because it's the right thing and expected of them, the intention for each is to help others in need and at the same time gain something for themselves.

According to Cornelius Pietzner, various types of philanthropists may give at different levels of philanthropy.[23] *Parochial* philanthropy is a limited-interest philanthropy; it comes and it goes. It is sympathetic and contextual. It is charity related to what you feel like at the moment—like giving to a beggar on the street. The next is called *paternalistic* philanthropy—instead of giving the proverbial fish to someone who is hungry and giving fish again the next day, the paternalist gives a fishing rod and instructions—and maybe a ride to the river. The third level of philanthropy is *production*—"problem-solving philanthropy." This form is issue-oriented rather than object-oriented, and the problem the philanthropist is trying to address occurs at the structural level in society. The philanthropist sees a need and wants to solve or rectify it. The production philanthropist deals more with situations, such as environmental degradation and illiteracy. This is the level where most major institutional funding occurs. The fourth and final level is *partnership*—

philanthropic giving connected to the deeper ideals and inner intentions of the donor. The motivation is sympathetic and it represents a mutual and creative process between the philanthropist and the recipient.

Although the major philanthropists continue to be corporations and tycoons, there are also less well-known individuals who can afford to give. The independent nonprofit sector gives much help in the form of volunteerism and philanthropy. Donors belong to service clubs, schools, or companies; they are known by reference to their philanthropic contributions or goals. Frequently, there are people who can barely afford to give yet still help others. Among these are the unsung heroes and altruists. Sometimes these unsung heroes are our neighbors.

Andrew Carnegie, Philanthropist

Andrew Carnegie is perhaps the most widely recognized philanthropist in U.S. history. A leading player in addressing social responsibility, his philosophy was that people should be engaged in humanitarian causes while they are alive and can direct their funds toward what they believe to be most important. Carnegie was inspired by the religious leader John Wesley, who said "gain all you can; save all you can; and then give all you can to do good to all men."

Carnegie was labeled a robber baron, yet he labored for the good of his fellow man and faithfully lived up to the charge of John Wesley by giving away 90 percent of his wealth, an amount well over $350 million.[24] Carnegie's importance to philanthropic history is part and parcel of the unique time in which he lived and the social conditions that shaped his character and allowed him unique opportunities.

Carnegie was born to Margaret and William Carnegie of Dunfermline, Scotland, on November 25, 1835. Of his parents' status at that time, Carnegie would later write, "Poor but honest, of good kith and kin."[25] His boyhood Scotland was a country in transition. The long-established institution of the aristocracy was the subject of harsh opposition by the rising liberal movement, and economic hardships on the lower class fueled the fires of their discontent. Carnegie's motto at that time was "death to privilege."

When the local textile industry mechanized, Carnegie's father was especially hard-hit and had to ask for financial help. It was clear to the boy that no child's father should be subject to such shame—and the root of his philanthropy took hold.

In July 1848, when Andrew was thirteen, the family moved from Scotland to the United States, a country undergoing metamorphosis; the population was growing and moving, the body of social thought was expanding, and the political climate was in transition. Gold had been discovered in the foothills of California's Central Valley, and the land rush west was in full swing; the country was following its natural westward drift in record numbers and at a greatly accelerated pace. The discovery of gold had touched off a national demand for transportation, and the railroads companies were responding.

It was this flexible, evolving society that Carnegie came to know and where he found his profit. Carnegie embraced the notion of the individual's right to opportunity, and from that was born his unique idea of the responsibility that accompanies opportunity. Those who have excelled in fair competition—and found fortune—have a responsibility to put back into society that which they extracted during their rise to success. This was the basis for Carnegie's ethic as it pertains to business, and it helps to explain his tremendous popularity with the workingman, even after he rose to power and prominence. His easy adaptation to the changing environment ensured his fame; his character ensured his destiny.

Carnegie's rise through the professional ranks was swift. He began his career in 1848 as a bobbin boy in a cotton mill earning $1.20 per week, then made $2 per week running a steam engine to fire a boiler in the cellar of another bobbin factory. The following year, he became employed as a messenger in a telegraph office and learned telegraphy; later he worked for the Pennsylvania Railroad as a secretary and telegrapher. Through successive promotions Carnegie became the superintendent of the Pittsburgh division of the railroad and began investing in oil and other financial interests. During the Civil War he served in the War Department and formed a company to produce iron railroad bridges. He later founded a steel mill and ultimately acquired controlling interests in other large steel mills. By the end of the nineteenth century he would control about 25 percent of all U.S. iron and steel production. In 1901 he retired and sold his company for more than $225 million.[26]

Though Carnegie had no formal education, he had a lifelong interest in books and education. His family's dependence on him fostered a strong sense of his own worth and maturity, which lent itself perfectly to his impression of the American character: individualistic, competitive, and self-reliant. He grew up working and taking advantage of the opportunities that presented themselves, and each chance turned in his favor. He worked hard and was reliable. His supervisors took notice.

In his autobiography, Carnegie describes his first such opportunity—the messenger-boy job—and its results: "From the dark cellar running a steam engine at two dollars a week, begrimed with coal dirt, without a trace of the elevating influences of life, I was lifted in to paradise, yes, Heaven, as it seemed to me, with newspapers, pens, pencils and sunshine all about me."[27]

Andrew Carnegie displayed a love of work and a love of philanthropy. Over the years, he gave to various educational, cultural, and peace institutions and set up special funds and institutes. His beneficiaries included Carnegie Hall in 1892, the Carnegie Institution in 1902, the Carnegie Hero Fund Commission in 1904, the Carnegie Foundation for the Advancement of Teaching in 1905, and the Carnegie Endowment for International Peace in 1910. His largest single gift was $125 million to establish the Carnegie Corporation of New York in 1911. In addition, more than 2,800 libraries bear his name, as do foundations for the advancement of medicine, science, and industry.

Carnegie was not unique in his tradition of philanthropy; he was in esteemed company. Other successful people such as Elizabeth Milbank Anderson, Diamond Jim Brady, William Colgate, Avery Fisher, Stephan Girard, Meyer Guggenheim, and Henry Huntington also practiced philanthropy during this era. It is Carnegie's *reasons* for giving that I wish to emphasize here. His generosity came from a sense of morality—a belief in an unspoken and unwritten contract with his fellow man. He believed that the social contract dictated that those who had the means should provide for those in need; members of society are responsible for each other's welfare, for each is a part of the whole. He illustrated this point by claiming that "the rich man who gives away his wealth while leading a virtuous life will find that his riches 'will not be a bar to heaven' . . . but that 'the man who dies rich dies disgraced.'"[28] In his lifetime and in the legacy he left behind, Andrew Carnegie set a standard for social responsibility, establishing the notion of welfare by the private individual.

Contemporary Philanthropy

We now focus on philanthropy today.[29] The new generation of wealthy philanthropists—the high-tech dot-com donors—has been the focus of many recent studies.[30] Do the cyber barons of the information age exhibit the same sorts of motives as did their predecessors?

Based on thirty-three face-to-face interviews with high-tech million-aires, one study concluded that this new breed is confident and energetic and motivated to seek out and attack social problems. Because of their back-grounds and education, "they generally believe that education and develop-ment of human capital provide the best solutions to society's problems."[31] Although their business practices may have been less than humanistic at the outset, once they accomplished their goals they relinquished their amassed sums to philanthropic causes such as libraries and museums.[32] This study utilized the work of sociologist Paul Schervish to explain motivation.

Schervish says there are two factors driving people to give away money: *individuality* and *principality*. The former deals with conceiving of oneself as having the ability and expectations to make a difference in the world, then having the confidence to act. The latter deals with world-building. These world-builders are what Schervish calls "hyper-agents," that is, those who are founders of the world, as opposed to most people, who are finders and expressionists of their place in the world. The simple scope of their char-ity—a total of nearly $550 million from Rockefeller and $21.8 billion so far from Bill Gates—can't help but change the world. Schervish says that for them it is an almost religious experience: "Wealth as an idol is an immoral task, but wealth as an instrument is a moral task."[33]

Richard Barrett provides us an additional view of corporate philan-thropy.[34] He has established seven levels of corporate giving, describing each level as a "consciousness" with an attached motivation. The first three levels are about self-interest, the main motivation being to get rather than give. The first is *survival consciousness,* in which the focus of the giving is simply to make more money. This level is a form of bribery, and the motivation is pure greed. The corporation is convinced that by giving some it will get more. The second is *relationship consciousness*, which establishes relations that serve the company's needs. It will offer support with the expectation that it will re-ceive favors in the future. You scratch my back; I'll scratch yours. The third addresses *self-esteem consciousness* in which the focus and motivation is to be the best and look good, especially when giving financial assistance to institu-tions or charities. The important thing is that the giver be in the pubic eye and find a form of self-promotion in the giving.

Barrett's next four levels shift to a more giving and prosocial attitude. *Transformation*, the fourth level, is directed to learning and growing, motivated by the desire to gain knowledge. This in turn leads to contributing to institutions that help to foster new ideas and help others grow in knowledge. The fifth level is *organizational consciousness*, which gives to the employees' spiritual, mental, emotional, and physical needs. This is motivated by employee fulfillment, but not in the sense of producing better employees and products, although that may be a by-product. The primary concern is to build a better world through creating better facilities and helping employees on a personal level—enhancing fitness or providing child care. *Community consciousness* is the sixth level. It extends to the community and helps employees as they give to community organizations and provides time off for employees to spend time volunteering or contributing to charity. The final level, *societal consciousness*, lends support to the world as a whole to make the world a better place. "Corporations at this level recognize that whatever contribution they can make to improving societal conditions will benefit everyone. They understand the interconnectedness of all life."[35]

Traditional philanthropy in the United States is a social institution made up of philanthropic elites. It implies status, power, social exclusivity, and a distinctive cultural identity. These individuals belong to special clubs and participate in fund-raising for their own specific purposes.[36] Contributions usually do not go directly to the poor; rather, they go to institutions that help to sustain and foster the culture—forms of art, theater, music, and museums—as well as to education. Furthermore, giving would not involve a hands-on experience; the philanthropist or donor writes a check and gets the prestige.

In past years corporate philanthropy donated to charities, and the charities in turn would spend the money the way they wanted. But this paradigm is changing toward working side-by-side with charities for the simple reason that it works better both for the donor and for the recipient. Employees want partnership in fulfilling social responsibilities; doing so as a group can improve staff motivation and create a better work environment.[37]

Corporate giving is a means of survival, and recipients will be selected by their capacity to provide survival means. If corporations can portray themselves as good, they can instill a positive attitude for the company and insure a longer life. What is needed for corporate philanthropy to be recognized is evidence that the corporation is giving to causes that are socially and environmentally responsible. Overall, there seems to be a trend in corporate involvement in philanthropic efforts.

A new hands-on approach to philanthropy and its application is being taught at the Haas School of Business at the University of California–Berkeley, where students are being educated to better understand philanthropy and charity.[38] The new class, "Contemporary Philanthropy," addresses issues of volunteer work, charitable giving, and nonprofit organizations, with the main focus on social responsibility. Professor Frances Van Loo says, "Everybody, whether they want to work in nonprofits or are in hardcore business, has to understand the responsibility."[39] This course is the first of its kind to be taught; its poignancy is due to the sudden surge of dot-com entrepreneurs entering the corporate world. They have attained their personal financial goals and now want to know what to do with the rest of their money.

The Philanthropic Elite

Sociologist Francie Ostrower conducted a study in New York City in 1995, interviewing almost ninety philanthropic donors.[40] For them, philanthropy is a distinct social and cultural way of life. Their involvement in it reflects their membership in the upper class. Giving involves an assertion of class identity along with the monetary contribution. In Ostrower's study, more than 75 percent of the donors sat on one nonprofit board, and more than 60 percent sat on multiple boards. Frequently, another elite or influential member induced the donor to participate. Philanthropy has high prestige among elites, and in order to belong to this group, one has to donate.

One of the attributes of philanthropy is that often it is given to public organizations and does not involve direct giving to the poor on the streets. Philanthropists contribute to those causes that enhance status—cultural events, operas, theater, and museums—as well as their preferred religious institutions and alma mater. More than 90 percent of all gifts were made in the areas of health, education, culture, and churches or temples.

Of the eighty-eight donors Ostrower interviewed, 59 percent were Jewish, 26 percent were Protestants and Catholic, and 10 percent had no specific religious affiliation. It is interesting that Jews contributed at a far higher rate than Protestants and Catholics. All donations given to Catholic schools were made by donors or relatives who attended the institutions. Donors also indicated the effect of peer pressure in their contributions and viewed contributing as debt and obligation, especially Jews.

It has been observed that the social elite in the United States has evolved into a closed caste, dominated by the white Anglo-Saxon Protestants, and that Jews have experienced an exclusion from both the social circles and institutions associated with the social elite. Looking at the donors, we find that 79 percent of Protestants, as compared to 25 percent of Catholics and only 19 percent of Jews, were socially elite at the time of the research in the late 1980s. This indicates that in New York City the elite is still of a Protestant character. Most of the Jewish members of the social elite did support the Jewish-affiliated fund, but not with major gifts. The major gifts were given to non-Jewish-affiliated organizations or institutions.

Otstrower finds that women were largely absent from top institutional positions of economic power in the United States. The norms of the upper class have dictated that women be distanced from the business and professional worlds; but those same norms direct women to charitable work where they join boards of charitable organizations, museums, symphonies, theaters, and so forth. These elite boards have attached prestige and require a certain number of hours of participation per month in order for the organizations to exist and flourish. Ostrower's study shows that a lot of giving is faith-based, from the rich and the less-than-rich.

Philanthropy has always stressed education and culture. Virtually everyone in Ostrower's sample contributed money to education—92 percent to universities or colleges alone—and 69 percent of the donors made at least one of their largest gifts to education. A number gave to their alma mater, suggesting again that sense of obligation and gratitude that is so often a motivation for giving. Elites support these organizations because they benefit society, but in addition they supported their chosen endeavors because they enjoyed good music or good art. Associating with culture and education are quite distinctive because such causes offer prestige and are frequently chosen as recipients of large gifts across diverse subgroups or donors. In other words, donors want to be associated with famous institutions because it is a form of prestige. Philanthropic gifts express the individual's relationship to and identify them with particular social groups. This identification is expressed through support.

Philanthropy is pervasive, important, and helps to sustain various institutions. The fact that it may also be beneficial to the social status of the philanthropist, as well as contributing to maintaining an upper class by justifying its position in society, may show it not to be completely altruistic. Yet the gift-granting institutions are generally beneficial to the general public.

Since the federal government legislated that philanthropists can deduct five percent of their taxable profits, they have been donating sizable funds, helping to establish philanthropic organizations or granting institutions. It is well to remember that philanthropic elites have lots of private monies and a negative attitude toward taxation. Ninety percent of them expressed opposition to the government taking over philanthropy because it smacked of socialism. Donors also expressed concerns with the limits of government, even though they acknowledge that in some instances, such as social welfare, the government should intervene.

Philanthropy is giving to promote human welfare. It is a deliberate attempt to establish procedures for giving to communities or organizations and individuals who are needy. There is no single motivating factor to explain philanthropic behavior; however, for me, it is not so important to pinpoint the motivations for giving as it is to acknowledge the results of giving to alleviate suffering.

The Judeo-Christian and Islamic traditions assert that society has a responsibility to those who are less able, that we are required to cloth the naked and feed the hungry. There is a connection between giving from the heart and receiving something in return, which in turn implies sustaining a moral self-image as a helper. Philanthropy implies voluntary helping and should always have a moral purpose. Above all, it must be beneficial for the recipients—individuals, organizations, or the community—and enable the recipients to maintain or restore dignity. Giving requires humility, courage, and sincerity. It must not be overtly attached to self-gain, publicity, or self-aggrandizement.

It is a longstanding belief that one must act selflessly on behalf of others for the act to be considered truly virtuous. John Stuart Mill, the English philosopher, said,

> Those only are happy . . . who have their minds fixed on some object other than their own happiness; on the happiness of others, on the improvement of mankind, even on some art or pursuit, followed not as a means, but as itself an ideal end. Aiming thus at something else, they find happiness by the way.[41]

It would seem that the quest for rightness with the world has helped to direct huge amounts of money toward a broad range of needs; that the wealthy, in seeking their own happiness, commit their wealth to helping others; that the fabric of society has been strengthened and beautified and warmed by the flow of dollars from the deep pockets of philanthropists.

9

❧

Finding the Best in Ourselves

Putting the Welfare of Others Alongside Our Own

One thing I know: the only one's among you who will be truly
happy are those who have sought and found how to serve.
                                                    —**Albert Schweitzer**

The great tragedy of September 11 showed us again that people can
and will demonstrate moral courage by their actions, by voluntarily
helping their fellow human beings. At the World Trade Center, at
the Pentagon, on the planes, and in the streets, ordinary people—secretaries,
bankers, stockbrokers, public service employees, firefighters, police officers,
waiters, tellers, clerks, custodians, and every other occupation, blue-collar
and white-collar, management and minion—did extraordinary things. None
was a superhero; they were the people of the neighborhood, city workers and
fellow workers, neighbors and strangers. Human beings from all walks of life
were moved and jolted by this event, and they found in themselves the capacity to show a compassionate face like never before.

By Halloween 2001, a mere two months afterward, the children's cos-
tume of choice was a public service uniform, either a police officer or a firefighter. Since September 11, children have become more understanding of
the adult world, even though in ways we might wish they could have been

195

spared. The fragmenting of those buildings seems to have welded the frag-
mentation of the populations. Not since the post–World War II years, when
the first baby boomers where youngsters, have we seen such an integrated
national presence. People more frequently greeted each other and became
engaged in conversation; others made being in close contact with their relatives a priority and built stronger relationships. People began to appreciate
firefighters and police officers as local heroes. Ordinary people who did not
know each other offered help to those in need. Actor Robert De Niro,
owner of the Tribeca Grill, located in the immediate area of the Twin Towers, brought food by boat to serve relief and rescue workers during the
cleanup of ground zero.

A *60 Minutes* segment that aired a few weeks after 9/11 depicted the dedication of the myriad volunteers and interviewed many of them about the
reasons for getting involved. An area of common ground was that their range
of emotions—shared by many of us—moved them to act. Only in this active
way could they fully share their empathy and concern. Volunteerism in the
form of heroic rescue or philanthropy is an indispensable part of human society that has shown itself rather dramatically in these tragic events; but there is
another indispensable form of volunteerism, a form that can be counted on
day in and day out to keep the complex needs of a diverse society met.

Long before 1988, when then–President George H.W. Bush inaugurated
his administration by calling upon every American to become one of a "thousand points of light," volunteerism was a well-established tradition. At a time
when shrinking budgets were required to meet expanding social needs, the
role of volunteers had become more and more crucial to the welfare of not
only our nation but also the increasingly interconnected global society.

Therefore, this chapter has a twofold purpose: first, to look at the research on motivations of volunteers in general; and second, to compare these
results with our recent findings on hospice volunteers—those who work
with people for whom death is near.

Looking Back

Since the establishment of the first European colony on the North American
continent, there has existed a tension between the values of individualism
and care for others. The communal culture of the indigenous peoples of
North America played an important role in the newcomers' survival. De-

spite the lack of gratitude of early colonists, the religious, political, and philosophical backgrounds of the colonists gave rise to a society that was "obsessed with the value of individual freedom and achievement, yet at the same time strongly committed to the welfare of [its] fellow citizens."[1] In 1830 the French writer Alexis de Tocqueville commented on the seeming contradiction between individualism and caring for others:

> Although private interest directs the greater part of human actions in the United States, it does not regulate them all. I must say that I have often seen Americans make great and real sacrifices to the public welfare, and I have remarked a hundred instances in which they hardly ever failed to lend faithful support to each other.[2]

Colonial America was settled and run by volunteers. Until the revolutionary period, charity, medical care, education, communication, public safety, and defense were provided on a voluntary basis. Although the colonists felt they were required to care for their own, their charity did have its limitations. In Puritan New England, for example, those who gave handouts to itinerants and beggars were viewed as fools who refused to acknowledge that a person's poverty was proof of failure to live correctly.

Gradually, as urban society became more complex, paid personnel replaced volunteers, and the nineteenth century saw the development of many institutions and organized charities. The care of the sick, indigent, and mentally ill was no longer left to families but was provided by the public sector or formal charitable organizations. Frequently, the motivation was less to give comfort and security to the unfortunate than it was to separate the unruly or dangerous from society and affirm the validity of the dominant—evangelical and religious—values.

The philosophies of social Darwinism, liberalism, and the social gospel promoted volunteerism in the late nineteenth century. The plight of those who needed help was seen as the result of a combination of poor morals, poor education, and poor genes, which could best be addressed through evangelic education. The Progressive movement of the early part of the twentieth century, the New Deal programs of the Great Depression years, and the Great Society programs of the 1960s resulted in an exponential growth in public welfare programs, which have augmented rather than replaced the voluntary sector.

A somewhat simplistic view is that the result of this augmentation is a two-tiered system: the public sector entrenched in bureaucracy and serving the unworthy poor in an inefficient manner; and the private voluntary sector serving the worthy poor in a highly efficient manner. Many who espouse a limited role for government also believe that volunteers can fill jobs just as well as professionals and that the social needs of society can be adequately met using volunteers. Others maintain that volunteers can assist the public sector only in meeting the needs of its citizens and that calling for the voluntary sector to replace government programs is nothing but an attempt to eliminate programs without seeming callous to voters. This debate has continued and likely will continue for decades. What seems clear is that volunteerism can be neither legislated nor banned.

Volunteers among Us

Despite the controversy over the role volunteerism plays in American society, the practice itself is prevalent. A 1988 Gallup Poll estimated that 80 million adults engaged in volunteering the previous year; more than one-fourth devoted five or more hours per week. It is estimated that more than 15 million hours of volunteer time are given annually to hospitals, schools, civic groups, rescue squads, and so on. If these volunteers were monetarily compensated for their work, they would collectively earn approximately $200 billion annually.

In recent years there has been great interest in the study of volunteerism to understand the nature and motivation of volunteers. In the course of this recent work, prior to September 11, I estimate that I have examined more than forty empirical studies conducted by social scientists between 1984 and 1999, using a combined sample of more than 6,000 respondents. This review of the literature has resulted in pinpointing a substantial number of overlapping motivating factors—a kind of quantification of caring. Among the motivating factors are: empathy; self-efficacy; emotional stability; a high internalized standard of morality; feeling more positive about self and others; high attribution of social responsibility; high self-esteem; high scores in moral development; a strong humanitarian attitude; learned nurturance; the need for recognition; altruism; social satisfaction; self-improvement; and social expectations.

Many Americans feel a sense of a moral imperative to help better their community. They also do it for personal growth—as an opportunity to do something worthwhile, creating an opportunity for relationships, making one feel better about oneself. Personal reasons include involving themselves with a prestigious group, achieving a sense of spirituality and religiosity, or generating a feeling of commonness with all humanity. People seem to want the meaning in their lives that they find in volunteering.

The common characteristics found among volunteers are compassion, coming from a loving home, having a volunteer model, being influenced by moral role models, and the adoption of the community's social attitudes.

Who Volunteers?

Older people are especially likely to volunteer. Studies conducted in geriatric communities found that social and cultural norms advocate helping, and motivation is based on egalitarian principles and a desire to keep the community safe. Many elderly people volunteer for more practical reasons. They have more free time to give to volunteer efforts, and they have supplemental income, allowing them to be able to afford to work as volunteers. An extensive British study found that motivating factors are reciprocal beneficence; religious motivation; recognition of personal obligation to help; idealism; social ability; courage; trust; hope; natural generosity; common ties with other people; fundamental human inclination; and altruistic human power.[3] Another study reports that there is something called an *imperative to volunteer*—a cultural theme stating that Americans have an obligation—even a divine obligation—to contribute to the betterment of their community.[4]

In these studies the most frequently mentioned motivating factors were empathy and compassion, followed by social responsibility, then a sense of moral obligation and spiritual and religious reasons. Self-enhancement was the least-mentioned. The motivator seems to be most in the heart, sometimes in the head, often in the memory of traditional religious instruction, and sometimes in the metaphoric wallet.

Volunteers practice nonspontaneous helping behavior for which they receive no material compensation. Volunteerism can be parochial (within one's social group) or nonparochial. Nonparochial volunteerism is a form of conventional altruism in that it is directed at others beyond one's immediate social group and is accompanied by no external reward. Multiple motivations exist for volunteering, and altruistic motivations may coexist with egoistic ones, such as learning a job for purposes of self-enhancement.

Volunteers generally score higher on measures of empathy, social responsibility, and moral development than do nonvolunteers.

The Hospice Movement and the Role of Volunteers

In 1967 Dr. Cicely Saunders, a British nurse who later became a physician, established St. Christopher's, a medical facility for the care of the terminally ill in London. The hospice model of care developed by Dr. Saunders and others was less a new innovation in health care than it was a return to an earlier model. The name "hospice" comes from the Latin word *hospes*, meaning "guest." Like other derivations of the root word such as "hospitality," "host," "hotel," and "hospital," it connotes the ideas of kindness and generosity to strangers and travelers.

Ancient and medieval hospices were sanctuaries for poor travelers, the sick and the dying, and religious pilgrims. In the medieval period hospices were generally run by religious orders who saw the care of the poor and sick as part of the Lord's work. For many centuries hospices and hospitals were one and the same. Life was thought of as a journey from this world to the next, and all travelers were in need of comfort, whether they were journeying from one land to another or from one life to the next.

During the past century the care of the sick and dying ceased being a private and religious function and became a public, governmental one in the West.[5] Advances in medical science and technology resulted in the total transformation of medical science from a palliative model to an aggressively therapeutic one. However, in the post–World War II years, some health care professionals began to suggest that although the system was well equipped to deal with acute life-threatening situations, it was not equipped to meet the special needs of terminally ill patients. Indeed, the terminally ill patient was considered a sign of medical failure and frequently shunned by medical personnel, who were at a loss to deal with patients to whom they could not offer any hope of recovery. This medical avoidance of death was accompanied by an increasing aversion to death because it was no longer so visible. No longer was death a part of everyday life. Few people died at home, and many died all alone in hospitals, separated from their families.

St. Christopher's hospice set out to address these problems by seeking to combine the old concept of hospitality with the medical skill and technology of the modern hospital.[6] Emphasis was placed on controlling pain and other adverse symptoms. Family were incorporated into the care plans for each patient. After the death of the patient, staff continued bereavement care for the patient's family.

The writings, of Dr. Saunders and others—among them the American Dr. Elisabeth Kübler-Ross, a psychiatrist who was among the first to raise the alarm at the appalling treatment dying patients were receiving—were well received here in the United States, and by 1974 the first hospice program was operating in New Haven, Connecticut. Since that time, more than 8,000 hospice programs have been established worldwide.[7] Of those, 3,200 are in the United States and served nearly 775,000 patients in 2001.[8] Hospice programs in this country vary considerably in design, ranging from those that rely on volunteer care and charge nothing for their services, to institutionalized programs with staff who are paid by third-party payers such as Medicare, private insurance carriers, and state and local governments. Although there are some in-patient hospices in this country, home care is the norm.[9]

Hospice Volunteers

Volunteerism is a nonspontaneous helping behavior for which one receives no material compensation. It can be parochial or nonparochial. Volunteers generally score high on measures of *empathy, social responsibility*, and *moral development*.[10] Individuals are more likely to volunteer if their parents did; their parents modeled volunteerism.[11] Few groups can provide a better example of this prosocial behavior than hospice volunteers, who devote their time on a regular basis to caring for the terminally ill and their families.

The fact that hospice programs have been able to provide a high level of personal care is due to the efforts of volunteers. Nearly every hospice program employs lay people and professionals as volunteers. These volunteers are interviewed by hospice staff and, if accepted, undergo orientation and training before being assigned to patients and their families. Volunteers meet regularly with each other and with staff to discuss patient care and the problems they themselves may be facing as part of their interaction with the terminally ill and their families.

Why Do They Volunteer?
Why do they volunteer? To answer this question, ninety-three hospice volunteers from Humboldt and Marin Counties in California and the Boston

area were interviewed. In addition, we obtained information from seventy-three nonhospice volunteers. Those who worked with hospice had many reasons for volunteering—from feelings of self-enhancement, empathy, wanting to make a difference, and living their ethics. The majority of the people we interviewed (sixty-eight) gave responses that can be interpreted as *self-enhancing*, including those describing a need to confront or learn more about death; a desire to feel needed and useful; a need to develop a sense of connection to the community; and a desire for job-related experience: "I was probably trying to fill a personal need"; "I was looking for something meaningful to do"; "I sought it out to become involved in something where I was needed."

Others wanted to feel better about themselves, fill up time, or feel less lonely. Eleven individuals described their motives as "selfish": "I had a purely selfish motive in that I thought it would be a good way to get into the community"; "I needed to get away from the rather shallow, glitzy life I lived in New York." Others described how this motivation was transformed by the hospice experience: "When I first went in as a volunteer, I was trying to fill a lot of stuff in me, and now I feel like I'm more sure of who I am, and I'm able to be there as a true person, to really be there."

But the most frequent response concerned the need to confront death, because of fear or lack of knowledge. Many of these individuals also remarked on how working with hospice had led to an acceptance of death:

> I think that part of our message is that dying is part of our whole life journey. The media tells us that we never have to grow old if we use certain products, we are told we can live forever if we have enough money . . . whatever they do, it's just not accepting this wonderful right of passage that is ours. It's a gift. We've lost it.

> I've lived most of my life, but I still have some time to go. . . . But identifying what's around the corner feels good to me, seeing that death is really not such a terrible thing, that it's really the last stage in life.

A similar percentage of both high- and low-level nonhospice volunteers (low-level volunteers spent less time volunteering; high-level volunteers spent more time volunteering) gave responses that could be categorized as *self-enhancing*. Most frequent were responses that referred to enjoyment, fulfillment, and reward, followed by references to a desire to feel helpful and needed. Seventy percent of the hospice volunteers gave responses that could be thought of as *empathic*, that is, they reflected an identification with hospice patients and their needs.[12]

The most frequent of all motivations was the death of a parent, spouse, or close friend. Thirty-seven percent of the hospice volunteers included this as a motivation. Those volunteers who indicated that the experience was a negative one and who wished to spare or mitigate that negative experience for others were categorized as empathic. One woman whose husband had died of cancer commented on how the painful experience led her to volunteer: "I felt I could do something for someone that I wished I could have had when my husband died. I wanted to offer what I would have liked to have had."

Other volunteers shared their reasons for volunteering: "I am a strong believer that I am my brother's keeper I would tell young people that I truly believe that caring people can be made, not born"; "It seems like the more I give to somebody, the more I get out of it."

Three of the hospice volunteers we talked to were cancer patients themselves who knew how it felt to suffer alone and wanted to spare others that solitary pain. One woman spoke of being in the hospital for her own cancer treatment and encountering a woman who was being forced to accept treatment against her will: "I felt so sorry for this woman. She seemed so alone. And I remembered going in there not knowing if I could do anything. . . . She was in a situation that nobody understood. Nobody even cared what she was feeling." Another volunteer, a registered nurse, related an experience from her early nursing career:

> I would see nurses virtually ignoring dying patients. Giving them
> their medication, changing their beds, but avoiding any real con-
> tact. I thought, what good are we if we can't give comfort to these
> people? Whenever I had a patient who was dying I would really
> try to spend whatever free time I had, giving them sips of water,
> back rubs . . . just holding their hand. But I always had to leave
> knowing the next shift would ignore them again.

Those who cited a personal experience with the death of a significant person in their lives were equally divided between the aforementioned categories—those who wished to spare others the difficulty they themselves had experienced, and those whose experience had involved hospice, who volunteered out of a sense of gratitude and a desire to share that positive experience ("I felt I owed them an obligation to contribute whatever I could"; "I wanted to continue my association with those marvelous people who did so much for her and me too").

Volunteering is a widely accepted activity in the United States, perhaps more so than any other Western country. Thus, we posit that many volunteer because of social expectations and pressure, that is, for *normocentric* reasons in which individuals internalize the norms and values of their community. Forty-four percent of the hospice volunteers gave responses congruent with behaviors that were encouraged and modeled by their parents and community.[13]

Hospice volunteers often referred to the importance of volunteering, reflecting societal norms that helping is part of the volunteer giving back to the community for the benefits the community has shown them: "I think as you get older, you start thinking, what am I doing for my community, and you start feeling the need to just do something, to put something back." Still others said that they were directly recruited: "Some people that I knew were volunteers, and they recruited me."

The category of *principled* responses were those reflecting underlying principles or beliefs of justice and fairness.[14] The responses arise out of abstract, ethical principles, which hold that all humanity is deserving of justice, fairness, and equity and that caring and compassion should be available to all—friends and family as well as other diverse groups. The most frequent response was a strong belief in the hospice concept, as seen in the following statements:

> I had seen on several occasions how inadequate the health care system was in taking care of dying patients. I felt there had to be a better way. Hospice has a philosophy that I am very comfortable with, that is, that people have a right to live until the second they die . . . a right to live as well as we can possibly make it for them.

> I guess I thought I could make a difference in the way people died and the way they went out of this lifetime, make it a little less difficult maybe. . . . It's nice to have someone there when you need them. I'm strong, I can help.

I believe we all need a hand getting into life and we all need a
hand getting out of life.

Other responses included in this category of helping reflected a more
generalized belief that not serving others is unjust and violates universally
moral principles of justice and fairness toward those who are in need. One
respondent said, "I think it is important for people to know they are part of
a society. So many people think that what they do doesn't affect other people. There isn't anyone like that. You affect everyone, every person who
touches you or the groups you touch."

The development of the caring, altruistic individual requires setting
boundaries between right and wrong, moral and immoral, and normative
and deviant behavior. In childhood, the hospice volunteers were more likely
to have been disciplined by reasoning and less by physical means than the
nonvolunteers—a finding that echoes many conversations with rescuers and
nonrescuers in Nazi-occupied Europe.

In addition, there appears to be a cultural theme in the United States
that we have an obligation—even a divine obligation—to contribute to the
betterment of the community.[15] Throughout U.S. history, the truest form of
charity in volunteering is found in local settings, in the building of one-on-
one relationships. There is evidence that Americans give and aid others because they want to help them, especially those with whom they share their
moral community.

Sociologist Amitai Etzioni focuses on the moral community and helping and feels that volunteering is an important element of human behavior.
He says some people make moral choices based upon internalized values.[16]
There is a sense of affirming these values by helping people who have the
same moral perspectives and are involved in the same moral choice. To ignore them—for instance, to renege on a promise or to pass by a tragedy such
as the World Trade Center—is an affront to one's moral choice and moral
voice. Most individuals hear their moral voice, albeit at different levels of intensity, and those who do not hear such a voice are, in sociological terms, so-
ciopaths, says Etzioni in *The Spirit of Community: The Reinvention of
American Society*. The moral voice has two main sources that are mutually
reinforcing: The inner voice of a person relies on shared values based on education, experience, and internal development; and the external voice stems
from others' encouragement to adhere to shared values. This finding is reflective in all groups of helpers discussed in this book.

The inner moral voice emanates from the acting self, and addressing that self urges the person to abide by his or her values and to refrain from behavior that violates them. Typically the inner voice's claim takes the form of statements such as "I ought to" rather than "I would like to." Etzioni says that the inner voice fosters moral behavior by according a special sense of self when a person adheres to his or her values and of disquiet when the person does not adhere to them. Yielding to such values as "I ought" is expressed in the following story:

> Despite the nature of the work, the weekend clean-up effort took on an almost festive air. The owners of a nearby bodega offered the workers free refreshments. Fire fighters from the local station came by and suggested that the crew use their larger garbage drums. The priest from the nearby St. Luke's School came out and blessed everyone in sight. To see a community so often plagued by apathy and neglect responding in a positive way, taking care of problems on its own, was uplifting for everyone.[17]

Value affirmation affects behavior deeply. No one need pressure a person to make the moral choice or to uphold the ideals of social responsibility; compliance is voluntary. Although the moral voice is part of the inner voice and may be partly the person's personality, it is also an expression of the community to which the person belongs. Balwina felt that despite the danger to her life she had to affirm her moral value that I, too, belonged to the human community and that she ought to help me. This, Etzioni maintains, is the significance of community for the communitarian paradigm. Communities often have strong moral voices and thus can maintain social order by drawing significantly on values, commitment, and voluntary compliance rather than compliance that is bought or forced. Communities are viewed by many as social webs in which people are attached to one another by crisscrossing relationships rather than by one-on-one relationships. That is why communities are often depicted as "warm and fuzzy" places. The moral voice is the main means by which individuals and groups in a good society encourage one another to adhere to behavior that reflects shared values and avoid behavior that offends or violates them.

Etzioni also maintains that a "deep connection between the two basic elements of community—social bonds and moral voices—comes into focus: Persons heed best the moral voice of others they care about, those to whom they are affectively attached—members of their community."[18] Good behavior in society takes place because people believe it is the right way to act, and those who share this perspective validate their moral perspectives.

I have found that bonding and attachment to others in a psychologically healthy way is strongly correlated with putting the welfare of another alongside one's own.

As Iris Murdoch, Amitai Etzioni, and Robert Coles have observed, the moral life is not something that emerges suddenly in the context of traumas; rather, it arises piecemeal in the routine business of living. It begins with parents who emphasize broadly inclusive ethical values, including caring and social responsibility, which they teach in the context of loving family relationships. Thus, assuming caring roles seems to require prerehearsed scripts and previously learned skills acquired in the ordinary activities of life. If we are serious about cultivating these characteristics, then we cannot leave the job to parents alone. Other social institutions—religious, educational, and professional—must reconsider their roles, their responsibilities, and their routine behaviors. Until social institutions accept responsibility to nurture inclusive ethical commitment in a context of caring environments, it is likely that no more than a fragment of the population can be counted on to engage in volunteering and performing acts of altruism.

There is no one way to diminish the number of bystanders, but among the suggestions I would make is that we need to celebrate, publicize, and appreciate the millions of people who already help and who might serve as moral role models.

In addition to publicizing and lauding these people for their kindness, I also believe that the school system can do much to raise awareness for the need of helping and caring for others. In the United States, we have approximately 80 million students at all levels who are, in a way, captive audiences. Would it not benefit us all to devote a few hours of instruction per week to a curriculum of caring in the community and reap the satisfaction and positive results that naturally ensue from such activities? Can we help parents show their children the meaning of helping others? Can we help children share with their parents the caring they learn? Can the workplace do more to encourage volunteering and helping? Can the churches, temples, and mosques get involved in ethical action and help those in need? Can we encourage a culture of altruism to all? Can we reverse the trends of alienation, separation, and violence by getting involved with caring, compassion, and love for humanity?

I have said it elsewhere before, and I want to reemphasize that it is not an impossible dream to produce a world with a caring human face. September 11, 2001 has shown us just how human we are, how vulnerable and strong, how moral and heroic, and how much we care about each other.

10

Building a World of Care

Questions Yet to Be Explored

I am sure that a person is born with the ability to respond to another's pain. I think that this feeling is inborn, given to us along
with instincts and a soul. But if this feeling is not used, is not ex-
ercised, it weakens and atrophies.
          —Danill Granin, Russian writer, "O miloserdii"[1]

In this book I have explored the behaviors of heroic (life-threatening)
and conventional (non–life threatening) altruism in a variety of situations. What do these eight groups—the 9/11 heroes, non-Jewish and
Jewish rescuers and resisters, Carnegie and military heroes, moral exemplars,
philanthropists, and volunteers—have in common? How do they model altruistic and heroic behavior in such a way as to help us nurture it? It was my
intention to understand the variety of ways that help is given and what motivates that help.

Among the common components of heroic and altruistic behavior are:
empathy, courage, compassion, social responsibility, efficacy, caring, loving
and kindness, virtuous behavior, a religious and spiritual predisposition to
help, risk-taking (especially among the younger helpers/rescuers); these
people have internalized the norm of their moral community.[2] It should be

obvious that not all of these motivating factors are discernable in all of the groups mentioned above. Still, some of them can be seen across all the groups discussed in this book.

What is the implication of these helpers/rescuers, and what can we learn from their rich narratives? Looking at the group of individuals we interviewed, I can say, first, that ordinary people are capable of both heroic and conventional altruism and that they are ordinary members of a moral community who have internalized the ethics of caring, virtue, and social responsibility from their loved ones, as well as being in contact with other moral leaders in a certain period of their life. They have internalized the notion that persecution, oppression, and the lack of helping others is not an acceptable part of their moral universe.

Second, although parents and other role models are vital in creating moral and caring individuals, it is also crucial that institutions such as churches, schools, the military, the government, and the workplace must incorporate in their routines the expectations and appreciation for acts of caring and moral behavior toward others. This is not an unrealistic vision or mission for the future. What it would take is a concerted effort and conviction that a caring society is possible if we act to make it real.

The pervasive question throughout the chapters was, how do we foster goodness and facilitate moral action? I, along with others (see Colby and Damon), found that some common characteristics of moral exemplars were optimism, certainty, a sense of moral autonomy, and moral behavior that comes out of an interest and concern for other people and by attaching oneself to others in healthy relationships. Throughout this book, I have maintained that socialization is important to the encouragement of both good and evil. We internalize the moral precepts modeled in our families and communities. Both conventional and heroic altruists exhibit self-control and discipline as aspects of morally relevant conduct.[3]

Moral development is associated with an individual's ability to differentiate between good and evil. Psychologists speak about a healthy and loving relationship between parents and children. It is important that parents teach, as well as model, moral values. Although self-esteem is not the most significant factor in aiding a rescuer to take action, it does help; we are more likely to feel positively toward others if we like ourselves. Empathy is also a core moral value, as is one's feelings of obligation to others. Empathy becomes part of altruistic behavior only when one acts on it; just thinking empathetically is not in itself altruistic. Martin Hoffman (1970) thinks that empathy is born in the infant and that there is an innate tendency to feel another's pain.[4]

Bonding and attachment are attributes of the altruistic person, just as loving nurturing is a very important aspect of caring for others. Some psychologists say that the difference between helping and not helping others is environmental. Studies of altruism show us the effect loving parents have on a healthy self-esteem and development of a strong moral code. Altruistic tendencies are learned early in life, so it is never too early to learn the joys of giving or too early to learn that it's wrong to hurt, it's wrong to oppress, it's wrong to neglect and exclude.[5]

An altruistic person is trained to accept diverse others, to be tolerant, to have a sense of justice and to be proactive on behalf of just and fair treatment for others. A person may be placed on the path of altruism through a spiritual upbringing of the universal kind that fosters ecumenicity and consists of the belief that everyone is a part of the common universe. Along such a path are many opportunities to help build a more caring world. By encouraging self-reliance and self-confidence in people, we may manifests the notion that "yes, I can make a difference. Yes, I shall stand upon my belief that I can make a difference." Mrs. Balwina Piecuch made just such a difference in my life, and I would like to think that the generosity and care she showed me has echoed out many times over in the years since that day when she shared her determination to see to it that I should live.

The stories of heroic altruists and conventional altruists used here demonstrate that goodness is possible and that it doesn't take any superhuman effort to inculcate in people the desirability of the moral road. I reemphasize that altruistic and heroic behaviors—kindness, true neighborliness, caring, empathy, love, and compassion—are all part of the human condition and is practiced around us every day.

There is no alternative to love, encouragement, and caring; it is the process that helps human beings to flourish rather than languish. The understanding and disseminating of altruistic love is the most important item on the agenda today. Fyodor Dostoevsky asked the question, "Should we fight evil with force of humble love?" Humble love, he says, is the most powerful force in the world today. Just as love is important in the survival of newborns, so it is necessary for the survival of the planet. Altruism and altruistic love may be one of the most important antidotes to war and human antagonism.

Goodness, like evil, is teachable, and the results of such teaching are measurable.

In my own teaching I try to share with students ample evidence that helping others and putting the welfare of others alongside their own is psychologically and physically healthy for them and that there are negative consequences of indifference to other people's plights.

How do we create a world where caring is the norm? How do we invest each of our social institutions with the values, procedures, and expectations that encourage cooperation and tolerance? How do we honor our heroes of popular culture without dishonoring our heroic altruists? Should we broaden our definition of "heroism" to include others among the heroes, such as mothers and fathers who love, care, nurture, and struggle on behalf of their offspring? Should we include other "noble" professions such as nursing, social work, and others who toil to help people cope with adversity? How about the 100 million–plus volunteers who give of their time and energy to help those in need? What about the protectors of the environment? Too often, in a complex society, one person's hero is another person's impediment or worse. Should we try somehow to convince the powerful media to commemorate, celebrate, and publicize random acts of kindness, in order to balance the daily potential of violence and selfishness in our evening news? A recent study from Oklahoma State University analyzed the number of hours children and adults watch television, and their findings conclude that children spend, on average, 1,500 hours per year watching television while they spend only 900 hours in school per year. Furthermore, children watch 200,000 acts of violence on television by the time they are eighteen years old, 16,000 of those being acts of murder. They are being bombarded with these images of violence and destruction.

Does bad news foster bad behavior? Would good news foster good behavior?

We need to model caring in the workplace, where tens of millions of us spend a third of our lives; in schools, where our children learn crucial life lessons along with their history, science, and math; in churches, where so many of history's bleakest chapters have been read; and in families, where it is too easy to strike out with anger and impatience at the one nearby.

I can only hope that people who share my vision for a more caring world will take this research and move it forward by designing caring curriculums, workplace procedures, and ways to invest their daily lives with good works. I can only hope that they will help young people select positive and moral models to emulate and help them find the goodness of right and the rightness of good. One of the heroic altruists that I interviewed had a poem prominently displayed on his desk. The poem seems to speak to my purpose in this book and to express some of my own feelings, I like to think:

I shall pass this way but once.
Any good that I can do, or any kindness
that I can show, let it be now.
Let me not defer or neglect it, for
I shall not pass this way again.

Albert Einstein expressed best my deep feeling about our craving for a better future:

A human being is a part of the whole, called by us "universe," a part limited in time and space. He experiences himself, his thoughts and feelings, as something separate from the rest— a kind of optical delusion of his consciousness. This delusion is a kind of prison for us, restricting us to our personal decisions and to affection for a few persons nearest to us. Our task must be to free ourselves from this prison by widening our circle of compassion to embrace all living creatures and the whole nature in its beauty.

I have seen and experienced a world of cruelty and uncaring. I also know that helping in hundreds of different ways is psychologically and physically beneficial to the helper. One can "feel well by doing good." As for myself, I have tried to live a caring life—and to be helpful to others. Perhaps my own personal losses have turned me in the direction of studying the nature of goodness, for that dark beginning made me yearn for light, and goodness is indeed the light of the world.

Bibliography

A&E Television Networks. 1996. *History Undercover: Diplomats for the Damned.* New York: New Video Group.

Abelson, Reed. 2000. "New Philanthropists Put Donations to Work." *New York Times*, July 6, pp. C1, C23.

Abramowitz, Molly. 1974. *Elie Wiesel: A Bibliography.* Metuchen, NJ: Scarecrow Press.

Adams, D. S. 1990. "Issues and Ideas in the Culture of American Volunteerism." Paper presented at the annual meeting of the American Sociological Association, Washington, DC. August.

Aikman, David. 1998. *Great Souls: Six Who Changed the Century.* Nashville, TN: Word Publishing.

Ainsztein, Reuben. 1974. *Jewish Resistance in Nazi-Occupied Eastern Europe.* New York: Barnes and Noble Books.

Al-Rashid, Moudhy. 1999. "Gibbon Lectures in Modern Heroism." *News* 120, 6, November 5. Retrieved June 18, 2001, http://www.lawrenceville.org/special/thelawrence/99/11_5_99/0.html.

Alderson, Bernard. 1905. *Andrew Carnegie: The Man and His Work.* Boston: Northeastern University Press.

Allen, N., and J. Phillippe Rushton. 1983. "Personality Characteristics of Community Mental Health Volunteers: A Review." *Journal of Voluntary Action Research* 12, 1: 36–49.

"The Amazon Still Needs Chico Mendes." 1998. Editorial. *San Francisco Chronicle*, December 31, p. A21.

American Legion. 2001. "Petition to Honor Rick Rescorla: One of the Heroes at the World Trade Center." Scottsdale, AZ: Sipe-Peterson Post 44. Retrieved May 9, 2002, http://www.post44.org/misc.rescorla. html.

Anand, Vidya. 1999. "Indian Heroes and Heroines of World War II." Retrieved August 21, 2000, http://www6.meer.net/Book/warHero. html.

Anderson, Leona. 1998. "Contextualizing Philanthropy in South Asia: A Textual Analysis of Sanskrit Sources." Pp. 57–78 in *Philanthropy in the World's Tradi-*

tions, edited by Warren F. Ilchman, Stanley N. Katz, and Edward L. Queen II. Bloomington: Indiana University Press.

Angers, Trent. 1999. *The Forgotten Hero of My Lai: The Hugh Thompson Story.* Lafayette, LA: Acadian House Publishing.

Arthur, Max. 2000. "Ganju Lama VC." *The Independent,* July 24, p.6.

Associated Press. 1998a. "Medals for My Lai Heroes Who Halted the Massacre." *San Francisco Chronicle,* March 7, p. A3.

————. 1998b. "Residents of an Apartment Watch a Fatal Beating." *New York Times,* March 29, p. A14.

————. 1999. "The Massacre at My Lai." *Newsweek,* March 8, p. 64.

Attenborough, Richard. [1986] 1998. "Mother Teresa." Videotape. Leonard Maltin, Producer. New York: Signet, a Division of Penguin Putnam.

BBC News. 2001. "Profile: Hero of the Twin Towers." December 15. Retrieved May 9, 2002, http://news.bbc.co.uk.

Bachner, Wilhelm. Interview with the author. July 15, 1982.

Bacon, Gary. 1982. *Essential Education: Drawing Forth the Golden Child.* Palo Alto, CA: Rainbow Bridge.

Banks, Judith M. 1994. "Decorated Commissioned Officers from the Vietnam War: A Study of Heroism." Ph.D. diss., Institute for Clinical Social Work, Chicago.

Barash, Ronit Kishon. 1995. "Factors Associated with Two Facets of Altruism in Vietnam War Veterans with Post-Traumatic Stress Disorder." UMI Microform # 9606908, Ann Arbor, MI.

Barkai, Meyer, ed. and trans. 1962. *The Fighting Ghettos.* New York: Tower Publications.

Barnett, Victoria J. 1999. *Bystanders: Conscience and Complicity in the Holocaust.* Westport, CT: Greenwood Publishing.

Baron, Lawrence. 1985–1986. "The Holocaust and Human Decency: A Review of Research on the Rescue of Jews in Nazi-Occupied Europe." *Humboldt Journal of Social Relations* 13, 1–2: 237–251.

————. 1988. "The Historical Context of Rescue." Pp. 13–48 in *The Altruistic Personality,* edited by Samuel P. Oliner and Pearl M. Oliner. New York: The Free Press.

————. 1992. "The Dutchness of Dutch Rescuers: The National Dimension of Altruism." Pp. 306–327 in *Embracing the Other: Philosophical, Psychological, and Historical Perspectives on Altruism,* edited by Pearl M.Oliner, Samuel P. Oliner, Lawrence Baron, Lawrence A. Blum, Dennis L. Krebs, and M. Zuzanna Smolenska. New York: New York University Press.

Barrett, Richard. 2000. "Seven Levels of Corporate Philanthropy: Making Money While Making a Difference." Article Excerpt. Waynesville, NC: Paraview.com. Retrieved July 11, 2001, http://www.paraview.com/pages/sectionarticlepages1/sevenlevels.htm.

Bartoszewski, W., M. Edelman, M. Halter, J. Karski, V. Meed, and I. Sendler. 1993. "Warsaw Ghetto Uprising." *Dimensions: A Journal of Holocaust Studies* (published by the Anti-Defamation League's Braun Center for Holocaust Studies) 7, 2: 3–39.

Baruch, Joel A.B. 1972. "Combat Death." *Suicide and Life-Threatening Behavior* 2, 3: 209–216.

Batson, C. Daniel. 1991. *The Altruism Question.* Hillsdale, NJ: Lawrence Erlbaum Associates.

Bauer, Yehuda. 1981. "Jewish Leadership Reactions to Nazi Policies." Pp. 173–192 in *The Holocaust as Historical Experience*, edited by Y. Bauer and N. Rotenstreich. New York: Holmes and Meier.

Bauer, Yehuda, and Nili Keren. 1982. *A History of the Holocaust.* New York: Franklin Watts.

Baum, Geraldine. 2002. *Running Toward Danger: Stories Behind the Breaking News of 9/11.* New York: Rowman and Littlefield.

Baumel, Judith Tydor. 1998. "The Parachutists' Mission from a Gender Perspective." Pp. 95–113 in *Resisting the Holocaust*, edited by Ruby Rohrlich. New York: Berg Publishers.

Beamer, Lisa. 2002. *Let's Roll: Ordinary People, Extraordinary Courage.* London: Tyndale Press.

Belenky, Gregory, Shabtai Noy, and Zahava Solomon. 1987. "Battle Stress, Morale, Cohesion, Combat Effectiveness, Heroism, and Psychiatric Casualties: The Israeli Experience." *Contemporary Studies in Combat Psychiatry: Contributions in Military Studies* 62: 11–20. Edited by Gregory Belensky. New York: Greenwood Press.

Bel Monte, Kathryn. 1998. *African-American Heroes and Heroines: 150 True Stories of African-American Heroism.* Hollywood, FL: Lifetime Books.

Berenbaum, Michael. 1993. *The World Must Know: The History of the Holocaust as Told in the United States Holocaust Memorial Museum.* Boston: Little, Brown.

Berenbaum, Michael, and Abraham J. Peck, eds. 1998. *The Holocaust, and History: The Known, The Unknown, The Disputed, and The Reexamined.* Bloomington: Indiana University Press. Published in association with the United States Holocaust Memorial Museum.

Berkowitz, Bill. 1987. *Local Heroes: Rebirth of Heroism in America.* Lexington, MA: Lexington Books.

Berkowitz, Leonard, and K. Luterman. 1968. "The Traditionally Socially Responsible Personality." *Public Opinion Quarterly* 32: 169–185.

Berkowitz, Leonard, and J. R. Macaulay, eds. 1970. *Altruism and Helping Behavior.* New York: Academic Press.

Bernstein, Richard. 2002. *Out of the Blue: A Narrative of September 11, 2001.* New York: Henry Holt.

Berson, Robin Kadison. 1999. *Young Heroes in World History.* Westport, CT: Greenwood Press.

Bertha, Carlos. 2001. "Moral Psychology in Times of War." Work in progress. Retrieved on April 25, 2001, http://www.usafa.af..mil/dfpfa/CVs/Bertha/Psyhero.html.

Blake, Joseph A. 1978. "Death by Hand Grenade: Altruistic Suicide in Combat." *Suicide and Life-Threatening Behavior* 8, 1: 47–59.

Blum, Lawrence A. 1980. *Friendship, Altruism, and Morality*. London: Routledge and Kegan Paul.

Blumenthal, David R. 1999. *The Banality of Good and Evil: Moral Lessons from the Shoah and Jewish Tradition*. Washington, DC: Georgetown University Press.

Blustein, Paul. 1994. "Japan's Savior of the Jews." *San Francisco Chronicle*, October 16, p. 6.

Breton, Mary Joe. 1998. *Women Pioneers for the Environment*. Boston: Northeastern University Press.

Brody, Seymour. 1996. *Jewish Heroes and Heroines of America: 150 True Stories of American Jewish Heroism*. Hollywood, FL: Lifetime Books.

Brown, Robert McAfee. 1983. *Elie Wiesel: Messenger to All Humanity*. Notre Dame, IN: University of Notre Dame Press.

Buckingham, Robert. 1983. *The Complete Hospice Guide*. New York: Harper and Row.

Burkeman, Steven. 1999. "An Unsatisfactory Company. . . ?" Lecture delivered to the Allen Lane Foundation. Retrieved July 11, 2001, http://www.allenlane.demon.co.uk/newpage2.htm.

CBS News Video. 2001. "Port Authority." Friday, October 19.

Calandra, Bob. 1999. "Why They Do It." P. 141 of "Heroes Among Us." *People Weekly*, November 22. Written by R. Jerome, S. Schindehette, N. Charles, and T. Fields-Meyer. New York: Time.

Campbell, Joseph. 1968. *Hero with a Thousand Faces*, 2nd ed., Bollingen Series XVII. Princeton, NJ: Princeton University Press.

Capri, D. 1977. "The Rescue of Jews in the Italian Zone of Occupied Croatia." Pp. 465–525 in *Rescue Attempts During the Holocaust: Proceedings of the Second Yad Vashem International Historical Conference*, edited by Y. Gutman and E. Zuroff. Jerusalem, April 8–11, 1974.

Carnegie, Andrew. [1920] 1986. *The Autobiography of Andrew Carnegie: With a New Foreword by Cecelia Tichi*. Reprint, Boston: Northeastern University Press.

Carnegie Hero Fund Commission. 1997. Pittsburgh, PA. Retrieved November 26, 1997, http://trfn.clpgh.org/carnegiehero.

————. 1999. Pittsburgh, PA. Retreived March 5, 1999, http://trfn.clpgh.org/carnegiehero.

Chang, Iris. 1997. *The Rape of Nanking: The Forgotten Holocaust of World War II*. New York: Penguin USA.

Charny, Israel, ed. 1999. *Encyclopedia of Genocide*, vols. 1–2. Santa Barbara, CA: ABC-CLIO.

Cnaan, Ram A., Amy Kasternakis, and Robert J. Wineburg. 1993. "Religious People, Religious Congregations, and Volunteerism in Human Services: Is There a Link?" *Nonprofit and Voluntary Sector Quarterly* 22, 1: 33–51.

Cohen, Rich. 2000. *The Avengers: A Jewish War Story*. New York: Alfred A. Knopf.

Colby, Anne, and William Damon. 1992. *Some Do Care: Contemporary Lives of Moral Commitment*. New York: The Free Press.

Coles, Robert. 1989. *The Call of Stories: Teaching and the Moral Imagination*. Boston: Houghton Mifflin.

_____. 2000. *Lives of Moral Leadership*. New York: Random House.

Congressional Medal of Honor Society. 1998a. "President Clinton Presenting James L. Day, MGen (Ret), USMC, the Medal of Honor. At the White House, January 20, 1998." Washington, DC. Retrieved May 31, 1999, http://www.awod.com/gallery/probono/cmhs/Day.htm.

_____. 1998b. "President Clinton Presenting Robert R. Ingram the Medal of Honor. At the White House, July 10, 1998." Washington, DC. Retrieved May 31, 1999, http://www.awod.com/gallery/probono/cmhs/ingram.htm.

_____. 1999. "World War II Black Medal of Honor Recipients." Washington, DC. Retrieved May 26, 1999, http://www2.army.mil/cmh-pg/mohb.htm.

"Courage at My Lai." 1998. Editorial. *San Francisco Chronicle*, March 6, p. A22.

Curtis, Bill. 1998. "The Angel of Bergen-Belsen." *Investigative Reports*. New York: A&E Television Networks.

Dalai Lama. 1984. *Kindness, Clarity, and Insight: The Fourteenth Dalai Lama, His Holiness Tenzin Gyatso*. Translated by Jeffrey Hopkins. Edited by Jeffrey Hopkins and Elizabeth Napper. Ithaca, NY: Snow Lion Publications.

_____. 1999. *Ethics for the New Millennium*. New York: Riverhead Books.

_____. 2001. *An Open Heart: Practicing Compassion in Everyday Life*. Boston: Little, Brown.

Dalai Lama and Howard C. Cutler. 1998. *The Art of Happiness: A Handbook for Living*. New York: Riverhead Books.

Davidson, Dennis. 1999. "Words of Faith: Dalai Lama Teaches Love, Kindness." *Desert Sun*, March 20, p. D6.

de Souza, Nick. 2001. "Sweet Charity." *World Link*, March/April: 42–43.

Doherty, Kiernan. 1998. *Congressional Medal of Honor Recipients*. Springfield, NJ: Enslow Publishers.

Drucker, Susan J., and Robert Cathcart, eds. 1994. *American Heroes in a Media Age*. Kresskill, NJ: Hampton Press.

Duckwitz, Georg Ferdinand. "Germany." Retrieved May 7, 2001, http://www.yad-vashem.org.il/right. . . many/duckwitz_georg_ ferdinand.html.

Duff, Eric. Interview with the author. January 10, 2000.

Eagly, Alice H., and Maureen Crowley. 1986. "Gender and Helping Behavior: A Meta-Analytic Review of the Social Psychological Literature." *Psychological Bulletin* 100: 283–308.

Edgerton, Robert B. 2001. *Hidden Heroism: Black Soldiers in America's Wars*. Boulder: Westview Press.

Eisenberg, Nancy. 1986. *Altruistic Emotion, Cognition, and Behavior*. Hillsdale, NJ: Lawrence Erlbaum Associates.

Eisenberg, Nancy, and Janet Strayer, eds. 1990. *Empathy and Its Development*, 2nd ed. Cambridge, MA: Cambridge University Press.

Electronic Telegraph Reporter, "Call for Israel to honour forgotten British hero." Issue 1317, January 2, 1999. Retrieved April 18, 2001 http://www.cnwl. igs.net/~zes/foleyspy.htm

Eliach, Yaffa. 1990. "Women of Valor: Partisans and Resistance Fighters." *Center for Holocaust Studies Newsletter* 4: 6.

_____. 1998. *There Once Was a World: A Nine-Hundred-Year Chronicle of the Shtetl of Eishyshok*. Boston: Little, Brown.

Elliott, Lawrence. 1997. "Heroine in Hell." *Readers Digest*, November, pp. 75–80.

Ellis, Susan J., and Katherine H. Noyes. 1990. *By the People: A History of Americans as Volunteers*. San Francisco: Jossey-Bass Publishers

Etzioni, Amitai. 1993. *The Spirit of Community: The Reinvention of American Society*. New York: Touchstone Books.

_____. 1996. *The New Golden Rule: Community and Morality in a Democratic Society*. New York: Basic Books.

Evans, Reverend Todd. Interview with the author. June 7, 2001.

Fischman, Walter Ian. 1964. "The Friar Who Saved 5,000 Jews." *Look Magazine*, December 1, pp. 67–71.

Fogelman, Eva. 1994. *Conscience and Courage: Rescuers of Jews During the Holocaust*. New York: Doubleday.

Ford, Joseph B., Michel P. Richard, and Palmer C. Talbutt. 1996. *Sorokin and Civilization: A Centennial Assessment*. New Brunswick, NJ: Transaction Publishers.

Forward, David C. 1994. *Heroes After Hours: Extraordinary Acts of Employee Volunteerism*. San Francisco: Jossey-Bass.

Foundation Center. 2001. Foundation Center Statistical Services. Retrieved May 21, 2001, http://fdncenter.org.

Free the Children. 2000. Ontario, Canada. Retrieved August 25, 2000, http://www. freethechildren.org/low/ftccraig.html.

Fried, Amy. 1997. "Gendered Heroism, Limited Politics." *Women and Politics* 17, 2: 43–75.

Fry, Varian. [1968] 1992. *Assignment: Rescue—An Autobiography*. With an introduction by Dr. Albert O. Hirschman. Published in conjunction with the United States Holocaust Memorial Museum. New York: Scholastic.

Gal, Reuven. 1987. "Combat Stress as an Opportunity: The Case of Heroism." Pp. 31–45 in *Contemporary Studies in Combat Psychiatry: Contributions in Military Studies*, Number 62, edited by Gregory Belenky. New York: Greenwood Press.

_____. 1995. "Personality and Intelligence in the Military: The Case of Military Heroes." Pp. 727–737 in *International Handbook of Personality and Intelligence*, edited by Donald H. Saklofske and Moshe Zeidner. New York: Plenum Press.

Gal, Reuven, and Richard Gabriel. 1992. "Battlefield Heroism in the Israeli Defense Force." *International Social Science Review* 57, 4: 232–235.

Gandhi Speaks . . . Selections from His Writings. Self-Realization Fellowship Lake Shrine pamphlet. Pacific Palisades, CA, p. 9.

Geier, Arnold. 1993. *Heroes of the Holocaust*. Miami, FL: Londonbooks/USA.

Gerard, David. 1985. "What Makes a Volunteer?" *New Society* 74: 1193.

Gershanik, Ana. 2001. "Hispanic Community Joins in Relief Effort." *Times-Picayune*, September 27. Retrieved October 22, Lexis-Nexus Academic Universe.

Gertel, Rabbi Elliot B. 1998. "See 'The Angel of Bergen-Belsen.'" *Post and Opinion*, March 11, p. NAT5.

Goldberger, Leo. 1987. *The Rescue of the Danish Jews: Moral Courage Under Stress*. New York: New York University Press.

Goldstein, Richard. 1999. "James Logan Is Dead at 78; Winner of the Medal of Honor." *New York Times*, October 14, p. A26.

Greenberg, Joel. 1999. "Crisis in the Balkans: Refugees; An Indebted Israel Shelters Family of Kosovo Albanians." *New York Times*, May 2, p. A1.

Grim, John. 1998. "A Comparative Study in Native American Philanthropy." Pp. 25–53 in *Philanthropy in the World's Traditions,* edited by Warren F. Ilchman, Stanley N. Katz, and Edward L. Queen II. Bloomington: Indiana University Press.

Gurin, G., P. Gurin, and B. M. Morrison. 1978. "Personal and Ideological Aspects of Internal and External Control." *Social Psychology* 41, 4: 275–296.

Gushee, David P. 1994. *The Righteous Gentiles of the Holocaust: A Christian Interpretation*. Minneapolis, MN: Fortress Press.

Gutman, Israel. 1985. *The Heroism of the Jewish People in the Second World War*. Translated by Dr. Meir Katz. Tel Aviv: International Quiz on Heroism of the Jewish People.

————. 1990. *Encyclopedia of the Holocaust*, vols. 3–4. New York: MacMillan Publishing.

Gutman, Israel, and Shmuel Krakowski. 1986. *Unequal Victims: Poles and Jews During World War II*. Translated by Ted Gorelick and Witold Jedlicki. New York: Holocaust Library.

Gutman, Y., and E. Zuroff, eds. 1977. *Rescue Attempts During the Holocaust*. Jerusalem: Yad Vashem.

Halberstam, David. 2002. *Firehouse*. New York: Hyperion.

Hallie, Philip. 1979. *Lest Innocent Blood Be Shed*. New York: Harper and Row.

Hastings, Max. 1987. *The Korean War*. New York: Simon and Schuster.

Hay, Peter. 1989. *Ordinary Heroes: The Life and Death of Chana Szenes, Israel's National Heroine*. New York: Paragon House.

Hellman, Peter. 1980. *Avenue of the Righteous*. New York: Atheneum.

Herzer, Ivo. 1989. *The Italian Refuge: Rescue of Jews During the Holocaust*. Washington, DC: Catholic University of America Press.

Hilberg, Raul. 1973. *The Destruction of the European Jews*. 1st New Viewpoints ed. New York: Franklin Watts.

Hill, Julia Butterfly. 2000. *The Legacy of Luna: The Story of a Tree, a Woman, and the Struggle to Save the Redwoods*. San Francisco: HarperCollins Publishers.

————. Interview with the author. March 3, 2000.

History Channel and MPR Film. "Hitler's Holocaust: The Final Toll." Videotape aired June 19, 2000. Und Furnesh Produktion.

Hoffman, Martin L. 1970. "Parents, Discipline, and Child's Consideration for Others." *Child Development* 34: 573–588.

Hogan, R. 1969. "Development of an Empathetic Scale." *Journal of Consulting and Clinical Psychology* 33: 307–316.

Hook, Sidney. 1943. *The Hero in History*. Boston: Beacon Press.

Horwitz, Gordon J. 1990. *In the Shadow of Death: Living Outside the Gates of Mauthausen*. New York: The Free Press.

Houtz, Jolayne. 2001. "Local Donations at $30.8 Million." *Seattle Times*. September 23.

Huneke, Douglas K. 1985. *The Moses of Rovno: The Stirring Story of Fritz Graebe, a German Christian Who Risked His Life to Lead Hundreds of Jews to Safety During the Holocaust*. New York: Dodd, Mead.

————. 1986. "The Lessons of Herman Graebe's Life: The Origins of a Moral Person." *Humboldt Journal of Social Relations* 13, 1–2: 320–332.

————. 1995. *The Stones Will Cry Out: Pastoral Reflections on the Shoah (with Liturgical Resources)*. Westport, CT: Greenwood Press.

Hunt, Morton. 1990. *The Compassionate Beast: What Science Is Discovering about the Humane Side of Mankind*. New York: William Morrow.

Ilchman, Warren, Stanley N. Katz, and Edward L. Queen II, eds. 1998. *Philanthropy in the World's Traditions*. Bloomington: Indiana University Press.

Ingram, Catherine. 1990. *The Footsteps of Gandhi: Conversations with Spiritual, Social Activists*. Berkeley: Parallax Press.

Jaffe, Carolyn, and Carol H. Ehrlich. 1997. *All Kinds of Love: Experiencing Hospice*. Amityville, NY: Baywood Publishing.

Jeffries, Vincent. 1998. "Virtue and the Altruistic Personality." *Sociological Perspectives* 41, 1: 151–166.

Jones, David H. 1999. *Moral Responsibility in the Holocaust: A Study in the Ethics of Character*. Lanham, MD: Rowman and Littlefield.

Jones, Stanley E. 1976. *Gandhi: Portrayal of a Friend*. Nashville, TN: Abingdon Press.

Karski, Jan. 1944. *Story of a Secret State*. Boston: Houghton Mifflin.

Kassof, Anita. *Varian Fry and the Emergency Rescue Committee: A Resource Guide for Teachers*. Washington, DC: Holocaust Teacher Resource Center. Retrieved May 5, 2000, http://www.holocausttrc.org/ fry.htm.

Kent, George. 1962. "200,000 Persecutions Prevented." *Together*, February, p. 169.

Kerrey, J. Robert. 2002. *When I Was a Young Man*. New York: Harcourt Publishers.

King, Dr. Martin Luther, Jr. 1963. *Strength in Love*. Philadelphia: Fortress Press.

————. [1963] 1997. *I Have a Dream*. New York: Scholastic Press.

Kirsch, Steve. 2000. "The State of Small Business: The Good-Deed Doer." *Inc Magazine*, May 15, p. 140.

Knauer, Kelly, ed. 1996. *Time: Great People of the 20th Century*. New York: Time Books.

Kohlberg, L. 1976. "Moral State and Moralization: The Cognitive-Development Approach." In *Moral Development and Behavior: Theory, Research, and Social Issues,* edited by T. Lickona. New York: Holt.

Kohn, Alfie. 1990. *The Brighter Side of Human Nature.* New York: Basic Books.

Konarzewski, K., and G. Zychlinska. 1978. "The Effect of Psychological Differentiation and Perceived Similarity on Allocentric Behavior." *Psychologia Wychowawcza* 1: 21–36 (in Polish).

Korczak, Janusz. 1978. *The Ghetto Diary.* New York: Holocaust Library.

_____. 1986. *King Matt the First.* Translated by Richard Lourie. New York: Farrar, Straus, and Giroux.

Kranzler, David. 2000. *The Man Who Stopped the Train to Auschwitz: George Mantello, El Salvador, and Switzerland's Finest Hour.* Syracuse, NY: Syracuse University Press.

Krebs, Dennis L., and Frank van Hesteren. 1992. "The Development of Altruistic Personality." Pp. 142–169, in *Embracing the Other: Philosophical, Psychological, and Historical Perspectives on Altruism,* edited by Pearl M. Oliner, Samuel P. Oliner, Lawrence Bacon, Lawrence A. Blum, Dennis L. Krebs, and M. Zuzanna Smolenska. New York: New York University Press.

Lampe, David. 1957. *The Danish Resistance.* New York: Ballentine Books.

Land-Weber, Ellen. 2000. *To Save a Life: Stories of Holocaust Rescue.* Urbana, IL: University of Illinois Press.

Langsam, Yehezkel, "American Gathering of Jewish Holocaust Survivors, " in *Together,* January 1999, 13, 1: p.16. See also David S. Wyman, 1998. *The Abandonment of the Jews: America and the Holocaust, 1941–1945.* New York: The New Press; Seymour Brody's (1996) *Jewish Heroes and Heroines of America: 150 True Stories of American Jewish Heroism.*

Latour, Anny. 1981. *The Jewish Resistance in France, 1940–1944.* Translated by Irene R. Ilton. New York: Holocaust Library.

Lazare, Lucien. 1994. *Rescue as Resistance: How Jewish Organizations Fought the Holocaust in France.* Translated by Jeffrey M. Green. New York: Columbia University Press.

Lesy, Michael. 1991. *Rescues: The Lives of Heroes.* New York: Farrar, Straus, and Giroux.

Levai, Jeno. [1948] 1988. *Raoul Wallenberg: His Remarkable Life, Heroic Battles, and the Secret of His Mysterious Disappearance.* Translated by Frank Vajda. Melbourne, Australia: WhiteAnt Occasional Publishing.

Liberman, Kenneth. 1986. "Tibetan Cultural Praxis: Bodhicitta Thought Training." *Humboldt Journal of Social Relations* 13, 1–2: 113–126.

Life, A Commemorative. 2001. *In the Land of the Free: September 11—And After.* New York: Time.

Lifton, Betty Jean. 1988. *The King of Children: A Biography of Janusz Korczak.* New York: Farrar, Straus, and Giroux.

Lifton, R. J. 1986. *The Nazi Doctors: Medical Killing and the Psychology of Genocide.* New York: Basic Books.

Lindenmeyr, Adele. 1998. "From Repression to Revival: Philanthropy in 20th Century Russia." Pp. 309–331 in *Philanthropy in the World's Traditions,* edited by Warren F. Ilchman, Stanley N. Katz, and Edward L. Queen II. Bloomington: Indiana University Press.

Lipson, Carol. 1999. "A Lesson in Courage." *Together*, January, p. 9.

Lois, Jennifer. 2000. "Heroic Efforts: The Emotional Culture of Search and Rescue Volunteers." Ph.D. diss., Department of Sociology, University of Colorado, Boulder.

LoMascolo, Anna F. 1999. "Toward a Sociological Understanding of Heroic Behavior: A Focus on Carnegie Heroes." Unpublished Master's Thesis, Department of Sociology, Humboldt State University, Arcata, CA.

Longman, Jere. 2002. *Among the Heroes: United Flight 93 and the Passengers and Crew Who Fought Back*. New York: HarperCollins.

Mark, Ber. 1976. *Uprising in the Warsaw Ghetto*. New York: Schocken Books.

Martin, Mike. 1994. *Virtuous Giving: Philanthropy, Voluntary Service, and Caring*. Bloomington: Indiana University Press.

Martin, William. 1991. *A Prophet with Honor: The Billy Graham Story*. New York: William Morrow.

Matter, Joseph Allen. 1974. *Love, Altruism, and World Crisis: The Challenge of Pitirim Sorokin*. Chicago: Nelson-Hall.

McFadden, Robert D. 1993. "Subway Hero Downplays Bravery." *New York Times*, May 18, p.7.

McGeary, Johanna, and Karen Tumulty 2001. "32 Years after Leaving Vietnam, Bob Kerrey Admits a Terrible Secret—And Stands Accused of Worse. The Tangled Tale Embodies the Madness of Vietnam." *Time.com*. Retrieved June 28, 2002, http://www.time.com/time/pacific/magazine/20010507/cover1.html.

Mehrabian, A., and N. A. Epstein. 1972. "A Measure of Emotional Empathy." *Journal of Personality* 40: 525–543.

Meyer, Ernie. 1989. "Rescue in Budapest." *Jerusalem Post International Edition*, October 7, pp. 9, 14.

Meyerhof, Walter. 1998. "Recognition of Varian Fry, the 'American Schindler'." *Stanford University Physics Newsletter*, November, p. 5. BBC Online, 2001. *The Artist's Schindler*, June 8. Retrieved June 10, 2001, http://www.bbc.co.uk/works/s3/fry.

Microsoft Encarta. 1995. "Mother Teresa of Calcutta (1910–1997)." Retrieved June 16, 1999, http://www.netsrq.com/~dbois/m-teresa.html.

Midlarsky, M. I. 1981. "Helping During the Holocaust: The Role of Political, Theological, and Socioeconomic Identifications." *Humboldt Journal of Social Relations* 13, 1–2: 285–305.

Mikaelian, Allen. 2002. *Medal of Honor: Profile of America's Military Heroes from the Civil War to the Present*. New York: Hyperion.

Mill, John Stuart. 1990. *The Autobiography of John Stuart Mill*. Garden City, NY: Doubleday.

Mille Lac Band of Ojibwe Indians. 1996. *A Hero's Voice*. Onamia, MN.

Miller, William Ian. 2000. *The Mystery of Courage*. Cambridge: Harvard University Press.

Mollison, Andrew. 2001. Cox Washington Bureau. "Sept. 11 Gifts Top $1 Billion, Much to Red Cross." *Atlanta Journal and Constitution*, October 18, p. A6.

Monroe, Kristin Renwick. 1996. *The Heart of Altruism*. Princeton, NJ: Princeton University Press.

Moore, Frank. 1997. *Women of the War: Two Stories of Brave Women in the Civil War*. Hartford, CT: Blue/Gray Book.

Murdock, Iris. [1970] 1985. *The Sovereignty of Good*. London: Ark Paperbacks.

Murphy, Dean E. 2002. *September 11: An Oral History*. New York: Doubleday.

Nakatsu, R. Russell. [1995] 2001. "Silent Warriors—Silent Heroes." Retrieved June 18, 2001, http://sun.kent.wednet.edu/KSD/SJ/ Nikkei/SilentHeroes.html.

New York Times. 2002. *Portraits 9/11/01*. New York: Times Books.

New Yorker Video. 1990. "A Film by Andrzej Wajda: Karzak." In Polish. New York: New Yorker Film Artworks.

Nielsen, Waldemar A. 1985. *The Golden Donors: A New Anatomy of the Great Foundations*. New York: Truman Talley Books/E.P. Dutton.

Nobel Peace Prize Conference. 1989. Citation presented October 5, Oslo, Norway.

Noble, Kathleen. 1994. *The Sound of Silver Horn: Reclaiming the Heroism in Contemporary Women's Lives*. New York: Fawcett Columbine.

Noddings, Nel. 1984. *Caring: A Feminine Approach to Ethics and Moral Education*. Berkeley: University of California Press.

Nolte, Carl. 2001. "Carlos C. Ogden Remembered for Daring Assault During Normandy." *San Francisco Chronicle*, June 24, p. A27.

O'Connell, Brian, ed. 1983. *America's Voluntary Spirit*. New York: Foundation's Center.

Odent, Michel. 1999. *The Scientification of Love*. London: Free Association Books.

Oliner, Pearl M., and Samuel P. Oliner. 1995. *Toward a Caring Society*. Westport, CT: Praeger Publishers.

Oliner, Pearl M., Samuel P. Oliner, Lawrence Baron, Lawrence A. Blum, Dennis L. Krebs, and M. Zuzanna Smolenska, eds. 1992. *Embracing the Other: Philosophical, Psychological, and Historical Perspectives on Altruism*. New York: New York University Press.

———. 1999. "Rescuers of Jews in Nazi Europe." Pp. 496–499 in *Encyclopedia Of Genocide, Volume II*, edited by Israel Charny. Santa Barbara, CA: Institute on the Holocaust and Genocide.

Oliner, Samuel P. 1993a. "The Altruistic Personality: Rescuers of Jews in Nazi Europe." Paper presented at the Prosocial Behavior Conference, University of Arkansas, Little Rock, Arkansas.

———. 1993b. "So That Others May Live: A Psycho-Historical Study of Heroic Jewish Rescue in Nazi-Occupied Europe." Paper presented to Rider College, Lawrence Hill, NJ, March.

———. 2000. *Narrow Escapes: A Boy's Holocaust Memories and Their Legacy*. St. Paul, MN: Paragon House.

———. 2002. "Extraordinary Acts of Ordinary People: Faces of Heroism and Altruism." Pp. 123–139 in *Altruism and Altruistic Love*, edited by Stephen G. Post, Lynn G. Underwood, Jeffrey P. Schloss, and William B. Hurlbut. New York: Oxford University Press.

Oliner, Samuel P., and Kathleen Lee. 1996. *Who Shall Live: The Wilhelm Bachner Story.* Chicago: Academy Chicago Publishers.

Oliner, Samuel P., and Pearl M. Oliner. 1988. *The Altruistic Personality: Rescuers of Jews in Nazi Europe.* New York: The Free Press.

Ostrower, Francie. 1995. *Why the Wealthy Give.* Princeton, NJ: Princeton University Press.

Paldiel, Mordecai. 1987. "Why They Risked Their Lives to Save Jews." *Jerusalem Post,* September 21, p. 8.

———. 1999. "Primo Levi's Hassid." *Yad Vashem Quarterly Magazine* 12: 14.

Pamplin, Dr. Robert, Jr., and Gary K. Eisler. 1995. *American Heroes: Their Lives, Their Values, Their Beliefs.* New York: Mastermedia.

Papanek, Ernst, with Edward Linn. 1975. *Out of the Fire.* New York: William Morrow.

Pasternak, Sean. 1995. "Craig Kielburger—12 Year Old Lobbyist." From *Thornhill Times,* December. Canada. Retrieved August 25, 2000, http://www.angelfire. com/on/pasternakpublishing/craigkielburger.html.

Peachtree Publishers. 1998. *The Escape of the Danish Jews.* Retrieved May 7, 2001, http://www.peachtreeonline.com/Ye. . . tar_no_art/Adults/ ecape.adult.htm.

Penkower, Monty Noam. 1983. *The Jews Were Expendable: Free World Diplomacy and the Holocaust.* Urbana: University of Illinois Press.

Penslar, Derek J. 1998. "The Origins of Modern Jewish Philanthropy." Pp. 197–214 in *Philanthropy in the World's Traditions,* edited by Warren F. Ilchman, Stanley N. Katz, and Edward L. Queen. Bloomington: Indiana University Press.

Percival, John. 1985. *For Valour, the Victoria Cross: Courage in Action.* London: Thames, Nethuen.

Perkins, Kenneth B., and Carole W. Metz. 1988. "Note on Commitment and Community among Volunteer Firefighters." *Sociological Inquiry* 58, 1.

Picciotto, Richard, with Daniel Paisner. 2002. *Last Man Down.* New York: Berkley Books.

Pietzner, Cornelius. 2000. "Perspectives on Philanthropy." Ethical Banking Conference. Basel, Switzerland, May 28. Retrieved July 23, 2001, http://www.camphillsoltane.org/news/philanthropy.htm.

Piliavin, Jane Allyn. 1994. "Feeling Good by Doing Good: Emotions and Volunteering." Paper presented at the American Sociological Association, Los Angeles, August 5–9.

Polster, Miriam. 1992. *Eve's Daughters: The Forbidden Heroism of Women.* San Francisco: Jossey-Bass.

Press Corner. 2001. "Topic WWII: Carl Lutz: The Swiss Consul Who in 1944 Saved 62,000 Jews in Budapest." Swiss Embassy, Washington, DC. Retrieved May 7, 2001, http://www.swissemb.org/press/ html/carl_lutz.html.

Prince, Russ Alan, and Karen Maru File. 1994. *The Seven Faces of Philanthropy: A New Approach to Cultivating Major Donors.* San Francisco: Jossey-Bass.

Purple Heart Home Page. 2001. "The Purple Heart—Then and Now." Retrieved June 26, 2001, http://www.purpleheart.org/history.htm.

Putnam, Robert. [2000] 2001. *Bowling Alone: The Collapse and Revival of American Community*. New York: Touchstone Publishers.

———. 2002. "Bowling Together: The United States of America." *American Prospect*, February, pp. 20–22.

Ray, Paul H., and Sherry Anderson. 2000. *The Cultural Creatives: How 50 Million People Are Changing the World*. New York: Harmony Books.

Revkin, Andrew. 1990. *The Burning Season: The Murder of Chico Mendes and the Fight for the Amazon Rain Forest*. Boston: Houghton Mifflin.

Reykowski, Janusz, and Jerzy Karylowski. 1984. "Part V Introduction." *In Development and Maintenance of Prosocial Behavior: International Perspectives on Positive Morality*, edited by Ervin Staub, Daniel Bar-Tal, Jerzy Karylowski, and Janusz Reykowski. New York: Plenum Press.

Riemer, Jeffrey W. 1998. "Durkheim's 'Heroic Suicide' in Military Combat." *Armed Forces and Society* 25, 1: 103–120.

Ring, Wendy, Dr. Interview with the author. January 14, 2000.

Rittner, Carol, and Sondra Myers, eds. 1986. *The Courage to Care*. New York: New York University Press.

Roche, George. 1998. *The Book Of Heroes: Great Men and Women in American History*. Washington, DC: Regnery Publishing.

Rohrlich, Ruby, ed. 1998. *Resisting the Holocaust*. New York: Berg Publishers.

Rosenberg, Morris. 1965. *Society and the Adolescent Self Image*. Princeton, NJ: Princeton University Press.

Rosenhan, David. 1970. "The Natural Socialization of Altruistic Autonomy." Pp. 251–268 in *Altruism and Helping Behavior,* edited by Jacqueline R. Macaulay and Leonard Berkowitz. New York: Academic Press.

Rosenthal, Abraham. 1969. "Thirty-Eight Witnesses." Pp. 284–296 in *Readings in Collective Behavior*, edited by Robert R. Evans. Chicago: Rand McNally.

Ross, Barbara. 2002. "Cop Finds Man Who Saved Her." *New York Daily News*, January 3. Retrieved from Lexis-Nexus Academic Universe, January 29, 2002, http://web.lexis-nexis.com/universe/document.

Roth, John K., and Elizabeth Maxwell, eds. 2001. *Remembering For the Future: The Holocaust in an Age of Genocide*, vols. 1–2. Hampshire, UK, and New York: Palgrave.

Rothbaum, Lawrence M. 1999. "Albania's Saving of Jews Is Little-Known Episode." *Martyrdom and Resistance*, January/February, p. 15.

Rotter, J. B. 1966. "Generalized Expectancies for Internal Versus External Control of Reinforcement." *Psychological Monographs* 80, 1.

Rubin, Talia. 2000. "Jan Karski, Alerted World to Shoah, 86." *Forward*, July 21, p. 8.

Rushton, J. Phillippe. 1980. *Altruism, Socialization, and Society*. Englewood Cliffs, NJ: Prentice-Hall.

Rushton, J. Phillippe, R. D. Chrisjohn, and G. Fekken. 1981. "The Altruistic Personality and the Self-Report Altruism Scale." Pp. 293–302 in *Personality and Individual Differences*, vol. 2. London: Pergamon Press.

Ryan, Michael. 1990. "A Simple Deed with Awesome Power." *Parade Magazine*, August 19, pp. 4–11.

Rysavy, Tracy, assist. ed. 2000. "Telling the Children's Story." *YES! A Journal of Positive Futures*. Retrieved August 25, 2000, http://www.futurenet.org/11powerofone/rysavy.html.

Sala, Harold J. 1998. *Heroes: People Who Made a Difference in Our World*. Uhrichsville, OH: Promise Press.

Sarbin, T. R. 1986. "The Narrative as a Root Metaphor for Psychology." Pp. 3–21 in *Narrative Psychology: The Storied Nature of Human Conduct*, edited by T. R. Sarbin. New York: Praeger Press.

Sauvage, Pierre. 1986. "Ten Things I Would Like to Know About Righteous Conduct." *Humboldt Journal of Social Relations* 13, 1–2: 252–259.

————. 1989. *Weapons of the Spirit: Friends of Le Chambon*. Video documentary. Los Angeles: Chambon Foundation.

————. 2000. "Dedication Ceremony for Varian Fry Outside U.S. Consulate in Marseille, France." Courtesy of the Chambon Foundation, October 18.

————. 2001. "Varian Fry in Marseille." *In Remembering for the Future: The Holocaust in an Age of Genocide*, edited by John K. Roth and Elizabeth Maxwell. Hampshire, UK: Palgrave.

Schervish, Paul, Mary A. O'Herlihy, and John J. Havens. 2001. *Agent-Animated Wealth and Philanthropy: The Dynamics of Accumulation and Allocation among High-Tech Donors*. Retrieved October 1, 2001, http://www.afpnet.org.

Schevitz, Tanya. 2000. "At UC Berkeley, Charity Begins in the Classroom." *San Francisco Chronicle*, September 7, pp. A1, A13.

Schroeder, David A., Louis A. Penner, John F. Dovidio, and Jane A. Piliavin. 1995. *The Psychology of Helping and Altruism: Problems and Puzzles*. New York: McGraw-Hill.

Seavey, Nancy, Jane S. Smith, and Paul Wagner. 1998. *A Paralyzing Fear: The Triumph over Polio in America*. New York: TV Books.

Sémelin, Jacques. 1993. *Unarmed Against Hitler: Civilian Resistance in Europe, 1939–1943*. Translated by Suzan Husserl-Kapit. Westport, CT: Praeger.

Senesz, Hannah. 1971. *Her Life and Diary*. London: Valentine Mitchell.

Shadmi, E. 1973. *Without Finding, Without Surrendering: Haviva Reik's Mission* (film). In Hebrew. Tel Aviv: Moreshet.

Shapiro, Gershon. 1988. *Under Fire: The Stories of Jewish Heroes of the Soviet Union*. Jerusalem: Yad Vashem Publications.

Shapiro, Irene. 1999. "A Synopsis of the Bialystok Ghetto Rebellion." *Together*, January, p. 25.

Shepard, Mark. 1987. *Gandhi Today*. Arcata, CA: Simple Productions.

Shepherd, Naomi. 1984. *A Refuge from Darkness: Wilfrid Israel and the Rescue of the Jews*. New York: Pantheon Books.

Showtime Cable Network. 2001. "Varian Fry's War." Feature film, June 4.

Sinisi, Christina S. 1993. "The Origins of Volunteerism: Socialization Antecedents and Personal Variables." Ph.D. diss., Department of Psychology, Kansas State University, Manhattan.

Smith, Dennis. 2002. *Report from Ground Zero*. New York: Viking Press.

Smith, Michael. 1999. *Foley: The Spy Who Saved 10,000 Jews*. London: Hodder and Stoughton.

Smith, Robert Barr. 1997. *Men at War: True Stories of Heroism and Honor*. New York: Avon Books.

Smolenska, M. Zuzanna, and Janusz Reykowski. 1992. "Motivations of People Who Helped Jews Survive the Nazi Occupation." Pp. 213–225 in *Embracing the Other: Philosophical, Psychological, and Historical Perspectives on Altruism*, edited by Pearl M. Oliner, Samuel P. Oliner, Lawrence Bacon, Lawrence A. Blum, Dennis L. Krebs, and M. Zuzanna Smolenska. New York: New York University Press.

Smoliar, Hersh. 1966. *Resistance in Minsk*. Translated by Hyman J. Lewbin. Oakland, CA: Judah L. Magnes Memorial Museum.

Sorokin, Pitirim A. 1941. *The Crisis of Our Age*. New York: Dutton Books.

_____. 1942. *Man and Society in Calamity*. New York: Dutton Books.

_____. 1950a. *The Ways and Power of Love*. New York: Bantam Books.

_____. 1950b. *Altruistic Love: A Study of "Good Neighbors" and Christian Saints*. Boston: The Beacon Press.

_____. 1950c. *Explorations in Altruistic Love and Behavior*. Boston: Beacon Press.

Stanley, Alessandra. 2000. "On a '44 Battlefield, a Salute for a Black Hero." *New York Times International*, July 16, pp. 1, 6.

Staub, Ervin. 1978 and 1979. *Positive Social Behavior and Morality*, vols. 1–2. New York: Academic Press.

Staub, Ervin, Daniel Bar-Tal, Jerzy Karylowski, and Janusz Reykowski, eds. 1984. *Development and Maintenance of Prosocial Behavior: International Perspectives on Positive Morality*. New York: Plenum Press.

Steele, Jason Kennedy. 1999. "Volunteering to Save Lives." *Times Standard*, May 23, no. 143.

Steinberg, Lucien. 1974. *Not as a Lamb: The Jews Against Hitler*. London: Saxon House.

Stewart, James B. 2002. *The Heart of a Soldier*. New York: Simon and Schuster.

Szymanski, Tekla. 2001. "Giorgio Perlasca: Italian Wallenberg." *World Press Review*, January, p. 35.

Tappan, Mark, and Lyn Midel Brown. 1991. "Stories Told and Lessons Learned: Toward a Narrative Approach to Moral Development and Moral Education." Pp. 171–192 in *Stories Lives Tell*, edited by Carol Witherell and Nel Nodding. New York: Teachers College Press.

Taylor, Michael. 1999. "Tracking Down False Heroes." *San Francisco Chronicle*, May 31, p. A1.

Tec, Nechama. 1986. *When Light Pierced the Darkness: Christian Rescue of Jews in Nazi-Occupied Poland*. Oxford: Oxford University Press.

_____. 1990. *In the Lion's Den: The Life of Oswald Rufeisen*. New York: Oxford University Press.

_____. 1993. *Defiance: The Bielski Partisans, The Story of the Largest Armed Rescue of Jews by Jews During World War II*. New York: Oxford University Press.

Terry, John, and Donna Woonteiler. 2000. "An Interview With Craig Kielburger, Founder of Free the Children." *CYD Journal* 1, 1. Retrieved August 25, 2000, http://www.cydjournal.org/2000winter/kielburger.html.

Tillich, Paul. 1968. *Love, Power, and Justice.* Reprint. London: Oxford University Press.

Tocqueville, Alexis de. 1956. *Democracy in America.* Translated and edited by Richard Heffner. New York: New American Library.

Tschuy, Theo. 2000. *Dangerous Diplomacy: The Story of Carl Lutz: Rescuer of 62,000 Hungarian Jews.* Grand Rapids, MI: William B. Eerdmans.

Tucker, Mary Evelyn. 1998. "A View of Philanthropy in Japan: Confucian Ethics and Education." Pp. 169–193 in *Philanthropy in the World's Transitions,* edited by Ilchman, Warren F., Stanley N. Katz, and Edward L. Queen II. Bloomington: Indiana University Press.

Tulving, E. 1983. *Elements of Episodic Memory.* New York: Oxford University Press.

Turniansky, Bobbie, and Julie Cwikel. 1996. "Volunteering in a Voluntary Community: Kibbutz Members and Voluntarism." *Voluntas* 7, 3: 300–317.

Underwood, Lynn G. 2001. "The Human Experience of Compassionate Love: Conceptual Mapping and Data from Selected Studies." In S. G. Post, L. G. Underwood, J. P. Schloss, and W. B. Hurlbut, eds., *Altruism and Altruistic Love: Science, Philosophy, and Religion in Dialogue.* New York: Oxford University Press.

United States Holocaust Memorial Museum. 1996. "Jewish Resistance during the Holocaust." Program brochure, October 29. Washington, DC: Miles Lerman Center for the Study of Jewish Resistance.

Vitz, P. C. 1985. *A Critical Review of Kohlberg's Model of Moral Development.* Unpublished report for the Department of Education, Washington, DC.

"Voices of the Century; World War II: Word from the Ghetto." 1999. *Newsweek,* March 8, p. 47.

Wagner, Meir. 2001. *The Righteous of Switzerland (Heroes of the Holocaust).* Edited by Andreas C. Fischer and Graham Buik. New York: Ktav Publishing House.

Washington, James M., ed. 1991. "I See the Promised Land." Speech given April 3, 1968, Memphis, TN. From *A Testament of Hope: The Essential Writings of Martin Luther King, Jr.* Retrieved September 4, 2001, from http://www.seto.org/king3.html, pp. 9–10.

———. 1992. *I Have a Dream: Writings and Speeches that Changed the World.* San Francisco: Harper San Francisco.

Webb, James. 2000. "Heroes of the Vietnam Generation." *American Enterprise* 11, 6: 22–24.

Werber, Jack. 1996. *Saving Children: Diary of a Buchenwald Survivor and Rescuer.* New Brunswick, NJ: Transaction Publishers.

Wiesel, Elie. 1986. *Night.* New York: Bantam Books.

———. [1982] 1995. *The Town Beyond the Wall: A Novel.* Translated by Stephen Becker. New York: Schocken Books.

Wilson, J. P., and R. Petruska. 1984. "Motivation, Model Attributes and Prosocial Behavior." *Journal of Personality and Social Psychology* 46: 458–468.

Wilson, Nicholas. 2000. "We Did It!" *Auto-Free Times,* issue 17, Spring: 35.

Witherell, Carol, and Nel Nodding, eds. 1991. *Stories Lives Tell.* New York: Teachers College Press.

Wood, E. Thomas, and Stanislaw M. Jankowski. 1994. *Karski: How One Man Tried to Stop the Holocaust.* New York: John Wiley and Sons.

Wuthnow, Robert. 1993. *Acts of Compassion: Caring for Others and Helping Ourselves.* Princeton, NJ: Princeton University Press.

Wyman, David S. 1998. *The Abandonment of the Jews: America and the Holocaust, 1941–1945.* New York: The New Press.

Zaret, Elliot. 2001. "Understanding the Titan of High-tech: Methods, Motivation of Gates Echo the Industrial Age." MSNBC. Retrieved July 9, 2001, http://www.msnbc.com/news/.

Zoberman, Rabbi Israel. 2001. "Some Swiss Were Heroes." *Post and Opinion* 67, 38, May 30: NAT 16.

Zuccotti, Susan. 1987. *The Italians and the Holocaust: Persecution, Rescue, and Survival.* New York: Basic Books.

Zuckerman, Marvin. 1978. "Sensation Seeking." *Dimensions of Personality,* edited by Harvey London and J. E. Exner Jr. New York: Wiley.

Internet Sources

American Liberty Partnership. "September 11, 2001 Victims." Retrieved September 13, 2002, http://www.september11victims.com/september11victims/STATIS-TIC.asp.

Association of Fund Raising Professional. "History Shows Giving Resilient in Crises." Retrieved October 5, 2001, http://www.afpnet. org/. . . folder_id=887 &content_item_id=344.

Bartleby.com Home Page. "Dr. Jonas Salk." http://www.bartleby.com/ 63/79/ 2879.html.

Daily Celebrations Home Page. "Dr. Jonas Salk." Retrieved August 7, 2002, http://www.dailycelebrations.com/100899.htm.

Elie Wiesel Foundation for Humanity Home Page. Retrieved August 7, 2002, http://www.eliewieselfoundation.org.

Equity Online: Women of Achievement. "Rachel Carson." Retrieved August 15, 2000. http://www. edc.org/WomensEquity/women/carson.htm.

Habitat for Humanity. "The History of Habitat for Humanity International." Retrieved September 6, 2002, http://www.habitat.org/ how/historytext.html.

Henry Hazlitt Foundation. "The Heroes of Flight 93: Thank You." Retrieved September 30, 2001. http://www.hazlitt.org/united/whotheywere2.html#Honor-Wainio.

Hospice Information Worldwide. Retrieved September 6, 2002, http://www.hospiceinformation.info/hospicesworldwide.asp.

King, Martin Luther, Jr. "I See The Promised Land." Retrieved September 4, 2002, http://www.seto.org/king3.html, p. 9–10.

_____. "Letter from Birmingham Jail." Retrieved September 5, 2002, http://www.ai.mit.edu/~isbell/HFh/black/events_and_people/.008.letter_from_jail.

National Hospice and Palliative Care Organization Home Page. Retrieved September 6, 2002, http://www.nhpco.org/public/articles/facts&figures9–2002.pdf.

Northwest Giving Project. "What Is Philanthropy?" Retrieved July 23, 2001, http://www.nwgiving.org.htm/whatis.htm.

Our Lady of Refuge. Home Page. "OLR Graduate from the Class of 1977, Stephen Driscoll NYPD, Among the Missing at the World Trade Center Attack." Retrieved September 12, 2002, http://www.ourladyofrefuge.com/news.htm.

"Pal Saluted for Last Act of Heroism, October 29, 2001." Retrieved September 12, 2002, http://www.pass.to/newsletter/pal_saluted_for_ last_act_of_hero.htm.

Sabin Vaccine Institute. "The Legacy of Albert B. Sabin." Retrieved August 7, 2002, http://www.sabin.org/who_legacy.htm.

San Jose State University Virtual Museum. "Albert B. Sabin." Retrieved August 31, 2000, http://www.sjsu.edu/depts/Museum/sabin.html.

White House Conference on Philanthropy. "Heroes Biography: Matel 'Mat' Dawson Jr." Retrieved August 20, 2002, http://clinton4. nara.gov/Initiatives/Millennium/Philan/html/bio_dawson.html.

White House Home Page. "Rachel Carson." Retrieved August 15, 2000, http://www.whitehouse.gov/WH/EOP/OVP/24hours/carson.html.

Women in Philanthropy (University of Michigan). Retrieved March 3, 2002, http://www.women-philanthropy.umich.edu/donors/.

Women's International Center. WIC Biography. "Dr. Jonas Salk." Retrieved August 31, 2000, http://www.wic.org/bio/jsalk.htm.

World Tibet Network News. "His Holiness the Dalai Lama's speech in New York, April 1994." Retrieved September 12, 2002, http://www.tibet.ca/wtnarchive/1994.5/3/–5_1/html.

Appendix A

Data, Methods, and Samples for this Book

For each chapter in this book, we reviewed the relevant literature to put us on the right track. The data was obtained from two sources: (1) existing recent published literature (including theoretical frameworks); and (2) actual interviews. We interviewed a variety of individuals in great depth using open-ended and closed-ended questions, and used a variety of scales. The social psychological scales we used are: the Social Responsibility scale, developed by L. Berkowitz and K. Luterman (1968); the Empathy scale, developed by A. Mehrabian and N. A. Epstein (1972); the Altruistic Personality scale, developed by J. Phillippe Rushton, R. D. Chrisjohn, and G. Fekken (1981); the Internal/External Locus of Control scale, developed by J. B. Rotter (1966) and modified by G. Gurin, P. Gurin, and B. M. Morrison (1978); the Sensation Seeking scale, developed by M. Zuckerman (1978); the Self Esteem scale, developed by M. Rosenburg (1965); the Diversity/Commonality scale, developed by S. Oliner and P. Oliner (1988); and the Daily Spiritual Experience (DSE) scale, developed by Lynn G. Underwood (2001).

We interviewed a sample of approximately 800 Christian respondents consisting of rescuers and bystanders, as well as rescued survivors (see Oliner et al. 1992, p. 361). We also interviewed 214 Carnegie heroes and 60 moral exemplars, all individuals living in various communities throughout the United States. In the volunteer chapter we interviewed 93 hospice volunteers and 73 nonhospice volunteers (those who volunteered in other settings). In all instances we used some of the questions and scales mentioned above.

Throughout the interviews, (that is, Christian rescuers, Carnegie heroes, moral exemplars, and hospice volunteers), we were trying to understand motivation using not only the scales mentioned above but also open-ended questions—the qualitative part of the interviews. All interviews were conducted either face-to-face or via telephone, tape-recorded, and transcribed; their narratives enabled us to gain insight about motivation.

We obtained the samples in the following manner: Christian rescuers were selected from Yad Vashem, the moral authority, which was established by the Holocaust Martyrs and Heroes Remembrance Law and adopted by the Israeli parliament in August 1953. The purpose of the Heroes Remembrance Law was to record and remember people during the Holocaust, and not just perpetrators and killers. They provided us with a list of authenticated rescuers, and we interviewed them in their own countries and languages. These countries consisted of Poland, France, Germany, Italy, Holland, and Norway, as well as rescuers who immigrated to the United States and Canada. They were compared with an equivalent, smaller sample of bystanders (nonrescuers). I established associates in each of the countries and trained the interviewers myself, and then the interviews were supervised by faculty in Europe, including Professor Janusz Reykowski in Poland, Professor Jurgen Falter in Germany, Professor André Kaspi in France, Dr. Michelle Sarfatti in Italy, Susan Schwartz in Norway, Professor Richard Van Dyck in Holland, and a team of trained interviewers who were paid to do the actual interviews and send the interviews to us at Humboldt State University, where the interviews were translated and feedback was given about the quality of the interviews.

The Carnegie heroes were chosen randomly from a list of more than 8,500 men and women, excluding the deceased, provided to us by Walter Rutkowski, the executive director and secretary of the Carnegie Hero Fund Commission. We interviewed 214 heroes on the telephone and tape-recorded the interviews. This was followed up by the mailed set of scales (the Social Responsibility scale, the Empathy scale, the Altruistic Personality scale, the Internal/External Locus of Control scale, the Sensation Seeking scale, and the Self Esteem scale), and provided with a self-addressed stamped envelope; the return rate was 99 percent.

The moral exemplars were chosen using the "reputational approach" as well as "expert nominators"—those who referred us to the individuals whom they felt were making a difference in their community. All of these individuals live in various communities throughout the United States.

The hospice volunteers sample was gathered by obtaining lists from directors of each of the hospice volunteer groups in Humboldt County in Northern California, the Boston area, and the San Francisco Bay area. The individuals were then randomly selected and interviewed face-to-face by skilled interviewers.

In all groups the open-ended questionnaire consisted of several parts. Part 1 dealt with the demographic background, including gender, age, educational attainment, occupation, religion, political affiliation, parental influences, the influences of any other significant individuals, and whether they knew the victim. Part 2 consisted of questions about attitudes, values, who or what motivated them to help, and was followed by actual details of why they rescued/helped. These narratives were considered a very important part of the data. We enlisted three independent raters in the Carnegie research, six in the Christian rescuers study, three in the hospice study, and three in the moral exemplar research. The reason for the multiple raters was to find reliability in what the narratives were saying. Common themes were then quantified. For the scales we used objective, statistical analysis. From these methodological approaches we were able to make some generalizations.

For the second part of our data collection we used secondary sources with some interviews. In each of the chapters, for example, the case of Jewish heroes (i.e., Jewish rescuers), we interviewed in great depth two individuals, Wilhelm Bachner (see Oliner and Lee 1996) and Jack Werber (see Chapter 4), who actually risked their lives to save Jews and non-Jews during the Nazi occupation. For data obtained on military heroes (Chapter 6), besides reading the literature on military heroism, we interviewed in-depth one military hero, Hugh Thompson. Among the moral exemplars-leaders (Chapter 7), we interviewed sixty individuals in several communities suggested to us by expert nominators and/or the reputational approach, who helped to explain what motivated them to be involved in their activities. We interviewed some philanthropists (see Chapter 8) and tried to capture their motivations, attitudes, and values, along with the available published literature.

In sum, the data from published materials, coupled with the rich interviews that we conducted, converged to try to better understand why people put the welfare of others alongside their own.

Appendix B

More Stories of Non-Jewish Rescuers
(See Chapter 3)

An empathic Polish rescuer of a Jewish prisoner said:

> In 1942, I was on my way home from town and was almost near home when M came out of the bushes. I looked at him in striped clothing, his head bare, shod in clogs. He might have been about thirty or thirty-two years old. And he begged me, his hands joined like for prayer—that he had escaped from Maldanek, and could I help him? He knelt down in front of me and said, "You are like the Virgin Mary." (It still makes me cry). "If I get through and reach Warsaw, I will never forget you." Well, how could one not help such a man? So I took him home and fed him because he was hungry . . . [and I gave him clothes, a bath, etc.].

In 1953 the Israeli parliament established the Yad Vashem Remembrance Authority, whose mission was to establish a memorial to the Righteous Among the Nations—those who risked their lives to save Jews. Since then more than 16,000 non-Jews have been recognized for their acts of valor and heroism. Despite the miserable failure of the major world powers, such as the United States and England, to save Jews, there were individuals, groups, and countries who did.

Among those individuals recognized by Yad Vashem were Aristides de Sousa Mendes, who issued visas to refugees; Paul Grueninger, who allowed hundreds of fleeing Jews to enter Switzerland even though his own government was against it; and Raoul Wallenberg, who saved tens of thousands of Hungarian Jews.

There are many others. Herman Langbein and Ludwig Worl went to Auschwitz to aid the Jewish prisoners there and worked to ease the wretched conditions. Julius Madrtsch and Raimund Titsch, who expressed concern for the Jewish interns employed in factories at the Plaszow Camp, obtained food supplements for them and defended them from the ill treatment of the sadistic commandant, Amon Goeth, and his murderous aides (as portrayed in the film *Schindler's List*). These Righteous human beings saved not only Jewish lives, but also the honor of humanity during the Holocaust. Their heroism and dedication to principle cannot be overstated.

A Gentile named Lorenzo Perrone helped the now famous author, Primo Levi, survive Auschwitz.[1] Lorenzo Perrone was an Italian mason who was hired by the Nazi authorities to do some masonry work. Completely by chance, Primo Levi, an Auschwitz prisoner, was assigned to be his assistant. Perrone was a civilian who could take off Sundays and take paid vacations, while Levi was, as were all Jews, a condemned prisoner. Paldiel tells us Perrone became very friendly with Levi and started bringing him food that he sneaked from the kitchen. For at least six months Levi was supplied with soup and sometimes bread. Levi attributes his and others' survival to Perrone's bringing food to them. Later, he testified that without the additional 400–500 calories that Perrone provided he would not have lasted.

Primo Levi wrote a number of books about his survival in Auschwitz, and painted a very deep and poignant picture of life in the "Auschwitz Kingdom." He wrote extensively about goodness and he found in Perrone "a good and simple human being." After the war his writings frequently mentioned this wonderful Italian Christian civilian who helped him. "Thanks to Lorenzo, I managed not to forget that I was myself a man."[2] Both Perrone and Levi are now dead, Levi committed suicide in 1987, but recently the Commission for the Designation of the Righteous bestowed the Righteous Among the Nations title on Lorenzo Perrone, following a request by Dr. Renzo Levi, Primo Levi's son, who was named after Perrone. A medal and a certificate were dispatched to the Israeli embassy in Italy, and Lorenzo Perrone's name will be in the Yad Vashem Garden of the Righteous to be remembered as one who made a difference and demonstrated compassion toward his fellow man.

A Franciscan friar named Rufino Niccacci headed an amazing rescue team in Italy, where authorities claim he and his group rescued 5,000 Jews during the Nazi occupation.[3] Based in the quiet town of Assisi, his rescue group grew to include almost 500 priests, plus half of the townspeople. Amateurs ran this venture, but they maintained a perfect record—not one of the Jewish victims who passed along this escape route was ever captured.

The smuggling operation began by accident in the summer of 1943 when nine Jews appealed to Bishop Brunacci of Assisi for sanctuary. Their names were already on the list of "undesirables" awaiting transportation to extermination camps. Impulsively, the bishop took them into his house and hid them while he cast about for escape routes. Two weeks later the group left Assisi disguised as religious pilgrims. Bishop Brunacci's underground friends had provided each with a forged identity card as proof of Aryan background. Escorted by friars, the nine of them set out toward the coast and their lives were saved. After this event Rufino Niccacci was chosen to continue assisting Jews to escape from Italy. In a simple plan the refugees were relayed into Assisi from outlying provinces, given forged identity, and then sent on their journey to safety.

Father Rufino was blessed with an innocent face and the Nazis believed he was too dumb to be capable of mounting such an operation. Even when he and his accomplices made horrible, naïve mistakes, like having refugees march around in the open or ferrying Jews out from right under the German noses, they were not found out. Eventually, when the stream of refugees increased to the point of overloading the monastery's facilities, townspeople took them in and also donated food and money. The danger of being discovered rose and everyone knew that the slightest slip of the tongue would result in torture by the Gestapo. Father Rufino was repeatedly questioned about his involvement with "those people."

Twenty years later, when Father Rufino was asked why he carried out this very dangerous mission, he said, "Need has no boundaries. In the final summing up, I am my brother's keeper. This has little to do with religion or race." Father Rufino was spiritually inspired by St. Francis of Assissi to help the innocent victims of Nazi persecution.

In 1940, when the Nazis invaded France and took Paris, an American named Varian Fry was a volunteer for the Emergency Rescue Committee in France, and was among the few non-Jewish Americans who understood the Nazi objective of a *Final Solution* for the Jews. After the invasion and occupation, the Germans established the Vichy government. Under German sovereignty, Marshall Pétain, a French military hero of WWI, was permitted to run the Vichy government and strongly encouraged to meet Gestapo demands to turn over any Jewish refugees.

Fry had no training in underground work, but he went to Marseilles and ran a refugee escape operation under the cover of relief work, despite the fact that the American Consulate strongly opposed the activity. He had a list of about 200 very prominent artists and intellectuals who were known to be in various places in Nazi-occupied Europe and who were in great danger due to their criticism of Hitler. His mission was to aid the escape of those at risk. Fry and his associates were under constant threat of arrest for forging documents, exchanging money on the black market, and operating an underground railroad to spirit people out.

Fry and his collaborators saved around 4,000 people during the fourteen months before he was deported by the Vichy government. Among them were artists Marc Chagall, Marcel Duchamp, and Max Ernst; political scientist Hannah Arendt; novelists Heinrich Mann and Franz Werfel; sculptor Jacques Lipchitz; and poet Andre Breton. Fry said he stayed because the refugees needed him, but it took courage, which he wasn't sure he possessed.

Emeritus Professor Walter Meyerhof of Stanford University, who was himself rescued by Fry, founded the Varian Fry Foundation Project of the International Rescue Committee in 1999. It is dedicated to publicizing the heroism of Varian Fry.[4]

Professor Meyerhof, his mother, and his father—a 1922 Nobel Prize winner in medicine—had been in exile in Paris where they felt there was safety. In 1940 that changed. The family was sent to an internment camp in southern France to await possible deportation back to Germany. With the assistance of Fry's organization, they were saved. Professor Meyerhof's parents walked over the Pyrenees to freedom in Spain; they had to wait six months for a U. S. visa before eventually escaping to the United States from Lisbon.

In 1967, Fry died alone and in obscurity. He had remained largely unrecognized in his country until Meyerhof dedicated himself to rescuing Fry's memory. To memorialize the extraordinary acts of this caring and heroic American, Meyerhof's foundation displays exhibits of Fry's rescue work around the United States; disseminates Fry's story to middle and high school students using a curriculum package containing a videotape narrated by Meryl Streep and a copy of Fry's book, *Assignment: Rescue*, (written shortly before his death in 1967). Varian Fry is, so far, the only American to be honored as a Righteous Among the Nations Gentile at Yad Vashem. Professor Meyerhof says, "His example shows how a single person can help people in need, even under the most adverse circumstances." It has been concluded by some that Fry was personally responsible for the rescue of some 2,000 people. This simple and unassuming person came with the conviction that injustice is not to be tolerated, and help should be given to people at all costs.

During World War II, Lamija Jaha's parents lived in Nazi-controlled Sarajevo. Not only did her parents save many Jews by hiding them in their home, but her father also concealed in his home the precious six-hundred-year-old *Sarajevo Haggadah*—a special prayer book used for Passover ritual. In 1999, when Lamija Jaha, her husband, her family, and thousands of other ethnic Albanians were being driven from their homes in Kosovo, in scenes reminiscent of the Holocaust, she carried a simple memento, a copy of a certificate engraved with her dead father's name. This certificate would be her ticket to safety.[5]

The certificate had been issued by the Yad Vashem Holocaust Memorial in Jerusalem honoring her parents, Dervis and Servet Korkut, both Muslims, for risking their lives to save Jews. It recognized them as "Righteous Among the Nations."

With their future unknown, Mrs. Jaha showed her father's commendation to officials of the Jewish community in Skopje, Macedonia. Thus, the Jaha family joined a planeload of Kosovar Albanian refugees on their way to be sheltered in the Jewish state. "I don't know how to express how much this means to me," Mrs. Jaha said in an interview. "My father did what he did with all his heart, not to get anything in return. Fifty years later, it returns somehow. It's a kind of a circle."[6]

Davor Bakovic, the son of a woman that Jaha's parents rescued, was there to greet Mr. and Mrs. Jaha when they arrived at the Ben-Gurion Airport. Mr. Bakovic told reporters, "It was an amazing discovery. I felt as if a sister had appeared from a faraway place. I felt close to these people even though I didn't know them at all. The circle of my life had become linked with Lamija and her family. To me it proved that people can't be divided up into nations and sects. They're human beings who can touch each other."[7]

Prime Minister Benjamin Netanyahu personally assured Mrs. Jaha that in recognition of her parents' deeds, she and her family would be welcome to stay in Israel and be eligible for citizenship. To a woman ripped from her home in the midst of an outrageous act of war, this is at the very least a miracle. Mrs. Jaha explained, "This is a big thing for us, because we have no home, we have nothing, and we've come to a country that won't turn us back."[8]

Marion Pritchard was a young Dutch citizen who became involved with the resistance movement at the beginning of the war when she recognized the intent of the Nazi occupation forces when they invaded the Netherlands in 1940.[9]

After witnessing children literally being thrown into German trucks by Nazi soldiers in Amsterdam, Pritchard knew she had to do something to thwart such atrocities. At great risk to herself she obtained Aryan identity cards for as many people as she could. She found people to take orphaned Jewish infants and children and helped to hide Jews in her home and in the homes of family friends, thus providing the basic necessities for survival. She relates the story of a Dutch Nazi policeman who had accompanied the Germans on an unsuccessful raid to look for concealed Jews and then returned alone to see if their prey had come out of hiding. Pritchard had a revolver and felt that she had no choice but to kill him. She says that the killing still bothers her, but she would do it again under similar circumstances.

Pritchard shares two stories of kindness amidst the horror of the Holocaust, one about the Dutch and the other about German soldiers. The first deals with a Dutch family who took Pritchard and a Jewish baby in after failing to find shelter for them. The family kept the baby and sent her away—in order to convince the villagers and allay suspicion—that Pritchard had had the baby out of wedlock and her punishment was that they keep the baby and send her on her way. Pritchard explains that this family's actions and those of many other Dutch rescuers of Jews were motivated by their Christian convictions and what God would want.

The second story involved German soldiers patrolling a bridge. Pritchard had a supply of food to use for bartering and trading with people on the other side of the Ijssel River. One evening German soldiers stopped her and confiscated everything she had brought with her. She was so tired and angry that she threw caution to the wind and vented her anger at the German soldiers, sharing her opinion of the war, Germans, Hitler, and the concentration camps. She took a big risk in doing this, but so did the German soldiers, for on the following morning they put her bike and goods into the back of a truck and drove her across the bridge. She does not know why, but speculates that there was some decency left in them, as within all people.

Speaking of her war experiences, she said,

> It did not occur to me to do anything other than I did. . . . I think you have a responsibility to yourself to behave decently. We all have memories of times we should have done something and didn't. And it gets in the way for the rest of your life. . . . Being brought up in the Anglican Church . . . imbued me early on with a strong conviction that we are our brother's keepers. When you truly believe that, you have to behave that way in order to be able to live with yourself.[10]

In 1983, Yad Vashem honored Marion P. van Binsbergen Pritchard for helping Jews during the Nazi occupation. She eventually moved to the United States and became a psychoanalyst.

Frank Foley, dubbed the "British Schindler," helped many Jews to escape, but has yet to be recognized by Yad Vashem. Michael Smith's compelling and moving book *The Spy Who Saved 10,000 Jews* tells the story of Foley, ostensibly a passport control officer during World War II, but in reality an M16 Head of Station.[11] Although the British Empire restricted the number of Jews allowed into Britain and Palestine, Foley, despite having no diplomatic immunity and operating in the most dangerous and unpredictable circumstances, went into the concentration camps to get Jewish prisoners out, hid them in his home, and procured for them forged passports and visas to Palestine.

It is reported that Foley also knew the Jewish underground operation to smuggle Jews out of Germany, but never reported it to the British authorities. In all, it is estimated that he saved tens of thousands of people during the Holocaust.

A report by the *Electronic Telegraph Reporter* found on the Internet reflects the urgency to include Foley as one of the Righteous Among the Nations.[12] Lord Janner, chairman of Britain's Holocaust Education Trust, documents survivors' stories and gathers accounts of Foley's aid in saving lives. There are many detailed documents supporting Foley's case.

Appendix C

More Stories of Jewish rescuers
(See Chapter 4)

Although the world should know the courage and deeds of Gentile rescuers like Herman Graebe, Raoul Wallenberg, Aristide Mendez, Giorgio Perlasca, Carl Lutz, Sempo Siguhara, Magda Trocmé, and thousands of less famous rescuers of Jews during the Holocaust, further research is required on Jewish rescuers of Jews.[1] In this regard, Nechama Tec's seminal work *In the Lion's Den* is a welcomed beginning, but I believe we need more individual narratives of heroic Jewish individuals or groups who actually hid, rescued, or transported other Jews to safety.

Mendele Groskopf
The story of Mendele Groskopf appears in the Brastycz Memorial Book, published in Israel. Groskopf was a learned Jew and cantor, a man who gave of himself to his community. Because of his active involvement in the community's affairs, the Germans, during their occupation of Poland, appointed him the head of the town's local Jewish council (*Judenrat*). Langsam writes, "When the Nazi commander ordered him to submit a list of Jews for slave labor, Mendele wrote down only one name, his own, and brought it to the Nazi command headquarters. He was shot and killed on the spot."[2]

Jewish Rescuers in France
French resistance during the German occupation was to liberate the country from Germans. Jewish resistance or parallel resistance focused more on the rescuing of

Jewish lives. Although Jews took part wholeheartedly in the celebration of French resistance, they should take pride in being overrepresented in resistance as a form of rescue. The Jewish resistance movement saved the lives of 10,000 children from the hands of Nazi assassins. Jewish rescuers literally snatched the children away from terrible jeopardy under dangerous circumstances and despite great risk. Many thousands of those who survived the war owe their lives to Jewish resistance organizations, which skillfully provided them with false identity papers, ration cards, lodging, hiding places from police searches, and smuggled them from camps in the south of France to Switzerland and Spain. Children were less lucky; the percentage of children who survived was less than that for adults. Statistics indicate that 27 percent of Jewish adults and 40 percent of Jewish children in France were murdered by the Nazis. In other words, loss and suffering of children was almost twice as heavy as adults.[3]

In the interviews we conducted and in the published materials, there is discernable, intense anger toward the enemy and a strong feeling of being betrayed by the bystanders, their countrymen. There was also anger about the loss of their loved ones and neighbors.

Appendix D

∽⥽

Carnegie Heroes Research and Data

(See Chapter 5)

In the spring of 1998, a relationship was established between the Carnegie Hero Fund Commission in Pittsburgh, Pennsylvania, and the Altruistic Personality and Prosocial Behavior Institute at Humboldt State University. The goal was to conduct research to gain a better understanding of why the individuals who had received the Carnegie Medal for heroic behavior had risked their lives. The purpose of this endeavor was to provide answers to the question: What factors prompt ordinary individuals to risk their lives on behalf of others in emergency situations? To find the answer, we carefully conducted structured interviews with those individuals.

The population of Carnegie heroes to be interviewed was identified and selected based on their criteria (see below) and the fact that the Carnegie Hero Fund Commission's selection criteria has been consistent from case to case and over time. Furthermore, the heroic characteristics are congruent with those identified in the research with rescuers of Jews in Nazi-occupied Europe. That is, the people who have received the Carnegie Medal for heroic behavior are ordinary individuals who risked their own lives in order to rescue others in emergency situations.

For this project, we conducted interviews with a sample of 214 Carnegie heroes using a questionnaire consisting of both open- and closed-ended questions. We elicited information focusing on the background of the respondents, including education, gender, age, religiosity, and the like. We also asked respondents how much they felt they had in common with other ethnic groups and who influenced them most when they were growing up. We then asked each respondent to give a detailed narrative of the rescue. These taped interviews were administered by trained interviewers via telephone and subsequently transcribed. Each respondent also filled out six personality scales—*Social Responsibility, Empathy, Altruistic Personality, Locus of Control, Self Esteem,* and *Sensation Seeking.*

While respondents provided the narrative of their rescue experience, open-ended queries were asked to discover why they engaged in this activity and what they believed to be the differences between people who respond heroically in emergency situations and those who do not. Once all the recorded interviews had been transcribed, printouts were distributed to three separate coders. Working with nine predefined motivational categories (*Normocentric, Social Responsibility, Empathy, Efficacy, Response/Reaction/Impulse/Instinct, Religiosity/Spirituality, Reciprocity, Principled Motivation,* and *Self Esteem*), each coder indicated which of these categories were perceived to be significant motivational factors for each individual rescuer.

The coders' results were then combined. For every individual rescuer, each motivational category had the possibility of receiving between zero and three checks, depending on how many coders indicated it as a salient factor. For example, if *Religiosity* was not indicated as a motivating factor by any of the coders, then a zero was entered in the *Religiosity* category for that rescuer; if it was indicated by one, two, or three of the coders, then a one, two, or three was entered.

In order to determine our coders' inter-rater reliability, we reasoned that if for any rescuer a motivational category had been checked either zero or three times, then there was complete coder agreement. If a particular rescuer received a zero in the *Religiosity* category, there was complete agreement that *Religiosity* was not a significant motivational factor in this person's rescue. If *Religiosity* was checked three times, this indicates to us that all of the coders agreed it was a salient factor motivating this person to engage in the rescue activity. To report our inter-rater reliability, we combined the percentage of times that either a zero or three had been entered for each of the nine motivational categories.

Thus, the inter-rater reliability scale measured the three researchers' combined indication of the nine particular motivational factors among the rescuers. Although it is true that complete inter-rater reliability did not exist when only one or two coders indicated that a particular rescuer displayed a specific motivational factor, it is safe to say that the factor was present to a lesser degree. When computed together, the coders achieved an overall inter-rater reliability result of 70 percent.[1]

The information collected from our sample resulted in a substantial amount of both qualitative and quantitative data. The data were analyzed using a variety of social scientific techniques in order to determine correlations both within and between data sets. This analysis brought forth a number of findings. (See Appendix E)

Appendix E

❧

Tables and Crosstabs

(See Chapter 5)

Table 1: Percentage Totals for the Number of Times that the Three Independent Coders Indicated Each Variable as a Significant Motivational Factor

Variable	Percentage Totals
Normocentric (Learned Values and Norms)	78.0%
Social Responsibility	65.8%
Empathy	42.2%
Efficacy	38.8%
Response/Reaction/Impulse/Instinct	27.3%
Religiosity/Spirituality	16.2%
Reciprocity	9.8%
Principled Motivation	4.4%
Self-Esteem	1.3%

Table 2: Percentages of Respondents within Each Ranking Per Scale

Scale	High	Moderate	Low
Social Responsibility	76.5%	23.5%	0.0%
Self-Esteem	66.7%	33.3%	0.0%
Locus of Control	21.6%	78.4%	0.0%
Sensation Seeking	12.7%	77.9%	9.3%
Altruistic Personality	22.1%	75.0%	2.9%

Appendix E

Crosstab 1: Respondent's Gender Correlated with Their Degree of Sensation-Seeking

Gender	High Sensation-Seeker	Moderate Sensation-Seeker	Low Sensation-Seeker	Total
Male	24 13.3%	145 80.6%	11 6.1%	180 100.0%
Female	2 8.3%	14 58.3%	8 33.3%	24 100.0%

- Significant at the .000 level with 2 degrees of freedom.

- Results show that *males* are much more likely than females to be ranked as *High Sensation-Seekers*, whereas *females* are much more likely to be ranked as *Low Sensation-Seekers*.

Crosstab 2: Respondent's Age at Time of Rescue Correlated with Their Score on the Sensation-Seeking Scale

Age at Time of Rescue	High Sensation-Seeker	Moderate Sensation-Seeker	Low Sensation-Seeker	Total
11 – 20 years old	11 48.8%	13 54.2%	0 0.0%	24 100.0%
21 – 30 years old	8 15.7%	38 74.5%	5 9.8%	51 100.0%
31 – 40 years old	2 3.0%	60 90.5%	4 6.15%	66 100.0%
41 – 50 years old	4 9.5%	31 73.8%	7 16.7%	42 100.0%
51 – 60 years old	1 7.7 %	10 76.9%	2 15.4%	13 100.0%
61 – 70 years old	0 0.0%	5 83.3%	1 16.7%	6 100.0%
71 – 80 years old	0 0.0%	2 100.0%	0 0.0%	2 100.0%

- Significant at the .000 level with 12 degrees of freedom.

- Results show that younger respondents were more likely to be ranked higher on the *Sensation-Seeking Scale*, whereas older respondents were more likely to be classified as having a *Moderate* or *Low* degree of *Sensation-Seeking*.

Crosstab 3: Respondent's Report of Prior Helping Behavior Correlated with Their Score on the Altruistic Personality Scale

	High Altruistic Personality	Moderate Altruistic Personality	Low Altruistic Personality	Total
Prior Helping Behavior Reported	43 25.4%	123 72.8%	3 1.8%	169 100.0%
No Prior Helping Behavior Reported	2 6.1%	28 84.8%	3 9.1%	33 100.0%

- Significant at the .006 level with 2 degrees of freedom.

- Results show that respondents who indicated prior helping behavior were much more likely to have been measured as having a *High Altruistic Personality* with an inverse relationship exhibited for those ranked as having a *Low Altruistic Personality*.

Crosstab 4: Respondent's Self-Reported Level of Religiousness/Spirituality Correlated with Their Sense of Commonality with Diverse Others

	High Commonality with Others	Moderate Commonality with Others	Low Commonality with Others	Total
Very or Somewhat Religious or Spiritual	56 33.1%	102 60.4%	11 6.5%	169 100.0%
Not Very or Not at All Religious or Spiritual	5 13.2%	25 65.8%	8 21.1%	38 100.0%

- Significant at the .003 level with 2 degrees of freedom.

- Results show that respondents who classified themselves as *Very* or *Somewhat Religious or Spiritual* were more likely to corresponding rank as having a *High Sense of Commonality with Diverse Others* than were respondents who reported that they were*Not Very* or *Not at All Religious or Spiritual.*

- Inversely, respondents who reported that they were *Not Very* or *Not at All Religious or Spiritual* were more likely to rank as having a *Low Sense of Commonality with Diverse Others* than were respondents who classified themselves as *Very* or *Somewhat Religious or Spiritual.*

Appendix F

∽

Hospice Volunteers Data

(See Chapter 9)

All hospice volunteers were interviewed by trained interviewers. The interviews were recorded and transcribed. Seventy-three nonhospice volunteers who may have volunteered in other settings and nonvolunteers were given an abbreviated version of the hospice volunteer questionnaire that they completed by themselves. This group was categorized by level of volunteering. Forty-three were classified as high-level volunteers—those who volunteered substantially more than six hours per week. The other thirty individuals either volunteered occasionally or not at all.

The questionnaire consisted of three sections, which included both open- and closed-ended questions. Section A dealt with the characteristics of the family milieu during the respondents' childhood and the relationship between family members. Section B explored the respondents' parental, educational, and occupational background, their political beliefs, religiosity, and values, and the disciplinary techniques used in their upbringing. Section C focused on such matters as the respondents' degree of closeness to parents and significant others, religious background and relative health of parents and significant others, whether parents or significant others volunteered, and how parents felt about their own volunteer experience. Also included in Section C were forty-two personality items composing four psychological scales:[1] (1) the Social Responsibility scale, developed by Berkowitz and Luterman (1968); (2) the Internal/External Locus of Control, developed by Rotter (1966) and modified by Gurin, Gurin, and Morrison (1978); (3) the Self Esteem scale developed by Rosenburg (1965); and (4) the Empathy scale developed by Mehrabian and Epstein

(1972) and modified by E. Midlarsky (1981). In addition, we included Oliner and Oliner's Diversity scale, which measures identification with nonparochial groups.[2]

In addition to the categorization of nonhospice volunteers by amount of time spent in volunteer activities, this sample was also separated into two groups based upon the nature of volunteer activity, that is, parochial or nonparochial volunteer behavior. Parochial volunteers limited their volunteer activities to their children's school, their church, club, or political group, whereas nonparochial volunteers volunteered beyond their own social group. The responses to closed-ended questions were analyzed by computer, and open-ended questions were read, assessed, and coded into categories for comparison.[3] The nature of the sample did allow for simple correlations and percentages.

The hospice sample was 73 percent female, and 88 percent of the sample was forty years old or older. It was overwhelmingly Caucasian (96.9 percent), and although only 57 percent identified with a Judeo-Christian religious tradition, 85 percent described themselves as "very" or "somewhat" religious. Within the hospice sample, 97 percent had prior voluntary experience. Seventy-five percent reported that their mothers had volunteered, 49 percent that their fathers had done so.

Within the high-level volunteers, 63 percent were female, 58 percent were over forty, and 83 percent were Caucasian. Seventy-six percent identified themselves as Protestant, Catholic, or Jewish, and 83 percent described themselves as "very" or "somewhat" religious. Of the high-level volunteers, 58 percent reported that their mothers had volunteered, 49 percent that their fathers were volunteers. Of the low-level and nonvolunteer group, 58 percent were female, 36 percent were over forty, and 80 percent were Caucasian. Ninety-two percent were either Protestant or Catholic, and 76 percent described themselves as "very" or "somewhat" religious.

Comparisons of hospice volunteers and nonhospice volunteers demonstrated no significant difference with regard to self-esteem or internal/external locus of control. Hospice volunteers and high-level volunteers scored significantly higher on measures of empathy and social responsibility, and hospice volunteer scores were higher than those of high-level volunteers on these two measures. Hospice volunteers scored significantly higher on measures of intrinsic religiosity; that is, religiosity that is implicit in its nature and in the personal orientation by which one lives. Low-level and nonvolunteers scored higher on measures of extrinsic religious orientation; that is, utilitarian, explicit, and self-justifying in nature.

In response to the question "What is the most important thing you learned from your mother?" the most frequent response among hospice volunteers was religion, followed by kindness, compassion, and empathy. Religion was also found to be the most frequent response in the nonhospice group, indicating that although religion plays an important role in one's life, it depends on the nature of religiosity—that is, intrinsic versus extrensic.

Hard work and honesty were the most frequent responses in both samples to the question "What is the most important thing you learned from your father?"

There was also little difference between the two groups when asked whom they most admired; parents and spouses were the most frequent responses of those who cited individuals known to them personally. The next most frequently admired response among hospice volunteers was hospice workers and administrators or hospice patients. From these results, it is easy to see that family and friends play an influential role in volunteer's lives, as well as other hospice workers.

Another question that sought to illustrate the respondents' values and beliefs asked what advice they would give to young people about what things are important in life.[4] The most frequently cited advice by hospice volunteers was to be true to oneself and respect others, followed by advice to follow your heart, to be aware of self and others, and to recognize one's connection to others. The most frequent responses to the question of advice to the young of high-level volunteers were similar, whereas the most frequent responses of low-level volunteers' and nonvolunteers' were to have faith in God, enjoy life, and be responsible.

The responses to this question were then classified as to extensivity, that is, whether they referred to the respondent's connection to others in terms of service, care, respect, and acceptance. Half of the hospice volunteers and high-level volunteers gave extensive responses, whereas in the low-level volunteers and nonvolunteers extensive responses were found in 25 percent or less of the responses. This tendency toward extensivity was also found to correlate when categorizing the nonhospice volunteers by the type of volunteering. Forty-five percent of nonparochial volunteers gave extensive responses, whereas only one-third of the parochial volunteers mentioned connection to others and putting the welfare of others before their own.

On the diversity scale, hospice volunteers and high-level volunteers responded that they felt they had more in common with diverse groups of people than did the low-level or nonvolunteer group. This included more favorable attitudes toward African Americans, Jewish Americans, homosexuals, and so forth. However, hospice volunteers did not appear to value certain other groups, as indicated by their responses regarding groups toward which they have strong negative feelings. Of the fifty-two hospice volunteers who admitted strong negative feelings toward a group, 96 percent identified groups such as the Ku Klux Klan, Aryan Nation, religious fundamentalists, bigots, or polarizing and intolerant groups.

Although there was no apparent difference in the history of discipline as a child—more than 95 percent responded that they were disciplined as children—

there did appear to be a difference in the type of discipline reported, whether physical or verbal. Physical discipline was reported by 39 percent of the hospice volunteers, whereas 60 percent of the high-level volunteers and 78 percent of the low-level and nonvolunteers reported physical discipline. Therefore, discipline of a certain nature does matter, that is, physical discipline has negative correlation, whereas speaking and explaining through the problems has positive outcomes for helping behavior.

Notes

Appendix B

1. Mordecai Paldiel, 1999. "Primo Levi's Hassid," *Yad Vashem Quarterly Magazine.* vol. 12: 14. See also Mordecai Paldiel, 1987. "Why They Risked Their Lives to Save Jews," *The Jerusalem Post*, September 21, p.8.

2. Ibid.

3. Walter Ian Fischman, 1964. "The Friar who Saved 5,000 Jews," *Look Magazine*, December 1, pp. 67–71.

4. Walter Meyerhof, 1998. "Recognition of Varian Fry, the 'American Schindler.'" *Stanford University Physics Newsletter*, November, p. 5. See also Pierre Sauvage, 2001. "Varian Fry in Marseille," *Remembering For the Future: The Holocaust in an Age of Genocide*, edited by John K. Roth and Elizabeth Maxwell. Hampshire, UK: Palgrave; Varian Fry, (1968) 1992. *Assignment: Rescue. An Autobiography.* New York: Scholastic, Inc ; Pierre Sauvage, 2000. "Dedication Ceremony for Varian Fry outside U.S. Consulate in Marseille, France." Courtesy of the Chambon Foundation, October 18; Showtime Television, 2001. "Varian Fry's War." Feature Film, June 4. On June 4, 2001, a video titled *Varian Fry's War* played on Showtime Cable Network. It portrays the struggles and intrigues the charismatic Fry employed to save Jewish intellectuals and others who he felt were scheduled for extermination, describing how Fry, arriving with funds in Vichy France, was able to ship some of these intellectuals to Spain, and subsequently to the United States; BBC Online, 2001. *The Artist's Schindler*, June 8. Retrieved June 10, 2001, http://www.bbc.co.uk/works/s3/fry/; Anita Kassof, *Varian Fry and the Emergency Rescue Committee: A Resource Guide for Teachers.* Washington, DC: Holocaust Teacher Resource Center. Retrieved May 5, 2000, http://www.holocaust-trc.org/fry.htm.

5. Joel Greenberg, 1999. "Crisis in the Balkans: Refugees; an Indebted Israel Shelters Family of Kosovo Albanians," *New York Times*, May 2, p. A1.

6. Ibid.

7. Ibid.

8. Ibid.

9. Rittner and Myers, *The Courage to Care,* pp. 28–31.

10. Ibid., p. 33; In 1983 Yad Vashem honored Marion P. van Binsbergen Pritchard for helping Jews during the Nazi occupation.

11. Michael Smith, 1999. *Foley: The Spy Who Saved 10,000 Jews*. London: Hodder and Stoughton.

12. Electronic Telegraph Reporter, "Call for Israel to honour forgotten British hero." Issue 1317, January 2, 1999. Retrieved April 18, 2001, http://www.cnwl. igs.net/~zes/foleyspy.htm

Appendix C

1. See Oliner and Lee, *Who Shall Live*. See also Michael Berenbaum and Abraham J. Peck (eds.), 1998. *The Holocaust and History: The Known, The Unknown, The Disputed and The Reexamined*. Bloomington, IN: Indiana University Press. Published in association with the United States Holocaust Memorial Museum.

2. Yehezkel Langsam, "American Gathering of Jewish Holocaust Survivors, " in *Together*, January 1999, 13, 1: p. 16. See also David S. Wyman, 1998. *The Abandonment of the Jews: America and the Holocaust, 1941–1945*. New York: The New Press; Seymour Brody's (1996) *Jewish Heroes and Heroines of America: 150 True Stories of American Jewish Heroism*.

3. See Lucien Lazare, 1996. *Rescue as Resistance: How Jewish Organizations Fought the Holocaust in France*. New York: Columbia University Press.

Appendix D

1. See Appendix A

Appendix F

1. (a) The *Social Responsibility Scale* was developed by L. Berkowitz and K. Luterman, 1968, ('The Traditionally Socially Responsible Personality,' *Public Opinion Quarterly*, 32:169–185), see Oliner and Oliner, 1988, p. 376. (b) The *Internal/External Locus of Control Scale* was developed by J. B. Rotter, 1966, ('Generalized Expectancies for Internal Versus External Control of Reinforcement,' *Psychological Monographs,* 80:1); we used an adaptation developed by G. Gurin, P. Gurin, and B. M. Morrison, 1978, ('Personal and Ideological Aspects of Internal and External Control,' *Social Psychology,* 41, 4:275–296. (c) The *Self-Esteem Scale* we used was developed by M. Rosenberg, 1965, (*Society and the Adolescent Self-Image,* Princeton, NJ: Princeton University Press), see Oliner and Oliner, 1988, p. 378. (d) The *Empathy Scale* was developed by A Mehrabian and N. A. Epstein, 1972, "A Measure of Emotional Empathy," *Journal of Personality* 40: 525–543.

2. Oliner and Oliner, *The Altruistic Personality,* p. 302. Using a Likert scale, we asked respondents whether they have something in common with diverse other people. The question asked was: Some people think that they have things in common with others. Please tell me if you have very much in common with the following groups, something in common, not very much in common, or nothing at all in common. This commonality scale was originally developed for the research on the rescuers of Jews in Nazi-occupied Europe, so the groups identified were rich people, poor people, Catholics, Protestants, Jews, Turks, Gypsies, and Nazis. For purposes of the hospice volunteer study, the list was amended to: rich people, poor people, Catholics, Protestants, Jews, Native Americans, Mexican Americans, Black Americans, and homosexuals.

3. For example, for question B19, which asked "What was the most important thing you learned from your mother?" responses could be grouped under headings such as religion, compassion, kindness, independence, getting ahead, etc.

4. · C35. If you had an opportunity to speak to a group of young people, what kinds of advice would you offer them? That is, what would you consider the most important thing about life?

Notes

Preface

1. Robert Putnam, ([2000] 2001), *Bowling Alone: The Collapse and Revival of American Community* (New York: Touchstone Publishers).

2. Robert Putnam (2002), "Bowling Together: The United States of America," *American Prospect*, February: 20–22.

3. Robert Coles (1989), *The Call of Stories: Teaching and Moral Imagination* (Boston: Houghton Mifflin).

Chapter 1

1. See Samuel P. Oliner (2000). *Narrow Escapes: A Boy's Holocaust Memories and Their Legacy.* (St. Paul, MN: Paragon House).

2. Yad Vashem is an organization established by the state of Israel in 1953 in order to honor and recognize non-Jewish heroes who risked their lives to save Jewish lives during the Nazi occupation.

3. See T. R. Sarbin (1986), "The Narrative as a Root Metaphor for Psychology," in T.R. Sarbin, ed., *Narrative Psychology: The Storied Nature of Human Conduct* (New York: Praeger), pp. 3–21; P. C. Vitz (1985). *A Critical Review of Kohlberg's Model of Moral Development.* Unpublished report for the Department of Education, Washington, D.C.; E. Tulving, (1983), *Elements of Episodic Memory,* (New York: Oxford University Press).

4. See http://www.pass.to/newsletter/pal_saluted_for_last_act_of_hero.htm.

5. Barbara Ross (2002), "Cops Finds Man Who Saved Her," *New York Daily News,* Thursday, January 3 (Lexis-Nexus Academic Universe, retrived January 29, 2002, http://www.lexis-nexis.com/universe/document).

6. Pitirim A. Sorokin (1942), *Man and Society in Calamity* (New York: Dutton Books), pp. 271–273. See also David Blumenthal (1999), *The Banality of Good and*

Notes

Evil: Moral Lessons from the Shoah and Jewish Tradition (Washington DC: Georgetown University Press).

Chapter 2

1. Since the Carnegie Hero Fund Commission was founded, its definition of a hero has gone largely unchanged from Andrew Carnegie's original conception; it is the same operational definition used in this study: "A civilian who knowingly risks his or her own life to an extraordinary degree while saving or attempting to save the life of another person." This definition is reflected in the New Testament verse that appears on each medal: "Greater love has no man than this, that a man lay down his life for his friends" (John 15:13). Taken from Anna F. LoMascolo (1999), "Toward a Sociological Understanding of Heroic Behavior: A Focus on Carnegie Heroes." Unpublished master's thesis, Department of Sociology, Humboldt State University, Arcata, CA.

2. BBC News (December 15, 2001), "Profile: Hero of the Twin Towers" (retrieved May 9, 2002, from http://news.bbc.co.uk). See also American Legion (2001), "Petition To Honor Rick Rescorla: One of the Heroes at the World Trade Center" (Scottsdale, AZ: Sipe-Peterson Post 44, retrieved May 9, 2002, from http://www.post44.org/misc.rescorla.html); *New York Times* (2002), *Portraits 9/11/01* (New York: Times Books), p. 416; Life: A Commemorative (2001), *In the Land of the Free: September 11—And After* (New York: Time); Dennis Smith (2002), *A Report from Ground Zero* (New York: Viking Press); Richard Picciotto (2002), *Last Man Down* (New York: Berkley Books); David Halberstam (2002), *Firehouse* (New York: Hyperion); Lisa Beamer (2002), *Let's Roll: Ordinary People, Extraordinary Courage* (London: Tyndale Press); Geraldine Baum (2002), *Running Toward Danger: Stories Behind the Breaking News of 9/11* (New York: Rowman and Littlefield); Richard Bernstein (2002), *Out of the Blue: A Narrative of September 11, 2001* (New York: Henry Holt); Dean E. Murphy (2002), *September 11: An Oral History* (New York: Doubleday); James B. Stewart (2002), *The Heart of a Soldier* (New York: Simon and Schuster); Jere Longman (2002), *Among the Heroes: United Flight 93 and the Passengers and Crew Who Fought Back* (New York: HarperCollins).

3. BBC News (December 15, 2001), "Profile: Hero of the Twin Towers."

4. Morton Hunt (1990), *The Compassionate Beast: What Science Is Discovering about the Humane Side of Mankind* (New York: William Morrow). See also Lawrence A. Blum (1980), *Friendship, Altruism, and Morality* (London: Routledge and Kegan Paul).

5. Iris Murdock (1985), *The Sovereignty of Good* (London: Ark Paperbacks). See also Paul Tillich (1968), *Love, Power, and Justice* (London: Oxford University Press, rpt.); Pitirim A. Sorokin (1950a), *The Ways and Power of Love* (New York: Bantam Books); Pitirim A. Sorokin (1950b), *Altruistic Love: A Study of "Good Neighbors" and Christian Saint*s (Boston: Beacon Press); Pitirim A. Sorokin (1950c), *Explorations in Altruistic Love and Behavior* (Boston: Beacon Press); Ronit Kishon Barash (1995), "Factors Associated with Two Facets of Altruism in Vietnam War Veterans with Post-

Traumatic Stress Disorder" (UMI Microform #9606908, Ann Arbor, MI); Joseph Allen Matter (1974), *Love, Altruism, and World Crisis: The Challenge of Pitirim Sorokin* (Chicago: Nelson-Hall); Joseph B. Ford et al. (1996), *Sorokin and Civilization: A Centennial Assessment* (New Brunswick, NJ: Transaction Publishers); Pitirim Sorokin (1941), *The Crisis of Our Age* (New York: Dutton Books).

6. Dennis L. Krebs and Frank Van Hesteren (1992), "The Development of Altruistic Personality," in *Embracing the Other*, edited by Pearl M. Oliner, Samuel P. Oliner, Lawrence Beacon, Lawrence A. Blum, Dennis L. Krebs, and M. Zuzanna Smolenska (New York: New York University Press), pp. 142–169. See also C. Daniel Batson (1991), *The Altruism Question* (Hillsdale, NJ: Lawrence Erlbaum Associates).

7. Samuel P. Oliner (2002), "Extraordinary Acts of Ordinary People: Faces of Heroism and Altruism," in *Altruism and Altruistic Love*, edited by Stephen G. Post et al. (New York: Oxford University Press), pp. 123–139. See also L. Berkowitz and J. R. Macaulay, eds. (1970), *Altruism and Helping Behavior* (New York: Academic Press), p. 3; J. Phillippe Rushton (1980), *Altruism, Socialization, and Society* (Englewood Cliffs, NJ: Prentice-Hall), p. 8; Krebs and Hesteren, "The Development of Altruistic Personality," pp. 142–169; Vincent Jeffries (1998), "Virtue and the Altruistic Personality," *Sociological Perspectives* 41, 1: 151–166; David Rosenhan (1970), "The Natural Socialization of Altruistic Autonomy," in *Altruism and Helping Behavior*, edited by Jacqueline R. Macaulay and Leonard Berkowitz (New York: Academic Press), pp. 251–268. See also Christina S. Sinisi (1993), "The Origins of Volunteerism: Socialization Antecedents and Personal Variables," Ph.D. diss., Department of Psychology, Kansas State University, Manhattan, pp. 79–80; J. P. Wilson and R. Petruska (1984), "Motivation, Model Attributes, and Prosocial Behavior," *Journal of Personality and Social Psychology* 46: 458–468.

8. *CBS News* Video (2001), "Port Authority" (Friday, October 19). See also American Liberty Partnership, "September 11, 2001, Victims" (retrieved September 13, 2002, from http://www.september11victims.com/september11victims/STATISTIC.asp).

9. See Miriam Polster (1992), *Eve's Daughters: The Forbidden Heroism of Women* (San Francisco: Jossey-Bass), who focuses on five major attributes that heroes possess: "(1) all heroes are motivated by a profound respect for life. (2) Heroes have a strong personal choice and effectiveness. (3) Their perspective on the world is original, going beyond what other people think is possible. (4) They are individuals of great physical and mental courage. (5) Heroes are not measured by publicity. Whether a heroic act received world-wide attention or occurs in an obscure setting and witnessed by a single witness, a heroic act is still heroic."

10. See "Our Lady of Refuge Home Page" (retrieved September 30, 2001, from http://www.ourladyofrefuge.com/news.htm).

11. See Jere Longman (2002), *Among the Heroes: United Flight 93 and the Passengers and Crew Who Fought Back* (New York: HarperCollins). The heroism of the passengers on Flight 93 is described in detail by Longman, a *New York Times* journalist.

12. See the Henry Hazlitt Foundation Home Page (retrieved September 31, 2001, from http://www.hazlitt.org/united/whotheywere2.html#HonorWainio).

13. Betty Jean Lifton (1988), *The King of Children* (New York: Farrar, Straus, and Giroux). See also Janusz Korczak (1978), *The Ghetto Diary* (New York: Holocaust Library); and Janusz Korczak (1986), *King Matt the First*, translated by Richard Lourie (New York: Farrer, Straus, and Giroux).

14. Lifton, *The King of Children*, p. 345.

15. For more information on heroes and heroic activity, see Sidney Hook (1943), *The Hero in History* (Boston: Beacon Press); Dr. Robert Pamplin Jr. and Gary K. Eisler (1995), *American Heroes: Their Lives, Their Values, Their Beliefs* (New York: Mastermedia); The Mille Lacs Band of Ojibwe Indians (1996), *A Hero's Voice* (Onamia, MN); Iris Chang (1997), *The Rape of Nanking* (New York: Penguin USA); Kathryn Bel Monte (1998), *African-American Heroes and Heroines: 150 True Stories of African-American Heroism* (Hollywood, FL: Lifetime Books); Susan J. Drucker and Robert Cathcart, eds. (1994), *American Heroes in a Media Age* (Kresskill, NJ: Hampton Press); Joseph Campbell (1968), *Hero with a Thousand Faces*, 2nd ed., Bollingen Series 17 (Princeton, NJ: Princeton University Press).

Chapter 3

1. Samuel P. Oliner and Pearl M. Oliner (1988), *The Altruistic Personality: Rescuers of Jews in Nazi Europe* (New York: The Free Press). We interviewed a sample of bona fide rescuers, as well as nonrescuers, who lived in Nazi-occupied Europe. These rescuers were recognized by Yad Vashem, an Israeli government organization that was established in 1953 to honor and memorialize non-Jews who rescued Jews during the Nazi occupation. Susan Zuccotti (1987), *The Italians and the Holocaust: Persecution, Rescue, and Survival* (New York: Basic Books); Eva Fogelman (1994), *Conscience and Courage: Rescuers of Jews During the Holocaust* (New York: Doubleday); Nechama Tec (1986), *When Light Pierced the Darkness: Christian Rescue of Jews in Nazi-Occupied Poland* (Oxford: Oxford University Press); D. Capri (1977), "The Rescue of Jews in the Italian Zone of Occupied Croatia," in *Rescue Attempts During the Holocaust: Proceedings of the Second Yad Vashem International Historical Conference,* edited by Y. Gutman and E. Zuroff (Jerusalem, April 8–11, 1974), pp. 465–525; Lawrence Baron (1988), "The Historical Context of Rescue," in *The Altruistic Personality*, pp. 13–48; Lawrence Baron (1992), "The Dutchness of Dutch Rescuers: The National Dimension of Altruism," in *Embracing the Other*, edited by P. Oliner et al. (New York: New York University Press), pp. 306–307; Victoria J. Barnett (1999), *Bystanders: Conscience and Complicity in the Holocaust* (Westport, CT: Greenwood); Lawrence Baron (1985–1986), "The Holocaust and Human Decency: A Review of Research on the Rescue of Jews in Nazi-Occupied Europe," *Humboldt Journal of Social Relations* 13, 1–2: 237–251. See also Philip Hallie (1979), *Lest Innocent Blood Be Shed* (New York: Harper and Row); Martin L. Hoffman (1970), "Parents, Discipline, and Child's Consideration for Others," *Child Development* 34: 573–588; R. Hogan (1969), "Development of an Empathetic Scale,"

Journal of Consulting and Clinical Psychology 33: 307–316; Ellen Land-Weber (2000), *To Save a Life: Stories of Holocaust Rescue* (Urbana: University of Illinois Press); Arnold Geier (1993), *Heroes of the Holocaust* (Miami: Londonbooks/USA); Israel Charny, ed. (1999), *Encyclopedia of Genocide*, 2 vols. (Santa Barbara, CA: ABC-CLIO); John K. Roth and Elizabeth Maxwell, eds. (2001), *Remembering for the Future: The Holocaust in an Age of Genocide*, 2 vols. (Hampshire, UK, and New York: Palgrave); M. Zuzanna Smolenska and Janusz Reykowski (1992), "Motivations of People Who Helped Jews Survive the Nazi Occupation," in *Embracing the Other*, pp. 213–225.

2. Janusz Reykowski and Jerzy Karylowski (1984), "Part V Introduction," in *Development and Maintenance of Prosocial Behavior: International Perspectives on Positive Morality*, edited by Ervin Staub, Daniel Bar-Tal, Jerzy Karylowski, and Janusz Reykowski (New York: Plenum Press). Based upon theoretical proposals developed in the work cited above, we were able to discern three kinds of catalysts that generally aroused a response. They were able to serve as catalysts because they were congruent with the ways rescuers characteristically made important life decisions. Rescuers who were characteristically *empathically* oriented responded to an external event that aroused or heightened their empathy. Rescuers who where characteristically *normocentrically* oriented responded to an external event that they interpreted as a normative demand of a highly valued social group. Rescuers who characteristically behaved according to their own overarching *principles*, in the main autonomously derived, were moved to respond by an external event that they interpreted as violating these principles.

3. The following narratives showing empathy, norms, religiosity, and principles of justice are taken from interviews for the Altruistic Personality and Prosocial Behavior Institute and the book *The Altruistic Personality*.

4. Paul Blustein (1994), "Japan's Savior of the Jews," *San Francisco Chronicle*, October 16. See also Peter Hellman (1980), *Avenue of the Righteous* (New York: Atheneum); Ivo Herzer (1989), *The Italian Refuge: Rescue of Jews During the Holocaust* (Washington, DC: Catholic University of America Press); Alfie Kohn (1990), *The Brighter Side of Human Nature* (New York: Basic Books); R. J. Lifton (1986), *The Nazi Doctors: Medical Killing and The Psychology of Genocide* (New York: Basic Books).

5. Israel Gutman, ed. (1990), *Encyclopedia of the Holocaust*, vol. 3 (New York: MacMillan Publishing), pp. 1262–1265, 1424. See also Jeno Levai ([1948] 1988), *Raoul Wallenberg: His Remarkable Life, Heroic Battles, and the Secret of His Mysterious Disappearance*, translated by Frank Vajda (Melbourne, Australia: White Ant Occasional Publishing); Samuel P. Oliner and Pearl M. Oliner (1999), "Rescuers of Jews in Nazi Europe," in *Encyclopedia Of Genocide*, vol. 2, edited by Israel Charny (Santa Barbara, CA: Institute on the Holocaust and Genocide), pp. 496–499; Naomi Shepherd (1984), *A Refuge from Darkness: Wilfrid Israel and the Rescue of the Jews* (New York: Pantheon Books).

6. A&E Television Networks (1996), *History Undercover: Diplomats for the Damned* (New York: New Video Group). See also Press Corner, "Topic WWII: Carl Lutz: The Swiss Consul Who in 1944 Saved 62,000 Jews in Budapest" (Swiss Em-

bassy, Washington, DC, retrieved May 7, 2001, from http://www.swissemb. org/press/html/carl_lutz.html); Theo Tschuy (2000), *Dangerous Diplomacy: The Story of Carl Lutz: Rescuer of 62,000 Hungarian Jews* (Grand Rapids, MI: William B. Eerdmans); David Kranzler (2000), *The Man Who Stopped the Train to Auschwitz: George Mantello, El Salvador, and Switzerland's Finest Hour* (Syracuse, NY: Syracuse University Press); Rabbi Israel Zoberman (2001), "Some Swiss Were Heroes," *Post and Opinion*, May 30, NAT 16; Meir Wagner (2001), "The Righteous of Switzerland," in *Heroes of the Holocaust*, edited by Andreas C. Fischer and Graham Buik (New York: Ktav Publishing House).

7. A&E Television Networks, *History Undercover: Diplomats for the Damned.* See also Georg Ferdinand Duckwitz (retrieved May 7, 2001, from http://www.yad-vashem.org.il/right-many/duckwitz_georg_ferdinand.html [address no longer on-line]); Peachtree Publishers (1998), *The Escape of the Danish Jews* (retrieved May 7, 2001, from http://www.peachtree-online.com/Yellow_ Star_no_art/Adults/escape.adult.htm); David Lampe (1957), *The Danish Resistance* (New York: Ballentine Books).

8. See also Leo Goldberger (1987), *The Rescue of the Danish Jews: Moral Courage Under Stress* (New York: New York University Press).

9. Gutman, *Encyclopedia of the Holocaust*, vol. 3, p. 1424.

10. Ernie Meyer (1989), "Rescue in Budapest," *Jerusalem Post International Edition*, October 7, pp. 9.

11. Tekla Szymanski (2001), "Giorgio Perlasca: Italian Wallenberg," *World Press Review*, January, p.35.

12. Meyer, "Rescue in Budapest," p. 14.

13. Ibid., pp. 9, 14.

14. Szymanski, "Giorgio Perlasca," p. 35.

15. Israel Gutman, ed. (1990), *Encyclopedia of the Holocaust*, vol. 4 (New York: MacMillan Publishing), pp. 1339–1340.

16. Taken from the Talmud.

17. Talia Rubin (2000), "Jan Karski, Alerted World to Shoah, 86." *Forward*, July 21, p.8. See also Douglas K. Huneke (1995), *The Stones Will Cry Out: Pastoral Reflections on the Shoah (with Liturgical Resources)* (Westport, CT: Greenwood Press).

18. *Newsweek* (1999), "Voices of the Century; World War II: Word from the Ghetto," March 8, p. 47. See also Thomas E. Wood and Stanislaw M. Jankowski (1994), *Karski: How One Man Tried to Stop the Holocaust* (New York: John Wiley and Sons).

19. *Newsweek*, "Voices of the Century," p. 188.

20. History Channel and MPR Film (2000), "Hitler's Holocaust: The Final Toll." Videotape, aired June 19, 2001, Und Furnesh Produktion; See also David S. Wyman (1998), *The Abandonment of the Jews: America and the Holocaust, 1941–1945* (New York: The New Press); Monty Penkower (1983), *The Jews Were Expendable: Free World Diplomacy and the Holocaust* (Urbana: University of Illinois Press).

21. Douglas K. Huneke (1985), *The Moses of Rovno: The Stirring Story of Fritz Graebe—A German Christian Who Risked His Life to Lead Hundreds of Jews to Safety During the Holocaust* (New York: Dodd, Mead). See also David P. Gushee (1994), *The Righteous Gentiles of the Holocaust: A Christian Interpretation* (Minneapolis, MN: Fortress Press); Douglas K. Huneke (1986), "The Lessons of Herman Graebe's Life: The Origins of a Moral Person," *Humboldt Journal of Social Relations* 13, 1–2: 320–332; Pierre Sauvage (1986), "Ten Things I Would Like to Know About Righteous Conduct," *Humboldt Journal of Social Relations* 13, 1–2: 252–259.

22. Huneke, *The Moses of Rovno*, p. 158.

23. Carol Rittner and Sondra Myers, eds. (1986), *The Courage to Care* (New York: New York University Press), pp. 100–107. See also Amy Fried (1997), "Gendered Heroism, Limited Politics," *Women and Politics* 17, 2: 43–75; K. Konarzewski and G. Zychlinska (1978), "The Effect of Psychological Differentiation and Perceived Similarity on Allocentric Behavior," *Psychologia Wychowawcza* 1: 21–36 (in Polish); Ervin Staub (1978), *Positive Social Behavior and Morality*, vol. 1 (New York: Academic Press); Ervin Staub (1979), *Positive Social Behavior and Morality: Socialization and Development*, vol. 2 (New York: Academic Press); Ervin Staub, Daniel Bar-Tal, Jerzy Karylowski, and Janusz Reykowski, eds. (1984), *Development and Maintenance of Prosocial Behavior: International Perspectives on Positive Morality* (New York: Plenum Press).

24. Rittner and Myers, eds, *The Courage to Care*, p. 107.

25. Philip Hallie (1979), *Lest Innocent Blood Be Shed* (New York: Harper and Row), p. 265. See also Pierre Sauvage (1989), *Weapons of the Spirit: Friends of Le Chambon*. Video documentary, Los Angeles, Chambon Foundation.

26. Hallie, *Lest Innocent Blood Be Shed*, p. 265.

27. Lawrence M. Rothbaum (1999), "Albania's Saving of Jews Is Little-Known Episode," *Martyrdom and Resistance*, January/February, p. 15.

Chapter 4

1. Lawrence Elliott (1997), "Heroine in Hell," *Reader's Digest*, November, pp. 75–80; See also Peter Hay (1989), *Ordinary Heroes: The Life and Death of Chana Szenes, Israel's National Heroine* (New York: Paragon House).

2. Rabbi Elliot B. Gertel (1998), "The Angel of Bergen-Belsen," *Post and Opinion*, March 11, p. NAT5. See also Bill Curtis (1998), A&E's *Investigative Reports*, video, "The Angel of Bergen-Belsen."

3. Carol Lipson (1999), "A Lesson in Courage," *Together*, January, p. 9; Reuben Ainsztein (1974), *Jewish Resistance in Nazi-Occupied Eastern Europe* (New York: Barnes and Noble Books); N. Tec (1990), *In the Lion's Den: The Life of Oswald Rufeisen* (New York: Oxford University Press); L. Baron (1988), "The Historical Context of Rescue," in *Altruistic Personality*, edited by P. Oliner and S. Oliner (New York: The Free Press), pp. 13–48; Michael Berenbaum (1993), *The World Must Know: The History of the Holocaust as Told in the United States Holocaust Memorial Museum* (Boston: Little, Brown); M. Berenbaum and A. Peck, eds. (1998), *The Holocaust and History: The Known, the Unknown, the Disputed, and the Reexamined*

(Bloomington: Indiana University Press), published in association with the United States Holocaust Memorial Museum; Hersh Smoliar (1966), *Resistance in Minsk*, translated by H.J. Lewbin (Oakland, CA: Judah L. Magnes Memorial Museum). There are several dozen books and articles about resistance in various parts of Europe. Only a few institutions in the United States, Israel, and Germany were helpful in providing the names of Jewish rescuers: the Moreshet Archives in Israel, the Vidal Sassoon International Center, the Tel Aviv University Wiener Library, Bet Lohamei Haghetaot Ghetto Fighters, the United States Holocaust Memorial Museum in Washington, the Fortunoff Video Archives for Holocaust Testimonies at Yale University, the Technische Universitat in Berlin, and the St. Louis Center for Holocaust Studies. In all of these cases only detailed searches can reveal the names of the Jewish rescuers.

4. Yehuda Bauer (1981), "Jewish Leadership Reactions to Nazi Policies," in *The Holocaust as Historical Experience*, edited by Y. Bauer and N. Rotenstreich (New York: Holmes and Meier), pp. 173–192. See also Lucien Steinberg (1974), *Not as a Lamb: The Jews Against Hitler* (London: Saxon House); Ruby Rohrlich, ed. (1998), *Resisting the Holocaust* (New York: Berg Publishers).

5. Rubin Ainsztein (1974), *Jewish Resistance in Nazi-occupied Eastern Europe* (New York: Barnes and Noble Books).

6. Yehuda Bauer and Nili Keren (1982), *A History of the Holocaust* (New York: Franklin Watts), p.247. See also Anny Latour (1981), *The Jewish Resistance in France, 1940–1944*, translated by Irene R. Ilton (New York: Holocaust Library); Lucien Lazare (1994), *Rescue as Resistance: How Jewish Organizations Fought the Holocaust in France*, translated by Jeffrey M. Green (New York: Columbia University Press); Jacques Sémelin (1993), *Unarmed Against Hitler: Civilian Resistance in Europe, 1939–1943*, translated by S. Hussert-Kapit (Westport, CT: Praeger); Meyer Barkai, ed. and trans. (1962), *The Fighting Ghettos* (New York: Tower Books); George Kent (1962), "200,000 Persecutions Prevented," *Together*, February, p. 169.

7. Although it has been estimated that 15 percent of Italian Jews lost their lives because Italians did not regard the Jews as the "other," the figure was 90 percent for Poland, which had a long tradition of anti-Semitism and experienced the harsh conditions of German occupation; see Baron, "The Historical Context of Rescue," pp. 25, 44. Jews who attempted to join partisan units were much less successful in Poland than in occupied Soviet Union, where they had Soviet support.

8. See Israel Gutman (1985), *The Heroism of the Jewish People in the Second World War*, translated by Dr. Meir Katz (Tel Aviv: International Quiz on Heroism of Jewish People); Y. Gutman and E. Zuroff, eds. (1977), *Rescue Attempts During the Holocaust* (Jerusalem: Yad Vashem).

9. See Rich Cohen (2000), *The Avengers: A Jewish War Story* (New York: Alfred A. Knopf).

10. Israel Gutman, ed. (1990), *Encyclopedia of the Holocaust*, vol, 3 (New York: Macmillan).

11. Israel Gutman and Shmuel Krakowski (1986), *Unequal Victims: Poles and Jews During World War II*, translated by Ted Gorelick and Witold Jedlicki (New York: Holocaust Library).

12. Jack Werber (1996), *Saving Children: Diary of a Buchenwald Survivor and Rescuer* (New Brunswick, NJ: Transaction Publishers).

13. Ibid., p. 98.

14. Ibid., p. 99.

15. Ibid., p. 104.

16. Israel Gutman, ed. (1990), *Encyclopedia of the Holocaust*, vol. 4 (New York: Macmillan), pp. 1455–1458. See also W. Bartoszewski et al. (1993), "Warsaw Ghetto Uprising," *Dimensions: A Journal of Holocaust Studies* (published by the Anti-Defamation League's Braun Center for Holocaust Studies) 7, 2: 3–39; Ber Mark (1976), *Uprising in the Warsaw Ghetto* (New York: Schocken Books).

17. Gutman, ed., *Encyclopedia of the Holocaust*, p. 1456.

18. Ibid.

19. Ibid., p. 1458.

20. See Irene Shapiro (1999), "A Synopsis of the Bialystok Ghetto Rebellion," *Together,* January, p. 25.

21. Ellen Land-Weber (2000), *To Save a Life: Stories of Holocaust Rescue* (Urbana: University of Illinois Press).

22. Ernst Papanek with Edward Linn (1975), *Out of the Fire* (New York: William Morrow).

23. Robin Kadison Berson (1999), *Young Heroes in World History* (Westport: CT: Greenwood Press). See also Yaffa Eliach (1990), "Women of Valor: Partisans and Resistance Fighters," *Center for Holocaust Studies Newsletter* 4: 6.

24. Jeno Levai ([1948] 1988), *Raoul Wallenberg: His Remarkable Life, Heroic Battles, and the Secret of His Mysterious Disappearance*, translated by Frank Vajda (Melbourne, Australia: White Ant Occasional Publishing).

25. See Judith Tydor Baumel (1998), "The Parachutists' Mission from a Gender Perspective," in *Resisting the Holocaust*, edited by Ruby Rohrlich (New York: Berg Publishers), pp. 95–113.

26. Baumel, "The Parachutists' Mission," p. 95 (from Hannah Senesz [1971], *Her Life and Diary* [London: Valentine Mitchell]). See also M. I. Midlarsky (1981), "Helping During the Holocaust: The Role of Political, Theological, and Socioeconomic Identifications," *Humboldt Journal of Social Relations* 13, 1–2: 285–305.

27. E. Shadmi (1973), *Without Finding, Without Surrendering: Haviva Reik's Mission* (in Hebrew) (Tel Aviv: Moreshet) (film).

28. United States Holocaust Memorial Museum (1996), "Jewish Resistance During the Holocaust," program brochure, p. 4. October 29, Washington, DC: Miles Lerman Center for the Study of Jewish Resistance.

29. Ibid., p. 5.

30. See David Kranzler (2000), *The Man Who Stopped the Train to Auschwitz: George Mantello, El Salvador, and Switzerland's Finest Hour* (Syracuse, NY: Syracuse University Press).

31. Ibid., p. xviii.

32. See Lucien Lazare (1994), *Rescue as Resistance: How Jewish Organizations Fought the Holocaust in France*, translated by Jeffery M. Green (New York: Columbia University Press).

33. Yaffa Eliach (1998), *There Once Was a World: A Nine-Hundred-Year Chronicle of the Shtetl of Eishyshok* (Boston: Little, Brown), p. 630

34. See Gershon Shapiro (1988), *Under Fire: The Stories of Jewish Heroes of the Soviet Union* (Jerusalem: Yad Vashem).

35. See Gutman, *The Heroism of the Jewish People.*

36. See Smoliar, *Resistance in Minsk.*

37. Eliach, *There Once Was a World,* p. 630

38. Nechama Tec (1993), *Defiance: The Bielski Partisans—The Story of the Largest Armed Rescue of Jews by Jews During World War II* (New York: Oxford University Press).

39. See Samuel P. Oliner and Kathleen Lee (1996), *Who Shall Live: The Wilhelm Bachner Story* (Chicago: Academy Chicago Publishers). In 1982 I interviewed Wilhelm Bachner as a rescued survivor. To my surprise, I found him to be a Jewish rescuer. P. M. Oliner and I decided then that when we finished *The Altruistic Personality* we would undertake research on Jewish rescuers, which we began in 1991 (see Appendix C).

40. Wilhelm Bachner interview, July 15, 1982.

41. Ibid.

42. Moudhy Al-Rashid (1999), "Gibbon Lectures on Modern Heroism," *News* 120, 6 November 5 retrieved June 18, 2001, from http://www.lawrenceville.org/special/thelawrence/00/11_05_99).

Chapter 5

1. Abraham Rosenthal (1969), "Thirty-Eight Witnesses," in *Readings in Collective Behavior,* edited by Robert R. Evans (Chicago: Rand McNally), pp. 284–296; see also Associated Press (1998), "Residents of an Apartment Watch a Fatal Beating," *New York Times,* March 29, p. A14.

2. For more information about Andrew Carnegie and the Carnegie Hero Fund Commission, in addition to the Carnegie Hero website (http://trfn.clpgh.org/carnegiehero), see also Andrew Carnegie ([1920] 1986), *The Autobiography of Andrew Carnegie,* with a New Foreword by Cecelia Tichi (Boston: Northeastern University Press, rpt.); Bernard Alderson (1905), *Andrew Carnegie: The Man and His Work* (Boston: Northeastern University Press); George Roche (1998), *The Book of Heroes: Great Men and Women in American History* (Washington, DC: Regnery Publishing); Michael Lesy (1991), *Rescues: The Lives of Heroes* (New York: Farrar, Straus, and Giroux).

3. Taken from Anna F. LoMascolo (1999), "Toward a Sociological Understanding of Heroic Behavior: A Focus on Carnegie Heroes." Unpublished master's thesis, Department of Sociology, Humboldt State University, Arcata, CA.

4. The Carnegie Hero Fund Commission decided not to recognize any individual heroes after the 9/11 tragedy. Instead, they recognized all individuals involved as heroes.

5. Carnegie Hero Fund Commission (1997) (retrieved November 26, 1997, from http://trfn.clpgh.org/carnegiehero).

6. Carnegie Hero Fund Commission (1999) (retrieved March 5, 1999, from http://trfn.clpgh.org/carnegiehero). See also Alice H. Eagly and Maureen Crowley (1986), "Gender and Helping Behavior: A Meta-Analytic Review of the Social Psychological Literature," *Psychological Bulletin* 100: 283–308.

7. Carnegie Hero respondent #072.

8. Carnegie Hero respondent #198.

9. Carnegie Hero respondent #012.

10. Carnegie Hero respondent #038.

11. Carnegie Hero respondent #045.

12. Carnegie Hero respondent #001.

13. Carnegie Hero respondent #030.

14. Carnegie Hero respondent #060.

15. Carnegie Hero respondent #072.

16. Carnegie Hero respondent #064.

17. Carnegie Hero respondent #024.

18. Carnegie Hero respondent #010.

19. Carnegie Hero respondent #078.

20. Carnegie Hero respondent #026.

21. Carnegie Hero respondent #011.

22. Carnegie Hero respondent #015.

23. Carnegie Hero respondent #135.

24. Carnegie Hero respondent #132.

25. Carnegie Hero respondent #138.

26. Carnegie Hero respondent #162.

27. Bob Calandra (1999), "Why They Do It." *People Weekly* ("Heroes Among Us"), November 22, p. 141 (written by R. Jerome, S. Schindehette, N. Charles, and T. Fields-Meyer) (New York: Time).

28. Carnegie Hero respondent #115.

29. Carnegie Hero respondent #013.

30. Carnegie Hero respondent #114.

31. In Frank Farley's recent interview, he also stated that heroes do feel fear but that sometimes they overcome this fear with powerful motives like religious beliefs. Taken from Calandra, "Why They Do It."

32. Carnegie Hero respondent #119.

33. Carnegie Hero respondent #012.

34. Carnegie Hero respondent #179.

35. Carnegie Hero respondent #184.

36. Carnegie Hero respondent #148.

Chapter 6

1. See Max Hastings (1987), *The Korean War* (New York: Simon and Schuster).

2. Johanna McGeary and Karen Tumulty (May 7, 2001), "32 Years After Leaving Vietnam, Bob Kerrey Admits a Terrible Secret—And Stands Accused of Worse. The Tangled Tale Embodies the Madness of Vietnam." *Time.com* (*The Fog of War,* retrieved June 28, 2002, from http://www.time.com/time/pacific/magazine/2001 0507/cover1.html).

3. J. Robert Kerrey (2002), *When I was a Young Man* (New York: Harcourt Publishers).

4. Associated Press (1999), "The Massacre at My Lai," *Newsweek*, March 8, p. 64. See also Associated Press (1998), "Medals for My Lai Heroes Who Halted the Massacre," *San Francisco Chronicle*, March 7, p. A3; *San Francisco Chronicle* (1998), editorial, "Courage at My Lai," March 6, p. A22.

5. Trent Angers (1999), *The Forgotten Hero of My Lai: The Hugh Thompson Story* (Lafayette, LA: Acadian House Publishing), p. 12.

6. Angers, *The Forgotten Hero of My Lai.*

7. Ibid., p. 167.

8. Carlos Bertha (2001), "Moral Psychology in Times of War." Work in progress (retrieved April 25, 2002, from http://www.usafa.af..mil/dfpfa/CVs/ Bertha/Psyhero.html).

9. Richard Goldstein (1999), "James Logan Is Dead at 78; Winner of the Medal of Honor," *New York Times*, October 14, p. A26.

10. See Gregory Belenky, Shabtai Noy, and Zahava Solomon (1987), "Battle Stress, Morale, Cohesion, Combat Effectiveness, Heroism, and Psychiatric Casualties: The Israeli Experience," *Contemporary Studies in Combat Psychiatry* 62: 11–20, edited by Gregory Belenky (New York: Greenwood Press), p. 15. See also Reuven Gal (1987), "Combat Stress as an Opportunity: The Case of Heroism," in *Contemporary Studies in Combat Psychiatry*, pp. 31–45; Reuven Gal (1995), "Personality and Intelligence in the Military: The Case of Military Heroes," in *International Handbook of Personality and Intelligence*, edited by Donald H. Saklofske and Moshe Zeidner (New York: Plenum Press), pp. 727–737.

11. Reuven Gal and Richard Gabriel (1992), "Battlefield Heroism in the Israeli Defense Force," *International Social Science Review* 57, 4: 232–235.

12. Judith M. Banks (1994), "Decorated Commissioned Officers from the Vietnam War: A Study of Heroism," Ph.D. diss., Institute for Clinical Social Work, Chicago, p. 86.

13. Joseph A. Blake (1978), "Death by Hand Grenade: Altruistic Suicide in Combat," *Suicide and Life-Threatening Behavior* 8, 1: 56; see also Joel Baruch (1972), "Combat Death," *Suicide and Life-Threatening Behavior* 2, 3: 209–216.

14. Jeffrey W. Riemer (1998), "Durkheim's 'Heroic Suicide' in Military Combat," *Armed Forces and Society* 25, 1: 104.

15. John Percival (1985), *For Valour—The Victoria Cross: Courage in Action* (London: Thames, Nethuen), p. xii. See also William Miller (2000), *The Mystery of Courage* (Cambridge, MA: Harvard University Press).

16. Percival, *For Valour*, p. 137.

17. Ibid., p. 230.

18. Ibid., p. 234.

19. See Vidya Anand (1999), "Indian Heroes and Heroines of World War II" (retrieved August 21, 2000, from http://www6.meer.net/Book/warHero.html).

20. Max Arthur (2000), "Ganju Lama VC," *The Independent*, July 24, p. 6.

21. See also Allen Mikaelianm (2002), *Medal of Honor: Profile of America's Military Heroes from the Civil War to the Present* (New York: Hyperion); Robert Barr Smith (1997), *Men at War: True Stories of Heroism and Honor* (New York: Avon Books).

22. See Michael Taylor (1999), "Tracking Down False Heroes," *San Francisco Chronicle*, May 31, p. A1. Taylor used the resources of the U.S. Army Center for Military History and the Congressional Medal of Honor Society in South Carolina for his documentation.

23. Ibid.

24. Ibid.

25. Ibid.

26. Ibid.

27. Ibid.

28. Ibid.

29. Cited from Congressional Medal of Honor Society (1998a), "President Clinton Presenting James L. Day, MGen (Ret), USMC, the Medal of Honor. At the White House, January 20, 1998," Washington, DC (retrieved May 31, 1999, from http://www.awod.com/gallery/probono/cmhs/Day.htm).

30. Ibid.

31. Cited from Congressional Medal of Honor Society (1998b), "President Clinton Presenting Robert R. Ingram the Medal of Honor. At the White House, July 10, 1998," Washington, DC (retrieved May 31, 1999, from http://www.awod.com/gallery/probono/cmhs/ingram.htm).

32. Ibid.

33. Alessandra Stanley (2000), "On a '44 Battlefield, a Salute for a Black Hero," *New York Times International*, July 16, pp. 1, 6. See also Robert Edgerton (2001), *Hidden Heroism: Black Soldiers in America's Wars* (Boulder: Westview Press); Congressional Medal of Honor Society (1999), "World War II Black Medal of Honor Recipients," (retrieved May 26, 1999, from http://www.www2.army.mil/cmh-pgf/mohb.htm).

34. Kieran Doherty (1998), *Congressional Medal of Honor Recipients* (Springfield, NJ: Enslow Publishers), p. 25.

35. R. Russell Nakatsu ([1995] 2001), "Silent Warriors-Silent Heroes" (retrieved June 18, 2001, from http://sun.kent.wednet.edu/KSD/SJ/Nikkei/SilentHeroes. html, p. 1 of 2.

36. Carl Nolte (2001), "Carlos C. Ogden Remembered for Daring Assault During Normandy," *San Francisco Chronicle*, June 24, A27.

37. James Webb (2000), "Heroes of the Vietnam Generation," *American Enterprise* 11, 6 September: 22–24. See also Ronit Kishon Barash (1995), "Factors Associated with Two Facets of Altruism in Vietnam War Veterans with Post-Traumatic Stress Disorder" (UMI Microform # 9606908, Ann Arbor, MI).

38. Purple Heart Home Page. "The Purple Heart—Then and Now" (retrieved June 26, 2001, from http://www.purpleheart.org/history.htm).

39. See also Frank Moore (1997), *Women of the War: Two Stories of Brave Women in the Civil War* (Hartford, CT: Blue/Gray Book); Kathleen Noble (1994), *The Sound of Silver Horn: Reclaiming the Heroism in Contemporary Women's Lives* (New York: Fawcett Columbine).

Chapter 7

1. Richard Attenborough ([1986] 1998), *Mother Teresa*. Videotape. Leonard Maltin, Producer. New York: Signet.

2. Author's interview with Dr. Wendy Ring, January 14, 2000.

3. Ibid.

4. Ibid.

5. Kristen Renwick Monroe (1996), *The Heart of Altruism* (Princeton, NJ: Princeton University Press), p. 17.

6. Robert Coles (2000), *Lives of Moral Leadership* (New York: Random House), pp. 52–53. See also Paul H. Ray and Sherry Anderson (2000), *The Cultural Creatives: How 50 Million People Are Changing the World* (New York: Harmony Books).

7. Anne Colby and William Damon (1992), *Some Do Care: Contemporary Lives of Moral Commitment* (New York: The Free Press), p. 29. These criteria, developed by Colby and Damon, give us some empirical insight into the nature of moral heroes and an approach to organizing insights about their motivations. They have identified a four-step process of reciprocity in the social influence and moral transformation that occurs between the actors and their supporters, leading to an influential development that may exist throughout a lifetime: (1) There is an understanding and match of goals between the two parties; (2) communication and sharing of new information and knowledge; (3) engaging in new activities; and (4) resulting in adopting and broadening new moral goals. See also Robert Coles (1989), *The Call of Stories: Teaching and the Moral Imagination* (Boston: Houghton Mifflin); L. Kohlberg (1976), "Moral State and Moralization: The Cognitive-development Approach," in *Moral Development and Behavior: Theory, Research, and Social Issues,* edited by T. Lickona (New York: Holt); John Stuart Mill (1990), *The Autobiography of John Stuart Mill* (Garden City, NY: Doubleday).

8. Colby and Damon, *Some Do Care*, p. 293.

9. Coles, *Lives of Moral Leadership*, pp. 191–192.

10. *Gandhi Speaks . . . Selections from his writings.* Self-Realization Fellowship Lake Shrine pamphlet. Pacific Palisades, CA, p. 9.

11. Mark Shepard (1987), *Gandhi Today* (Arcata, CA: Simple Productions), p. 3.

12. Quoted in Catherine Ingram (1990), *The Footsteps of Gandhi: Conversations with Spiritual Social Activists* (Berkeley: Parallax Press), p. 14. See also Stanley E. Jones (1976), *Gandhi: Portrayal of a Friend* (Nashville, TN: Abingdon Press).

13. Gary Bacon (1982), *Essential Education: Drawing Forth the Golden Child* (Palo Alto, CA: Rainbow Bridge), p. 204

14. Shepard, *Gandhi Today*, p. 1.

15. See World Tibet Network News, "Reflections on the Challenges of the 21st Century," speech given in New York City, April 27, 1994 (retrieved September 12, 2002, from http://www.tibet.ca/wtnarchive/1994/5/3–5_1.html).

16. Kenneth Liberman (1986), "The Tibetan Cultural Praxis: Bodhicitta Thought Training," *Humboldt Journal of Social Relations* 13, 1–2: 113–126.

17. Dalai Lama and Howard C. Cutler (1998), *The Art of Happiness: A Handbook for Living* (New York: Riverhead Books), p. 114.

18. Ibid.

19. Ibid., p. 89.

20. Dalai Lama (1999), *Ethics for the New Millennium* (New York: Riverhead Books).

21. Nobel Peace Prize Conference (1989), citation presented October 5 in Oslo, Norway.

22. Dalai Lama and Cutler, *The Art of Happiness,* p. 71.

23. Dennis Davidson (1999), "Words of Faith: Dalai Lama Teaches Love, Kindness," *Desert Sun*, March 20, p. D6. See also Dalai Lama (2001), *An Open Heart: Practicing Compassion in Everyday Life* (Boston: Little, Brown); Dalai Lama (1984), *Kindness, Clarity, and Insight: The Fourteenth Dalai Lama, His Holiness Tenzin Gyatso,* translated by Jeffrey Hopkins, edited by Jeffrey Hopkins and Elizabeth Napper (Ithaca, NY: Snow Lion Publications).

24. Davidson, "Words of Faith."

25. Ibid.

26. Dalai Lama, *An Open Heart,* p. 131.

27. Davidson, "Words of Faith."

28. See James M. Washington, ed. (1991), "I See the Promised Land," speech given April 3, 1968, Memphis, TN, taken from *A Testament Of Hope: The Essential Writings of Martin Luther King, Jr.* (retrieved September 4, 2002, from http://www.seto.org/king3.html), pp. 9–10.

29. Dr. Martin Luther King Jr. ([1963] 1997), *I Have a Dream* (New York: Scholastic Press), p. 19.

30. See This Event in Black History, "Letter from a Birmingham Jail" (written April 16, 1963) (retrieved September 5, 2002, from http://www.ai.mit.edu/~isbell/HFh/black/events_and_people/.008.letter_from_jail).

31. King, *I Have a Dream,* pp. 25–31. See also Dr. Martin Luther King Jr. (1963), *Strength in Love* (Philadelphia: Fortress Press); James Washinton (1992), *I Have a Dream: Writings and Speeches that Changed the World* (San Francisco: Harper San Francisco).

32. David Aikman (1998), *Great Souls: Six Who Changed the Century* (Nashville, TN: Word Publishing), p. 76.

33. Ibid., p. 78.

34. Ibid., p. 61.

35. Ibid., p. 101.

36. Samuel P. Oliner (1993a), "The Altruistic Personality: Rescuers of Jews in Nazi Europe." Paper presented at the Prosocial Behavior Conference, University of Arkansas, Little Rock.

37. Elie Wiesel (1986), *Night* (New York: Bantam Books), p. 32.
38. Ibid., p. 36.
39. Ibid., p. 32.
40. Gordon J. Horwitz (1990), *In The Shadows of Death: Living Outside the Gates of Mathausen* (New York: The Free Press).
41. Robert McAfee Brown (1983), *Elie Wiesel: Messenger to all Humanity* (Notre Dame, IN: University of Notre Dame Press), as quoted in Aikman, *Great Souls,* p. 315. See also Molly Abramowitz (1974), *Elie Wiesel: A Bibliography* (Metuchen, NJ: Scarecrow Press).
42. Aikman, *Great Souls,* p. 354.
43. See the Elie Wiesel Foundation for Humanity (retrieved August 7, 2002, from www.eliewieselfoundation.org).
44. Dr. Robert Pamplin Jr. and Gary K. Eisler (1995), *American Heroes: Their Lives, Their Values, Their Beliefs* (New York: Mastermedia), p.146. See also Bill Berkowitz (1987), *Local Heroes: Rebirth of Heroism in America* (Lexington, MA: Lexington Books); Michael Ryan (1990), "A Simple Deed with Awesome Power," *Parade Magazine,* August 19, pp. 4–11; Elie Wiesel ([1982] 1995), *The Town Beyond the Wall,* translated by Stephen Becker (New York: Schocken Books), p.159.
45. Aikman, *Great Souls,* p. 366.
46. Ibid., p. 212.
47. Ibid., p. 220
48. Ibid., pp. 192–193.
49. Ibid., p. 193
50. Ibid., p. 194.
51. Ibid., p. 196. See also Microsoft Encarta (1995), "Mother Teresa of Calcutta (1910–1997)" (retrieved June 16, 1999, from http://www.netsrq.com/~dbois/m-teresa.html).
52. Colby and Damon, *Some Do Care.* See also William Martin (1991), *A Prophet with Honor: The Billy Graham Story* (New York: William Morrow); Mark Tappan and Lyn Midel Brown (1991), "Stories Told and Lessons Learned: Toward a Narrative Approach to Moral Development and Moral Education," in *Stories Lives Tell,* edited by Carol Witherell and Nel Nodding (New York: Teachers College Press), pp. 171–192.
53. Harold J. Sala (1998), *Heroes: People Who Made a Difference in Our World* (Uhrichsville, OH: Promise Press), p. 37.
54. Nancy Seavey, Jane S. Smith, and Paul Wagner (1998), *A Paralyzing Fear: The Triumph over Polio in America* (New York: TV Books).
55. Kelly Knauer, ed. (1996), *Time: Great People of the 20th Century.* New York: Time Books.
56. See Daily Celebrations Home Page, "Dr. Jonas Salk" (retrieved August 7, 2002, from http://www.dailycelebrations.com/100899.htm).
57. See Women's International Center, "Dr. Jonas Salk" (retrieved August 31, 2000, from http://www.wic.org/bio/jsalk.htm).
58. See Daily Celebrations Home Page, "Dr. Jonas Salk" (retrieved August 7, 2002, from http://www.dailycelebrations.com/100899.htm).

59. See Bartleby.com Home Page, "Dr. Jonas Salk" (retrieved August 7, 2002, from http://www.bartleby.com/63/79/2879.html).

60. See San Jose State University Virtual Museum, "Albert B. Sabin" (retrieved August, 31, 2000, from http://www.sjsu.edu/depts/Museum/sabin.html).

61. See Sabin Vaccine Institute, "The Legacy of Albert Sabin" (retrieved August 7, 2002, http://www.sabin.org/who_legacy.htm).

62. Mary Joe Breton (1998), *Women Pioneers for the Environment* (Boston: Northeastern University Press), p. 99.

63. See Equity Online: Women of Achievement, "Rachel Carson" (retrieved August 15, 2000, from http://www.edc.org/WomenEquity/women/carson/htm).

64. See White House Home Page, "Rachel Carson" (retrieved August 15, 2000, from http://www.whitehouse.gov/WH/EOP/OVP/24hours/carson.html).

65. Andrew Revkin (1990), *The Burning Season: The Murder of Chico Mendes and the Fight for the Amazon Rain Forest* (Boston: Houghton Mifflin), p. 4.

66. *San Francisco Chronicle* editorial (1998), "The Amazon Still Needs Chico Mendes," December 31, p. A21.

67. Ibid.

68. Nicholas Wilson, "We Did It!" *Auto-Free Times* 17, Spring 2000: 35.

69. Author's interview with Julia Hill, March 3, 2000.

70. Julia Butterfly Hill (2000), *The Legacy of Luna: The Story of a Tree, a Woman, and the Struggle to Save the Redwoods* (San Francisco: HarperCollins).

71. Author's interview with Julia Hill, March 3, 2000.

72. Ibid.

73. Hill, *The Legacy of Luna*, p. 246.

74. Author's interview with the Reverend Eric Duff, January 10, 2000.

75. Ibid.

76. Sean Pasternak (1995), "Craig Kielburger—12 Year Old Lobbyist," *Thornhill Times* (Canada) December (retrieved August 25, 2000, from http://www.angelfire.com/on/pasternakpublishing/craigkielburger.html); See also John Terry and Donna Woonteiler (2000), "An Interview With Craig Kielburger, Founder of Free the Children," *CYD Journal* 1, 1 (retrieved August 25, 2000, from http://www.cydjournal.org/2000winter/kielburger.html).

77. Tracy Rysavy, ed. (2000), "Telling the Children's Story." *YES! A Journal of Positive Futures* (retrieved August 25, 2000, from http://www.futurenet.org/11powerofone/rysavy.html).

78. Ibid.

79. Ibid.

80. David H. Jones (1999), *Moral Responsibility in the Holocaust: A Study in the Ethics of Character* (Lanham, MD: Rowman and Littlefield). See also Nel Noddings (1984), *Caring: A Feminine Approach to Ethics and Moral Education* (Berkeley, CA: University of California Press); Michel Odent (1999), *The Scientification of Love* (London: Free Association Books); Pearl M. Oliner et al, eds. (1992), *Embracing the Other: Philosophical, Psychological, and Historical Perspectives on Altruism* (New York: New York University Press).

81. Ibid., p. 60.

82. Ibid., p. 242. For further examples, see also Samuel P. Oliner and Pearl M. Oliner (1988), *The Altruistic Personality: Rescuers of Jews in Nazi Europe* (New York: The Free Press), and Nechama Tec (1986), *When Light Pierced the Darkness: Christian Rescue of Jews in Nazi-Occupied Poland* (Oxford: Oxford University Press.

83. Samuel P. Oliner (1993b), "So That Others May Live: A Psycho-historical Study of Heroic Jewish Rescue in Nazi-Occupied Europe." Paper presented to Rider College, Lawrence Hill, New Jersey; Samuel P. Oliner and Kathleen Lee (1996), *Who Shall Live: The William Bachner Story* (Chicago: Academy Chicago Publishers).

Chapter 8

1. See Northwest Giving Project, "What Is Philanthropy?" (retrieved July 23, 2001, from http://www.nwgiving.org/htm/whatis.htm). A detailed discussion of philanthropy in other world traditions can be found in Warren F. Ilchman, Stanley N. Katz, and Edward L. Queen II, eds. (1998), *Philanthropy in the World's Traditions* (Bloomington: Indiana University Press).

2. See White House Conference on Philanthropy, "Heroes Biography: Matel 'Mat' Dawson, Jr." (retrieved August 20, 2002, from http://clinton 4.nara.gov/Initiatives/Millennium/Philan/html/bio_dawson.html).

3. Ibid.

4. Ibid.

5. Mike W. Martin (1994), *Virtuous Giving: Philanthropy, Voluntary Service, and Caring* (Bloomington: Indiana University Press).

6. Ibid., p. 1 (emphasis added).

7. Ibid.

8. See Leona Anderson (1998), "Contextualizing Philanthropy in South Asia: A Textual Analysis of Sanskrit Sources," in *Philanthropy in the World's Traditions,* edited by Warren F. Ilchman, Stanley N. Katz, and Edward L. Queen II (Bloomington: Indiana University Press), pp. 57–78.

9. John Grim (1998), "A Comparative Study in Native American Philanthropy," in ibid., p. 25.

10. Ibid.

11. Reed Abelson (2000), "New Philanthropists Put Donations to Work," *New York Times,* July 6, pp. C1, C23; see also Derek Penslar (1998), "The Origins of Modern Jewish Philanthropy," in *Philanthropy in the World's Traditions.*

12. Jolanye Houtz (2001), "Local Donations at $30.8 Million," *Seattle Times,* September 23.

13. Francie Ostrower (1995), *Why the Wealthy Give* (Princeton, NJ: Princeton University Press).

14. Ibid., p. 101.

15. Steven Burkeman (1999), "An Unsatisfactory Company. . . ?" Lecture delivered to the Allen Lane Foundation (retrieved July 11, 2001, from http://www.allen-lane.demon.co.uk/newpage2.htm), p. 2.

16. Ibid., p. 1.

17. Ibid., p. 3.

18. Waldemar A. Nielsen (1985), *The Golden Donors: A New Anatomy of the Great Foundations* (New York: Truman Talley Books/E. P. Dutton). See also the Foundation Center Statistical Services (retrieved May 21, 2001, from http://fdncenter.org).

19. Kristen Renwick Monroe (1996), *The Heart of Altruism* (Princeton, NJ: Princeton University Press).

20. Ibid., p. 43.

21. Ibid., p. 52.

22. Russ Alan Prince and Karen Maru File (1994), *The Seven Faces of Philanthropy: A New Approach to Cultivating Major Donors* (San Francisco: Jossey-Bass).

23. Cornelius Pietzner (2000), "Perspectives on Philanthropy," Ethical Banking Conference (Basel, Switzerland, May 28, retrieved July 23, 2001, from (http://www.camphillsoltane.org/news/philanthropy.htm).

24. George Roche (1998), *The Book of Heroes: Great Men and Women in American History* (Washington, DC: Regnery Publishing).

25. From Andrew Carnegie ([1920] 1986), *The Autobiography of Andrew Carnegie*, with a New Foreword by Cecelia Tichi (Boston: Northeastern University Press, rpt.).

26. Roche, *The Book of Heroes*, p. 214.

27. Carnegie, *Autobiography*, pp. 37–38.

28. Roche, *The Book of Heroes*, pp. 214–215.

29. Philanthropic giving is devoted to domestic help and frequently field-specific, that is, philanthropists most frequently offer funds to medical research and education.

30. Paul Schervish, Mary A. O'Herlihy, and John J. Havens (2001), *Agent-Animated Wealth and Philanthropy: The Dynamics of Accumulation and Allocation Among High-Tech Donors* (retrieved October 1, 2001, from http://www.afpnet.org).

31. Ibid., p. 51

32. Ibid. See also Elliot Zaret (2001), "Understanding the Titan of High-Tech: Methods, Motivation of Gates Echo the Industrial Age." MSNBC (retrieved July 9, 2001, from http://www.msnbc.com/news/).

33. Ibid., pp. 8–9.

34. Richard Barrett (2000), "Seven Levels of Corporate Philanthropy: Making Money While Making a Difference" (retrieved July 11, 2001, from http://www.paraview.com/pages/sectionarticlepages1/sevenlevels.htm).

35. Ibid., p. 2.

36. Ostrower, *Why the Wealthy Give.*

37. Nick de Souza (2001), "Sweet Charity," *World Link*, March/April: 42–43.

38. Tanya Schevitz (2000), "At UC Berkeley, Charity Begins in the Classroom." *San Francisco Chronicle*, September 7, pp. A1, A13.

39. Ibid.

40. Ostrower, *Why the Wealthy Give.*

41. Martin, *Virtuous Giving*, p. 161.

Chapter 9

1. Susan J. Ellis and Katherine H. Noyes (1990), *By the People: A History of Americans as Volunteers* (San Francisco: Jossey-Bass), p. 365.

2. Alexis de Tocqueville (1956), *Democracy in America*, translated and edited by Richard Heffner (New York: New American Library), p. 193.

3. David Gerard (1985), "What Makes a Volunteer?" *New Society* 74, 1193: 236–238.

4. David S. Adams (1990), "Issues and Ideas in the Culture of American Volunteerism." Paper presented at the American Sociological Association, Washington, DC, August. See also Jennifer Lois (2000), "Heroic Efforts: The Emotional Culture of Search and Rescue Volunteers." Ph.D. diss., Department of Sociology, University of Colorado, Boulder.

5. R. Buckingham (1983), *The Complete Hospice Guide* (New York: Harper and Row), p. 12. See also Carolyn Jaffe and Carol H. Ehrlich (1997), *All Kinds of Love: Experiencing Hospice* (Amityville, NY: Baywood Publishing).

6. Buckingham, *The Complete Hospice Guide*, p. 13.

7. Hospice Information Worldwide. Retrieved September 6, 2002, from http://www.hospiceinformation.info/hospicesworldwide.asp.

8. NHPCO Website. Retrieved September 6, 2002, from http://www.nhpco.org/public/articles/facts&figures9–2002.pdf.

9. Buckingham, *The Complete Hospice Guide*, p. 15.

10. N. Allen and J. Phillippe Rushton (1983), "Personality Characteristics of Community Mental Health Volunteers: A Review," *Journal of Voluntary Action Research* 12, 1: 36–49.

11. J. Piliavin (1994), "Feeling Good by Doing Good: Emotions and Volunteering." Paper presented for the American Sociological Association, Los Angeles, August 5–9.

12. This figure compares with 12 percent for the high-level volunteers and 5.5 percent for the low-level volunteers.

13. Only 7 percent of high-level volunteers gave normocentric responses, and none of the low-level volunteers gave responses that could be interpreted as normative.

14. This was cited by 30 percent of the hospice volunteers.

15. See Adams, "Issues and Ideas in the Culture of American Volunteerism."

16. Amitai Etzioni (1996), *The New Golden Rule: Community and Morality in a Democratic Society* (New York: Basic Books).

17. Ibid., p. 120.

18. Ibid., p. 125.

Chapter 10

1. From Adele Lindenmeyr (1998), "From Repression to Revival: Philanthropy in 20th Century Russia," in *Philanthropy in the World's Traditions*, edited by

Warren F. Ilchman, Stanley N. Katz, and Edward L. Queen II (Bloomington: Indiana University Press, p. 309.)

2. See Nancy Eisenberg and Janet Strayer, eds. (1990), *Empathy and Its Developmen,* (2nd ed.), Cambridge, MA: (Cambridge University Press).

3. Pearl Oliner and Samuel P. Oliner (1995), *Toward a Caring Society* (Westport, CT: Praeger Publishers).

4. See Martin L. Hoffman (1970), "Parents, Discipline, and Child's Consideration for Others," *Child Development* 34: 573–588; Nancy Eisenberg (1986), *Altruistic Emotion, Cognition, and Behavior* (Hillsdale, NJ: Lawrence Erlbaum Associates); Ervin Staub (1978), *Positive Social Behavior and Morality,* vol. 1 (New York: Academic Press); and E. Staub (1979), *Positive Social Behavior and Morality: Socialization and Development,* vol. 2 (New York: Academic Press); Robert Wuthnow (1993), *Acts of Compassion: Caring for Others and Helping Ourselves* (Princeton, NJ: Princeton University Press).

5. See David A. Schroeder, Louis A. Penner, John F. Dovidio, and Jane A. Piliavin (1995), *The Psychology of Helping and Altruism: Problems and Puzzles* (New York: McGraw-Hill).

Index